I0827717

IMAGES
of America

WARREN TOWNSHIP

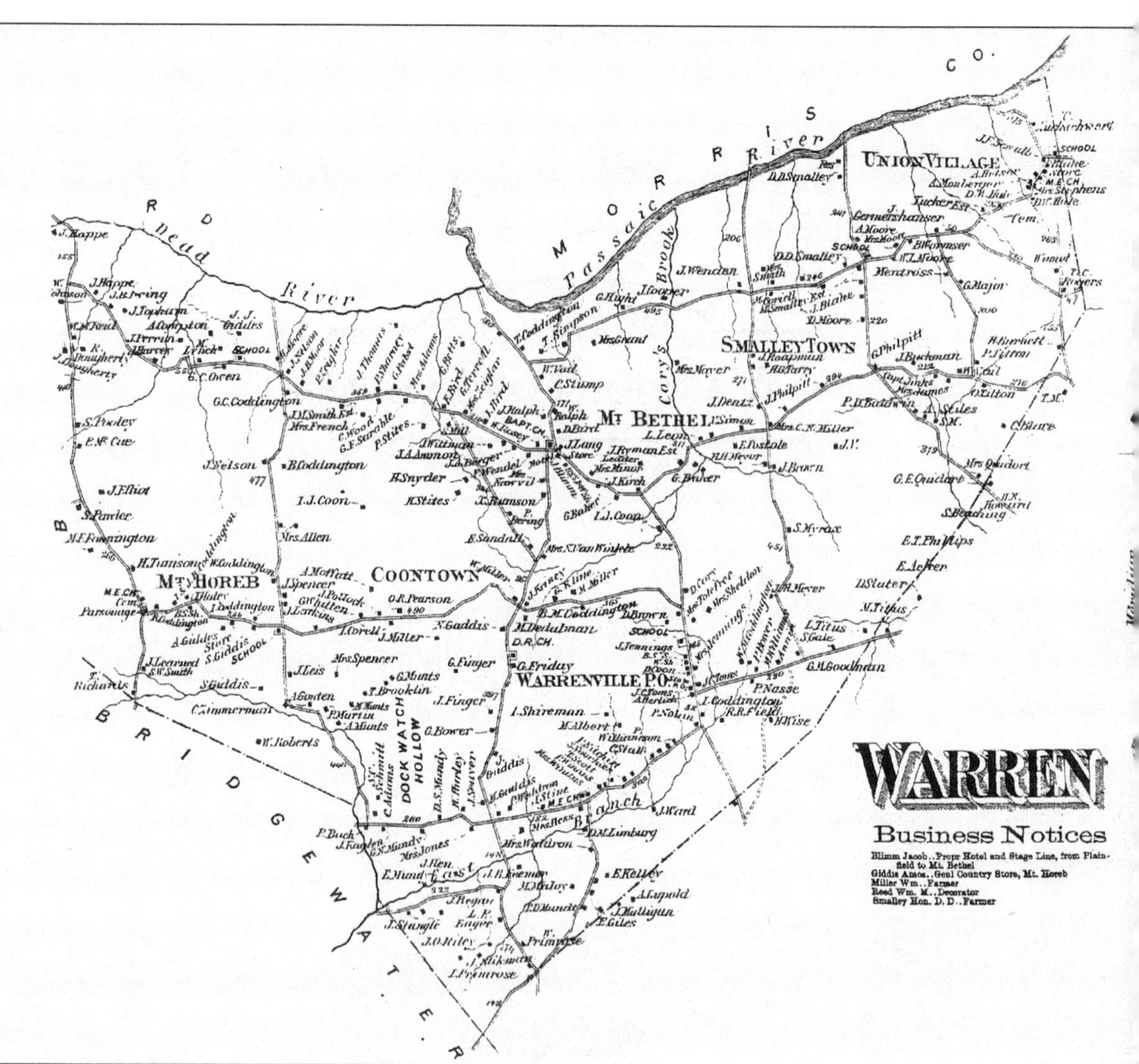

Warren Township, from the *Atlas of Somerset County, N.J.* (1873).

IMAGES
of America

WARREN TOWNSHIP

Alan A. Siegel

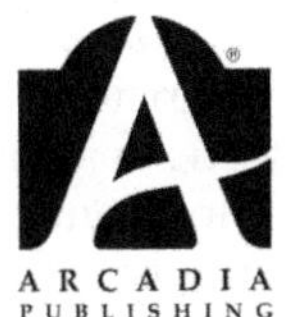

ISBN 978-1-5316-6017-8

Published by Arcadia Publishing
Charleston, South Carolina

For all general information contact Arcadia Publishing at:
Telephone 843-853-2070
Fax 843-853-0044
E-mail sales@arcadiapublishing.com
For customer service and orders:
Toll-Free 1-888-313-2665

Visit us on the Internet at www.arcadiapublishing.com

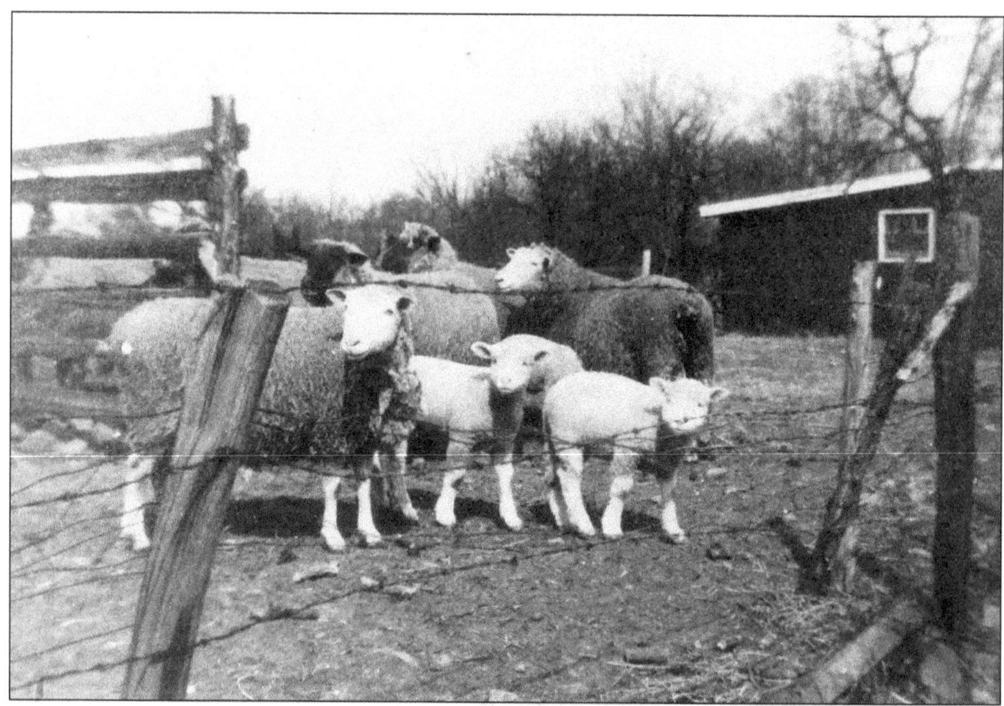

"The industries of the township are chiefly agricultural, including stock- and grain-raising and dairying," wrote a historian in 1880. When an anonymous photographer snapped these sheep in the pasture at Bowers' Cedar Hill Farm on Mountainview Road, *c.* 1900, Warren Township still had another half century to go before its farms began disappearing.

Contents

Acknowledgments

The author wishes to express his gratitude to all those friends of Warren history whose photographs made this book possible, including: American Legion Post 293; Richard Bachert, Schwaebische Alb; George Bebbington; Dina Wagner Bowers; Susie Boyce; Francis W. Brain; Ted Christiansen; Donald Christie; Community Volunteer Fire Company; Carol DeFilippis; Charlotte DeHaan; Clarence and Hugo Duderstadt; *Echoes-Sentinel*; Judy Fairless; Jack Farrell, William Farrell, Dick and Mary Farrell; Kathleen Flanagan; Frank R. Freehauf; Sylvia Gerken; Alan Grossweiler; William T. Halsey; Mildred Harold; Zoltan Haydu; Marion Helmstetter; Russell Horster; Mr. and Mrs. Glenn Kennedy; Ruth L. Komorek; Ilse Landau; Michael Lach, Police Chief; Joyce LaPoint; Dee Lortie, Township Clerk; Lucent Technologies; Joan W. Macaulay; Eleanor Mathews; Gus Mobus; Elsie Monica; Mount Bethel Baptist Church; New Jersey Room, Newark Public Library; Noye Newton; Marian Pagano; Paul Ratner; John Roser, Warren Hills Lodge No. 2252, B.P.O.E.; Frank Salvato; Jean Smalley; Special Collections and Archives, Rutgers Universities Libraries; Martha Sage Sweezy; Hildegard Touchon; Dorothy Mundy Trupo; Walter Tucker, Washington Valley Volunteer Fire Company; Leonard Visotski; Mrs. E.A. Waldorf; Margaret Waldron; Jane Wallace; Mary Lou Weller; William Wittreich; Warren Yarrington; and members of the Warren Township Historical Society.

A special word of thanks is due to Frank Freehauf and George Bebbington who reviewed this work in manuscript, to Jack Farrell who put me in touch with so many longtime residents, and to the folks at Arcadia Publishing who conceived the idea of publishing the Images of America series.

Alan A. Siegel
Warren Township, New Jersey
May 15, 1996

A Brief History of Warren Township

Called by one early author "the greenest place in New Jersey," Warren Township stretches from the crest of the First Watchung Mountain across Washington Valley to the Second Mountain and beyond, ending at the Dead and Passaic Rivers. Now encompassing an area of 19.3 square miles, Warren was half again as large before 1872, the year the communities now know as North Plainfield, Green Brook, and Watchung were carved from its land mass.

The Watchung Mountains, whose natural beauty characterizes the township, came into being 125 million years ago when volcanic eruptions to the west covered the area with two thick lava flows that later were tilted upwards 20 degrees. Then, gradually, imperceptibly, during the millions of years that followed this massive shifting of the earth, water eroded away the land, exposing the jutting edges of the buried lava. These exposed basaltic edges, now much weathered, are the First and Second Mountains; between them lies a broad, fertile valley through which flows the Middle Brook.

The Lenape Indians roamed these parts for thousands of years before the Europeans came, but they left little history: a few arrowheads and grinding stones have been found along the Passaic River; Dock Watch Hollow is the only locale that bears an Indian name.

English and Scots-Irish from Turkey (now New Providence) and Scotch Plains first settled the township in the 1720s. Farmers from New Providence followed the Passaic River into what is now Union Village and Smalleytown. To the south, pioneers from the lowlands moved through Lincoln Gap (Somerset Street, Watchung) and into Washington Valley. Philip Cox may have arrived here as early as 1727, the year he bought 200 acres "betwixt the first and second mountain called the Blue Hills. . . ." Until 1743, when the borders of Somerset County shifted northward, Warren was part of Elizabeth Borough in Essex County.

By the time of the American Revolution, fewer than a hundred families lived in what would become Warren, eking out a living from the stone-scattered fields. There were saw and grain mills on Cory's Brook, in Dock Watch Hollow, and elsewhere. A Baptist church on Old Church Road and a schoolhouse on Mount Bethel Road were the centers of community life. Twenty or so men from Warren served in the state militia. One of them, David Smalley, rose to the rank of captain.

Not until 1806 was Warren Township created from portions of Bridgewater and Bernards. Named in honor of Joseph Warren, hero of the Battle of Bunker Hill, Warren grew slowly. In the 1830s Germans settled in Washington Valley, soon followed by French and Swiss and later by Italians, all of whom turned their industrious hands to whatever work there was to do. The Civil War divided the township sharply. Fifty or so men joined the Northern ranks, many of them draftees, while at home County Freeholder Daniel Cory was jailed by the federal government for disloyalty.

Throughout the late nineteenth century and into the early twentieth, the principal industries were livestock, fruit and grain raising, dairy farming, and logging. Land values were low and the population static. Indeed, the population actually declined from 1,097 in 1875 to 1,083 in 1920. By 1933, when Warren finally sold its one-room schoolhouses after Central School opened, the population had only reached 1,500.

World War II had an enormous impact on the community. Almost all able-bodied young men (and some women, too) served in the armed forces. The post-war demand for housing spurred a flurry of new construction—the number of homes increased 45 percent during the years 1946-48. New schools and paved roads inevitably followed, encouraging even more construction.

A second building boom in the 1960s drove the population to 8,592 by 1970. A shopping center, the town hall, and a cluster of commercial buildings made Warrenville the new "downtown." To many old timers, it seemed that the township had been transformed beyond recognition. But when Route 78 finally opened to its full length in 1986, still another wave of building crested over the remaining farmland. In 1992 alone, the town approved nearly one thousand new homes. A luxury hotel that opened in 1989 and AT&T's multi-million-dollar complex on King George Road (finished in 1996) completed the transformation. Population now exceeds 12,000. As late as 1982 there were still 150 working farms in the township. Now most of them are but a memory, the victims of progress.

Almost from its beginning, Warren was a scattering of small villages, often mere crossroads. Centered about a church or school, even in their heyday these villages boasted only a post office and general store, perhaps a blacksmith shop and a few houses. Their names—Mount Horeb, Coontown, Mount Bethel, Union Village, Smalleytown, Warrenville and Springdale—evoke pleasant memories still. While enough of old-time Warren remains to hint at what once was, much has been lost during the last forty years. The photographs we present here preserve the past, offering a visual history that will stir the memories of longtime residents and encourage a sense of pride in those new to Warren Township.

One

Union Village

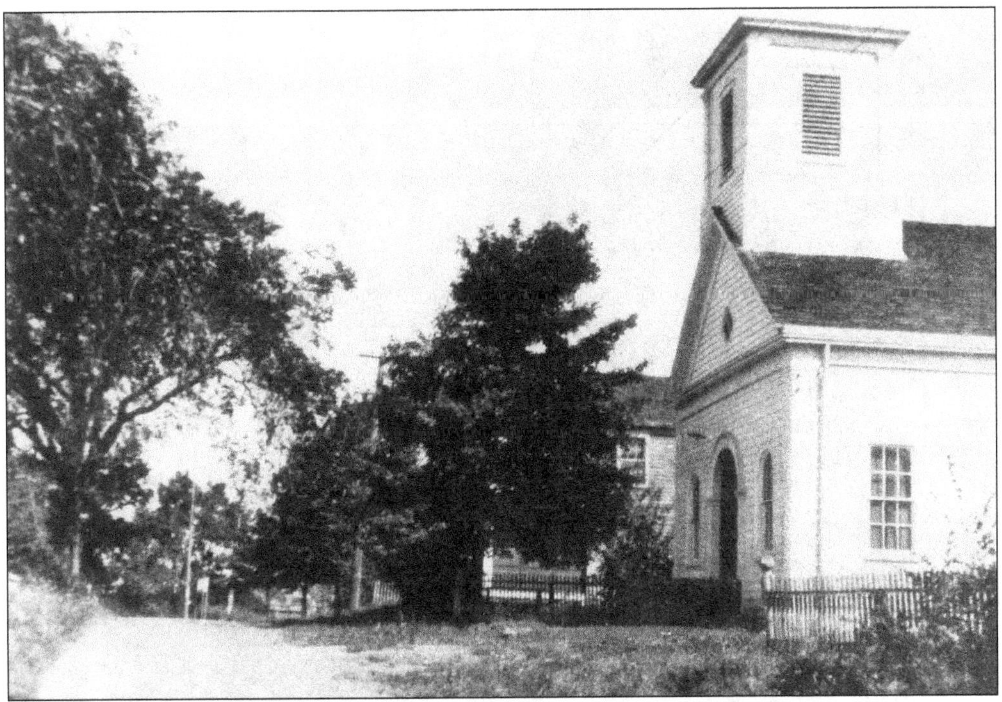

Situated at the intersection of Hillcrest Road and Mountain Avenue, Union Village is one of Warren's oldest settled areas, occupying a portion of a 3,000-acre tract acquired by William Dockwra in 1690. Settlers from New Providence moved into the area along the "Pasaick River" in the late 1720s, but it was not until July 4, 1824, when residents erected a liberty pole, that the place was named Union Village in honor of the American Union. In this scene looking east on Mountain Avenue 1900, the Union Village Methodist Church is at the right, the liberty pole at the far left.

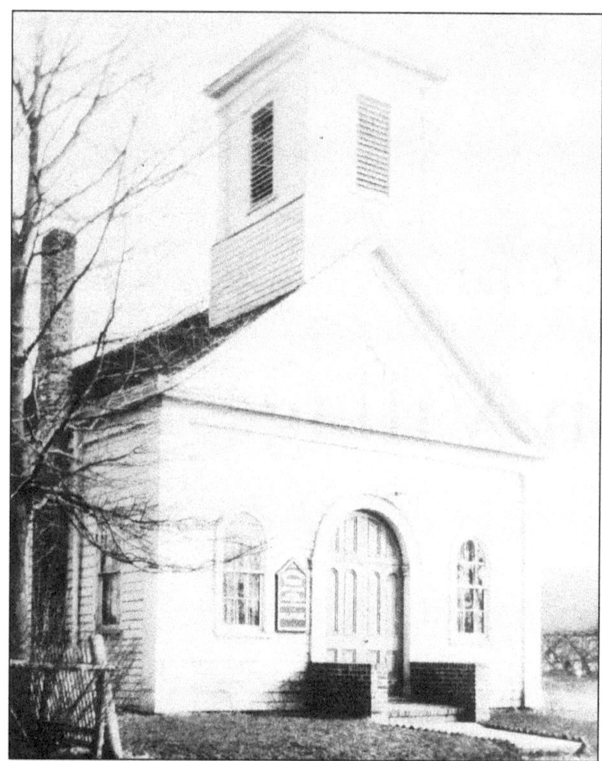

Known affectionately as "The Little Church by the Wayside," the Methodist church was dedicated in December 1825. Built on land next to Elam Genung's general store and post office, the building remained in use until 1960 when a new sanctuary on Hillcrest Road replaced it. After serving as home of the Stony Hill Players for a number of years, the church became a private residence.

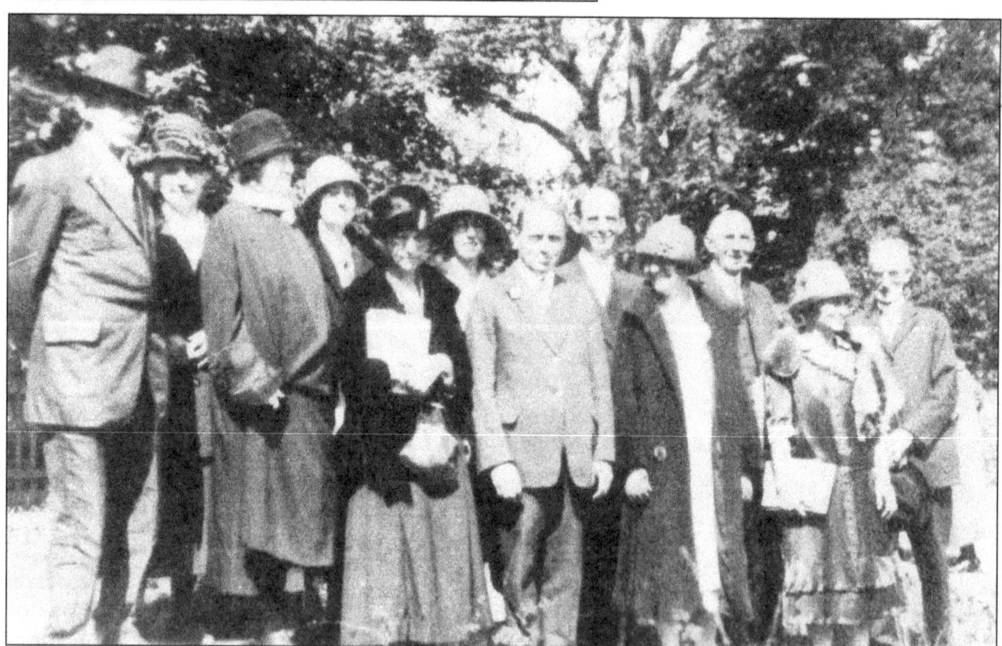

The Methodist church celebrated its centennial in October 1926. In honor of this event, a committee led by Mrs. W.S. Duguid and Mrs. A.D. Creveling was joined by former pastors S.H. Jones, C. Bowers, David Smalley, J.S. Burton, W.A. Molyneaux, and W.S. Coyeman (all pictured here) for sacred music on the banjo, violin, and piano and a supper of boiled ham, baked beans, and doughnuts.

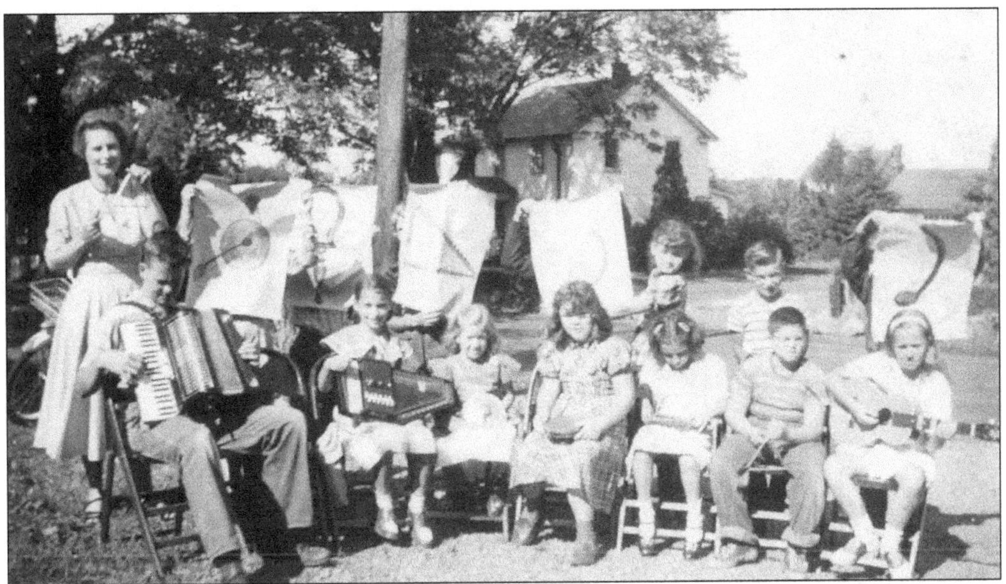

The church entered its period of greatest growth after World War II. Nearly 175 pupils were enrolled in Sunday school by 1953 when this photograph of the Summer Vacation Bible School Band was taken. Included in this picture are Herb Belin, Carol Werner, Melinda Weber, Susan Shaffer, Nancy O'Brien, Ms. Fisher, and Priscilla Pratt.

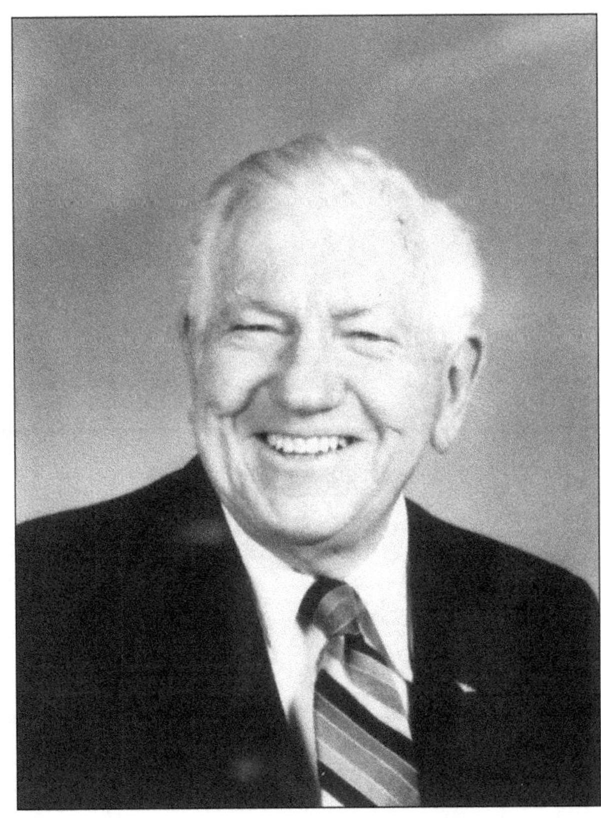

Henry J. McKinnon began his pastorate at the Union Village church in 1948 while he was still a student at Drew University. When he left in 1971, church membership had reached one thousand and a new sanctuary had been built.

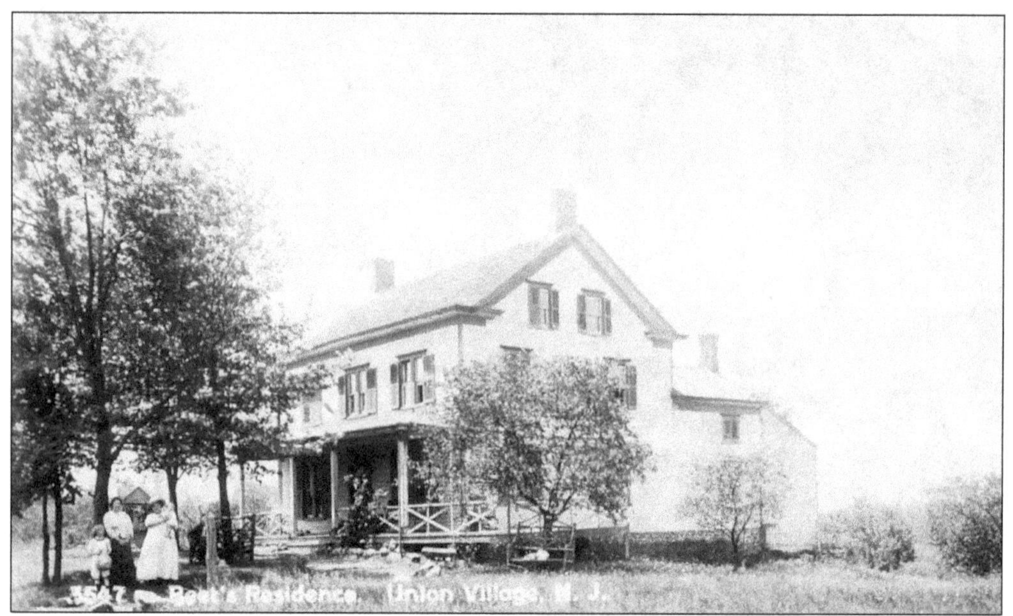

Union Village changed little over the years. An 1881 visitor described it as "a small hamlet, containing one store, a blacksmith shop, a wheelwright shop and a Methodist Church." The Beet home on Mountain Avenue was typical of the farmhouses that dotted that street.

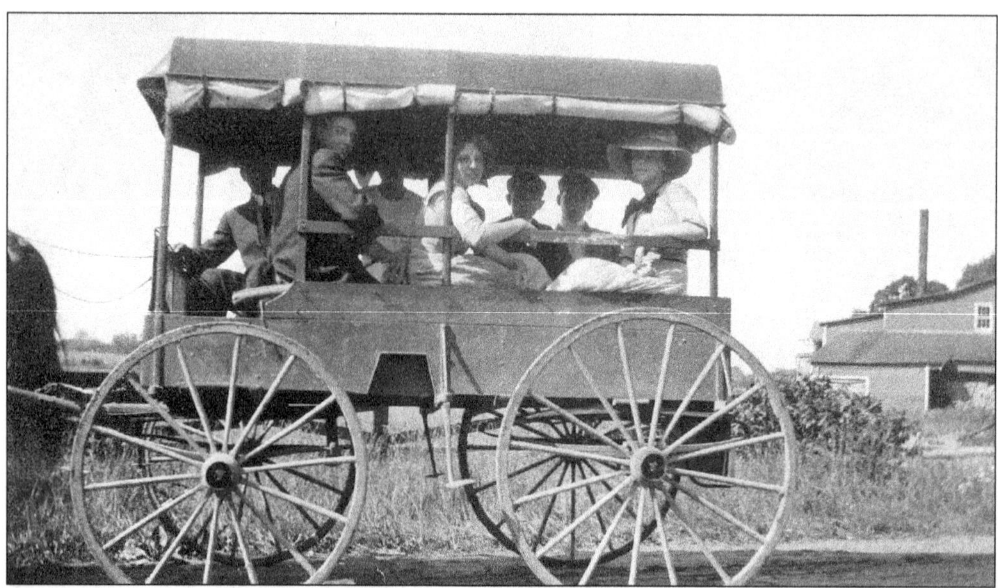

A horse-drawn coach like this one—used to take children on a Sunday school outing *c.* 1915—was also used to transport students to and from schools. There were few automobiles in Warren until the twenties, and paved roads were a rarity until the forties.

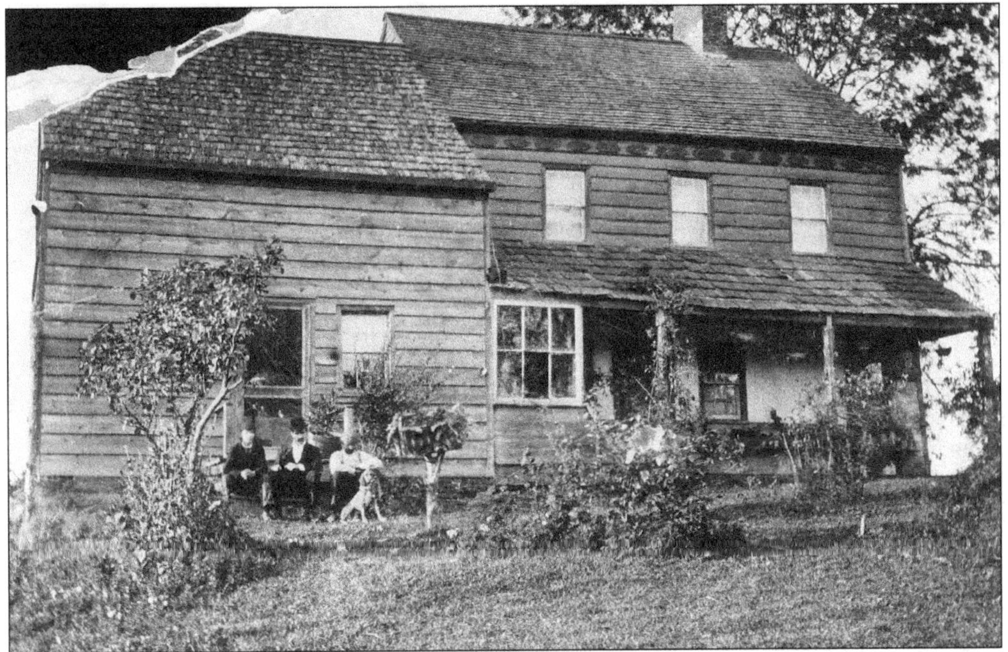

The Tucker house still stands at 51 Mountain Avenue, a mile or so west of Union Village. Built about 1800, probably by John Tucker, the home passed to John's son, Joseph (who held Methodist services here until the church was built) , and later, to the Sage family. Nearby is the Tucker family cemetery, a small patch of woods that holds the remains of Union Village's pioneers.

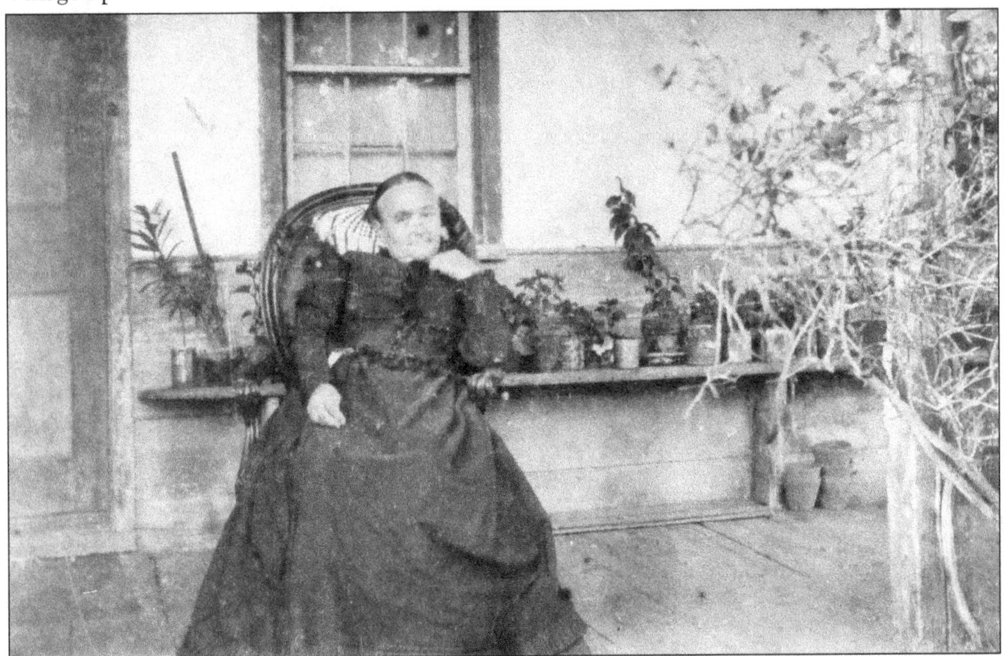

Charles and Mary Sage moved to Warren in 1878, buying the Tucker place. Their sons Edmund and Frederick occupied the home after their parents died. Mary E. Sage (1837-1907), whose hobby was clearly gardening, poses on her front porch in this turn-of-the-century photograph.

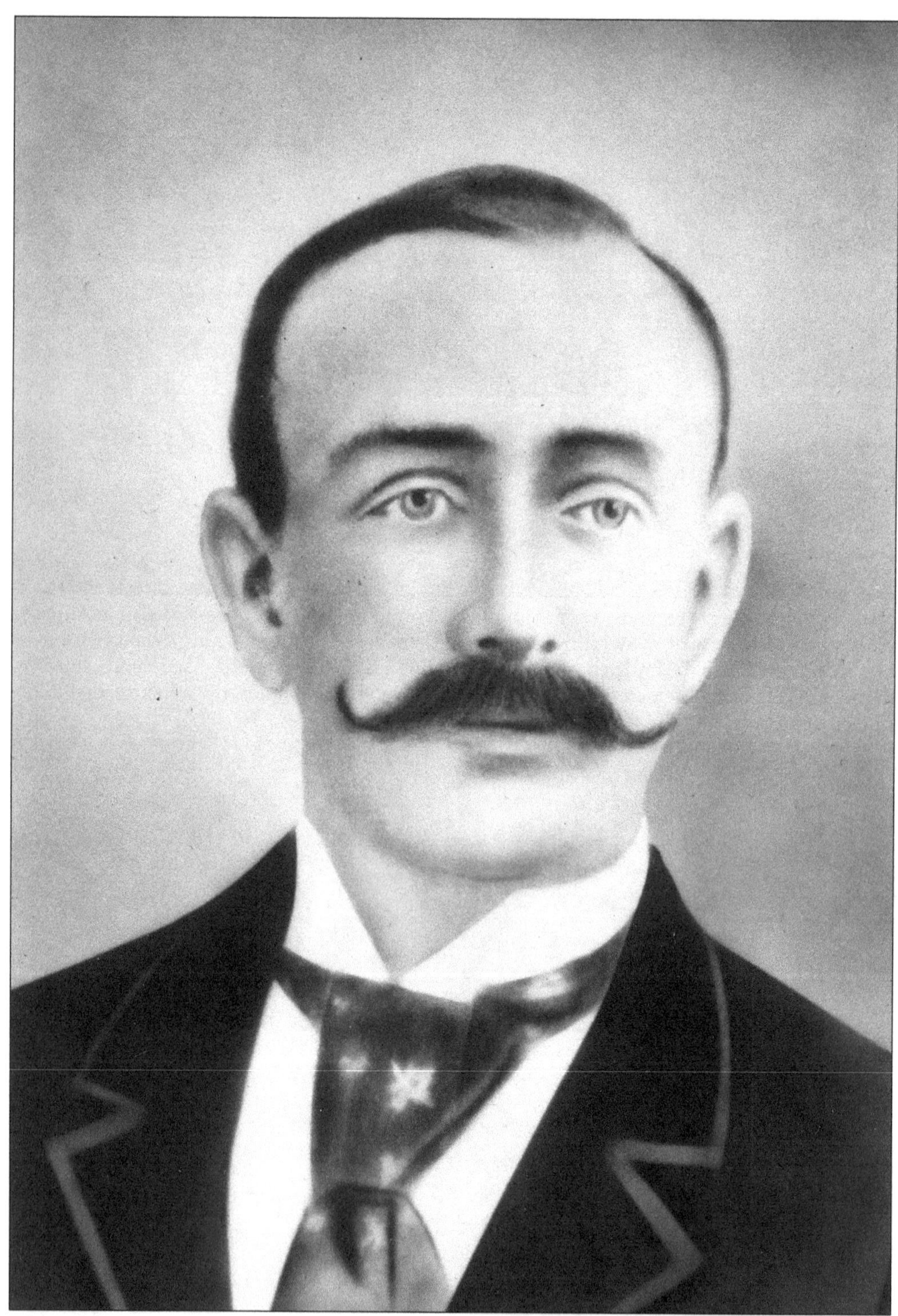

Edmund E. Sage (1871-1944) was a graduate of the Trenton State Normal School. Hired to teach at the South Stirling School in 1901 for the princely sum of $35 per year, he served as supervisor of schools from 1911 to 1916, and later as township tax assessor.

Two

Smalleytown/ South Stirling

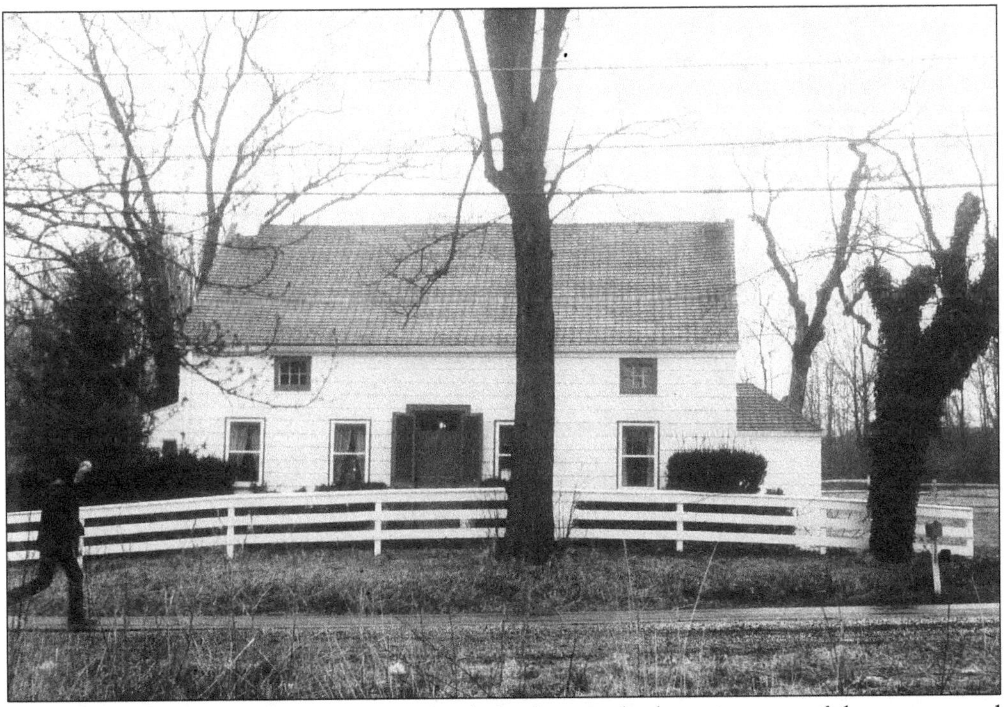

Smalleytown, more recently known as South Stirling, is the historic name of the area around the intersection of Mountain Avenue and Stirling Road. During the late eighteenth and early nineteenth centuries, members of the Smalley family owned most of the land thereabouts. The Smalley-Wormser house, at 84 Mountain Avenue, the only privately-owned structure in Warren on the State and National Registers of Historic Places, was built *c.* 1775 by David Smalley, a captain in the Revolution. Bartholomew Wormser bought it in 1847, doubling it in size a few years later. Indoor plumbing arrived in 1946.

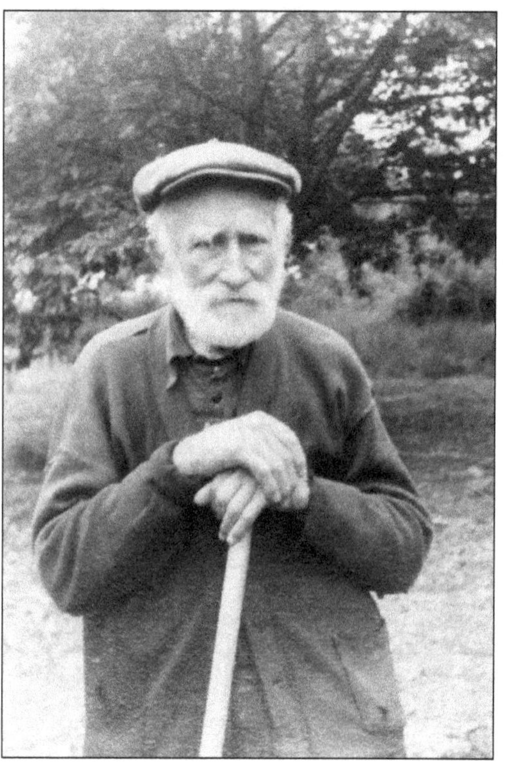

Bartholomew Wormser (1847-1938) was born the year his parents bought the Smalley house and farm. A farmer like his father before him, Wormser also operated a quarry near his Mountain Avenue property, using an ox cart to draw stones to nearby building projects.

Warren's land values remained depressed throughout the nineteenth century. Wormser's 38 acres were valued at $1,000 and taxed at $15.90 in 1885. For working on the roads near his home, Wormser received a tax credit of $1.25.

THE PERCENTAGE IS $10.80 TO THE $1,000.

PLEASE PRESENT THIS NOTICE WHEN YOU PAY YOUR TAX.

TAXES FOR 1885 IN WARREN TOWNSHIP.

Mr Bartholomew Wormser Jr.

Your Taxes for the year 1885 are now due and payable to me on or before the 20th day of December next. If not paid then, they will be returned to a Justice of the Peace, and 12 per cent. interest added.

Number of Acres.	*Valuation of Real Estate.*		
38	$ 1000	*Poll Tax,*	$ 1.00
		Dog Tax,	.72
		County Tax,	3.78
Valuation of Personal Property,	$ 50	*Township Tax,*	2.94
Mortgages,	$	*School Tax,*	1.57
Total Valuation,	$	*Poor Tax,*	3.05
Deduction,	$	*Road Tax,*	2.84
		Special School Tax,	
Amount Taxed for,	$ 1050	*Whole amount of Tax,*	$ 15.90
Received Payment,		*Cr. for work on Road Deducted,*	1 25
George Terrell *Collector.*		*Amount Due,*	$14.65

N. B.—The Commissioners of Appeal, in cases of taxation, will meet at Mt. Bethel Hotel on the Fourth Tuesday of November next, at 10 A. M.

For the convenience of Tax Payers, I will be at Mt. Bethel Hotel to receive taxes on Tuesday, December 8, 1885, from 10 A. M. to 3 P. M. At Bornman's Store on Thursday, December 10, 1885. At David E. Mundy's Store on Saturday, December 12, 1885. At Mt. Bethel Hotel, Saturday, December 19, 1885.

All taxes on real estate not paid by Feb. 1, 1886, will be returned to the County Clerk's Office, as required by law, and remain a first lien upon the property assessed.

GEORGE TERRELL, *Collector.*

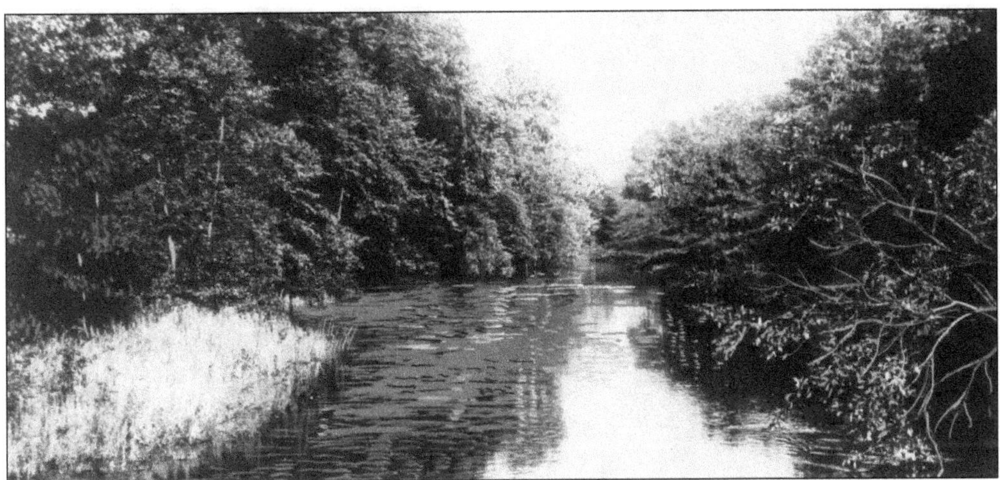

The Passaic River, seen here in 1920, borders Union Village on the north. The township's lowest elevation is found at the point where the river flows into Berkeley Heights. Its loftiest point is nearly 7 miles away, at the top of the 580-foot mountain opposite Dock Watch Hollow quarry.

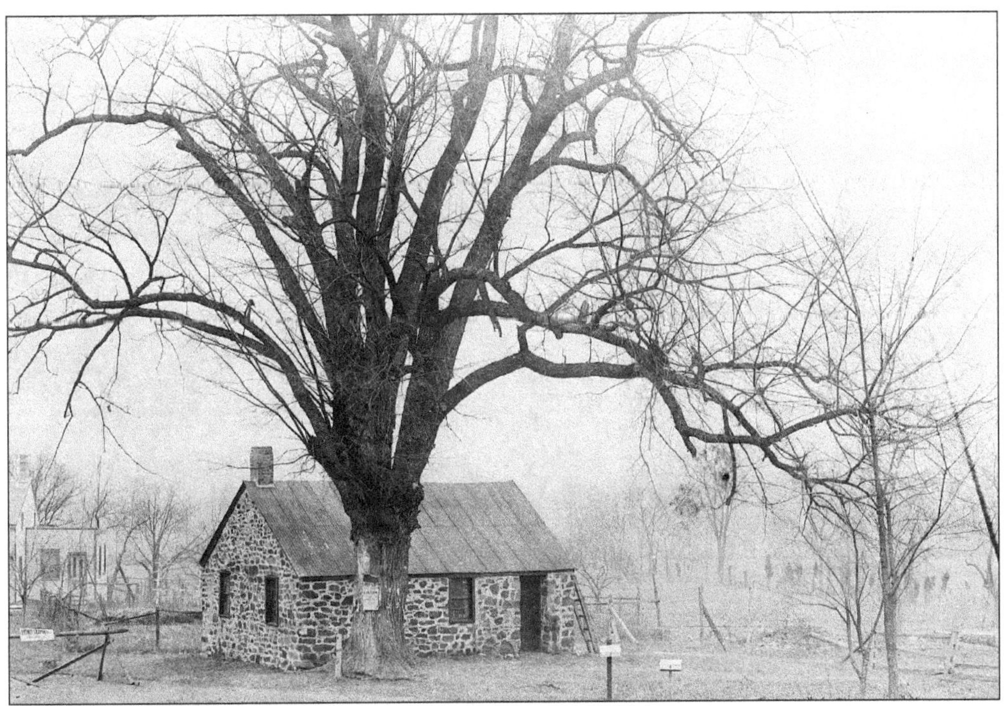

The old Smalleytown School was built of fieldstone *c.* 1800. The large elm shown in this *c.* 1900 view was planted as "guardian" of the pupils who studied there in 1842, the year the township acquired the land. The structure to the left was a stagecoach stop *c.* 1790.

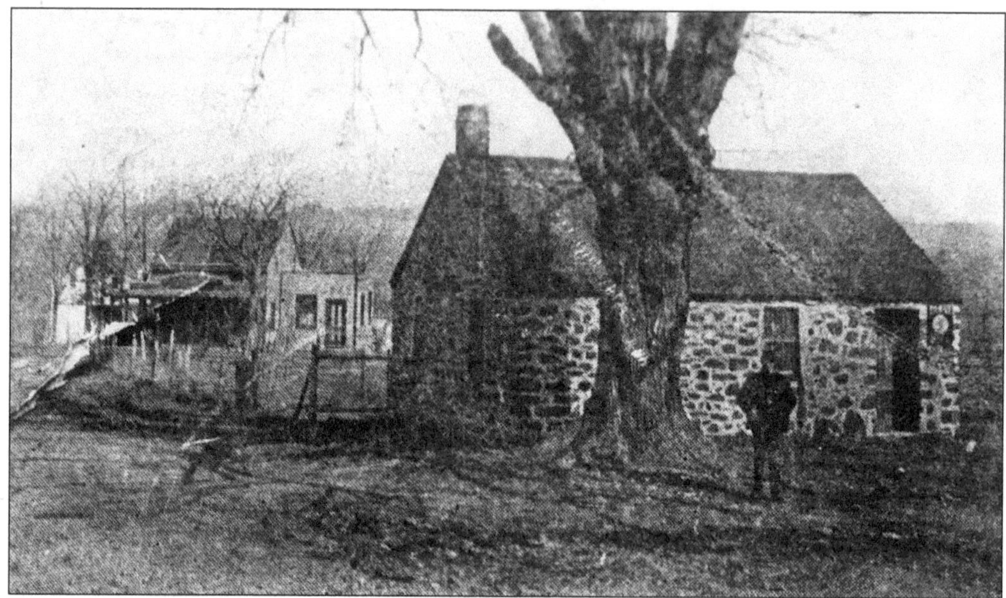

During the 1870s and 1880s, the Reverend David D. Smalley III taught forty pupils in this one-room schoolhouse. Closed in 1885, the building was a private home until it was removed in 1976 to Olde Towne Village in Piscataway.

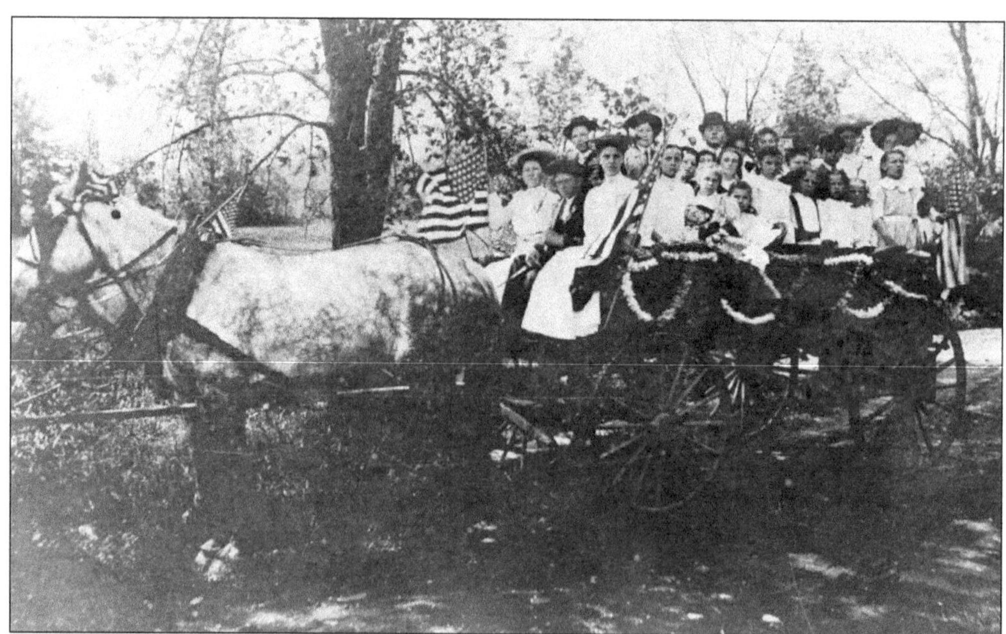

South Stirling students, dressed in their finest, prepare for a July 4th outing in this turn-of-the-century photograph. Their parents were farmers and dairymen, many of them working farms their parents and grandparents had worked before them.

The South Stirling School replaced the old stone schoolhouse in 1885. There was a school in Warren before the Revolution, but not until 1829 were taxes raised to support education. That year $86 was spent for school purposes. Tuition was $1 per student per quarter until 1846 when free public school education became the law.

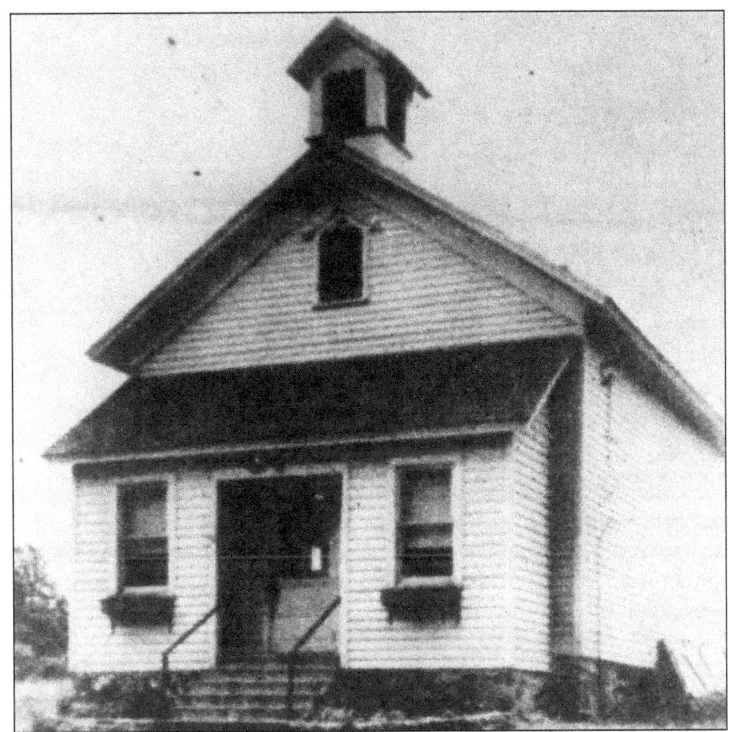

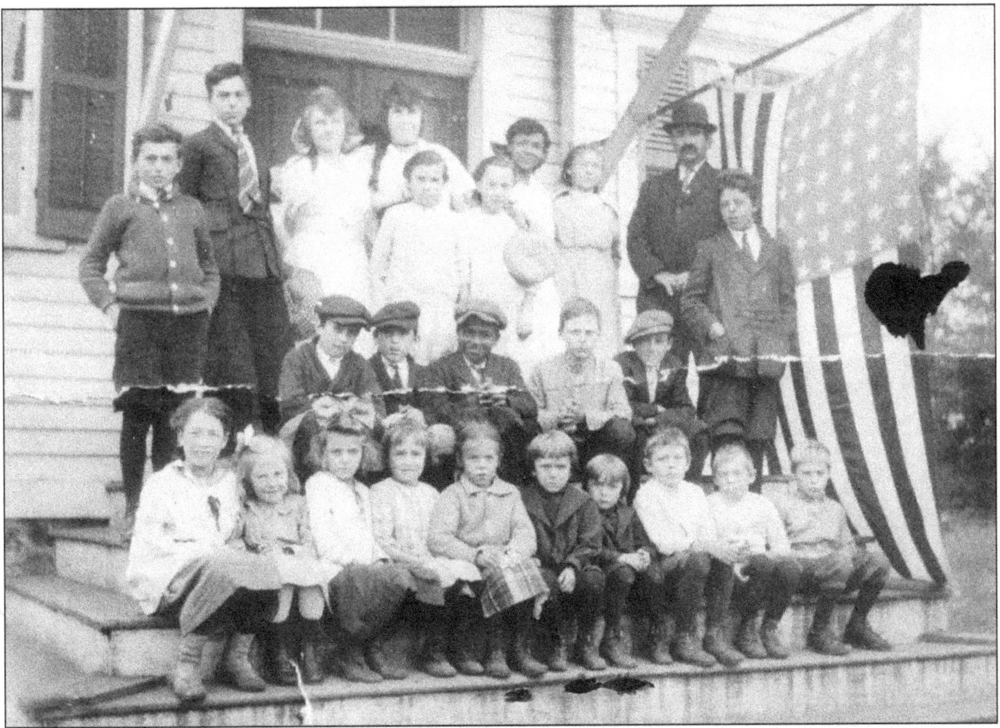

Edmund E. Sage taught grades one through eight at the South Stirling School when this 1917 picture was snapped. Students included George, May, Edmund, and Willis Sage; Sarah, Anna, Tony, and Hilda Arrighi; Bill Frank; and James and Mary Stiles.

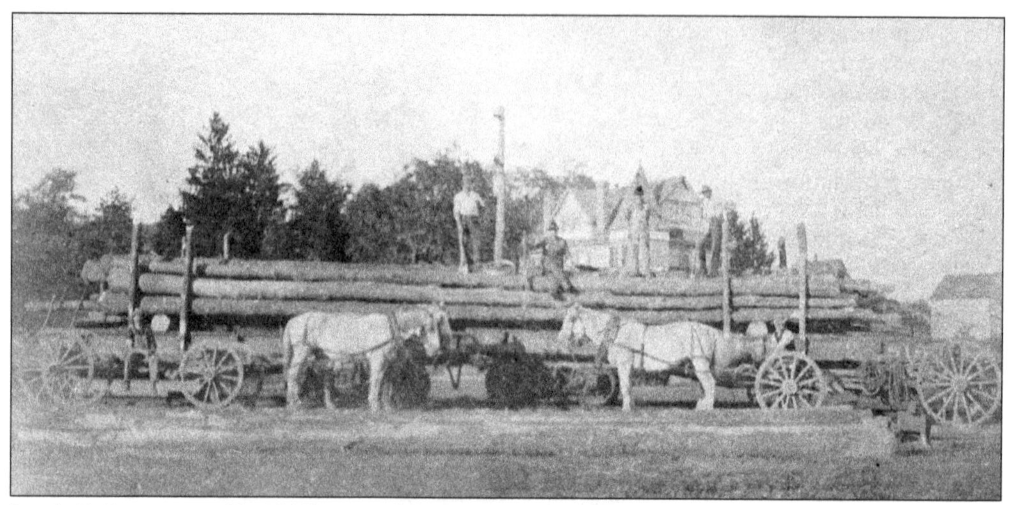

Jacob E. Reinmann (d. 1911) owned 88 acres on Reinman Road west of Smalleytown where he grew corn, oats, and buckwheat and cultivated apples, pears, and peaches. He also hauled timber from Warren to railroad flat cars in Millington. Transported to New York City, the poles were used to build the city's piers.

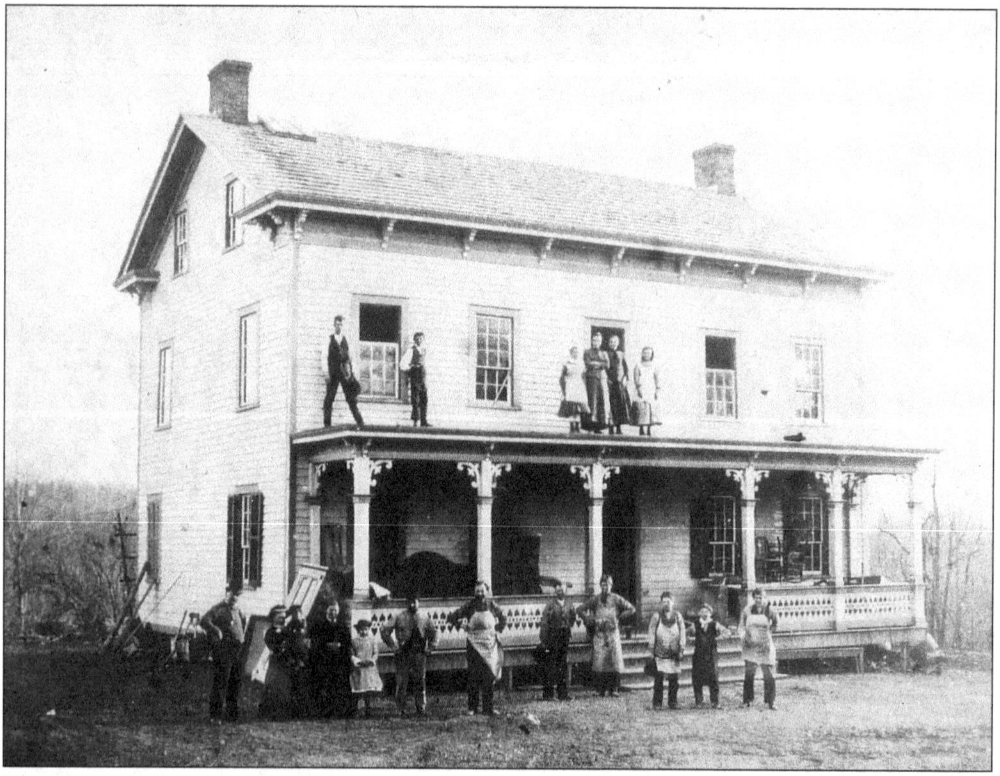

The Casenove house, pictured here on what appears to be moving day, c. 1890, stood proudly on Reinman Road midway between Cory's Brook and Old Stirling Road. A summer boarding house and sometime flower pip factory, the house and its 53 acres were acquired by the Grundel and Cazeneuve families in 1876.

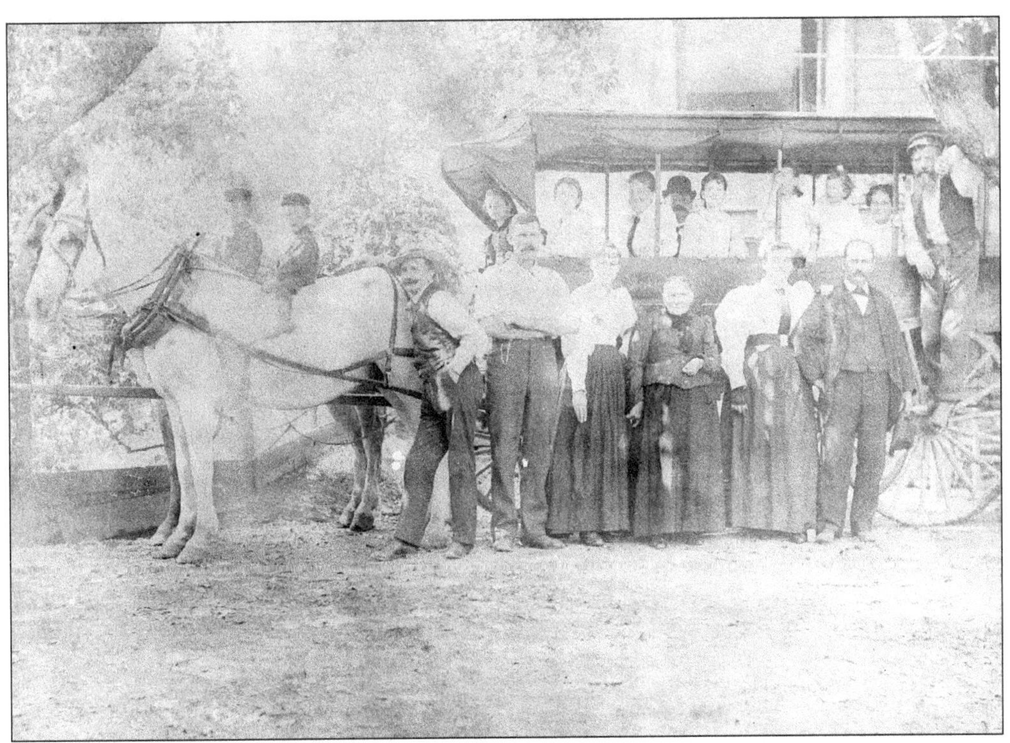

Besides hauling logs to Millington, Jacob Reinmann ran a stagecoach that brought summer boarders to Warren from the railroad depot in Plainfield. Reinmann's property was sold in 1928 and divided into building lots. Plainfield Gardens is the name of his farm today.

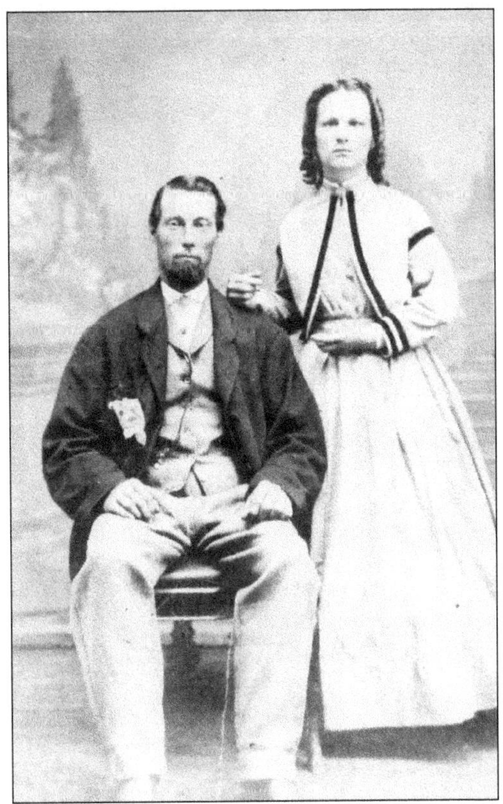

Jonathan Willet (1735-1811) built one of Warren's first sawmills on Cory's Brook prior to the Revolution. His son, Thomas (1759-1831), operated it until his death. Lewis Willet and his wife, Sarah, pictured here *c.* 1860, farmed near Reinman Road.

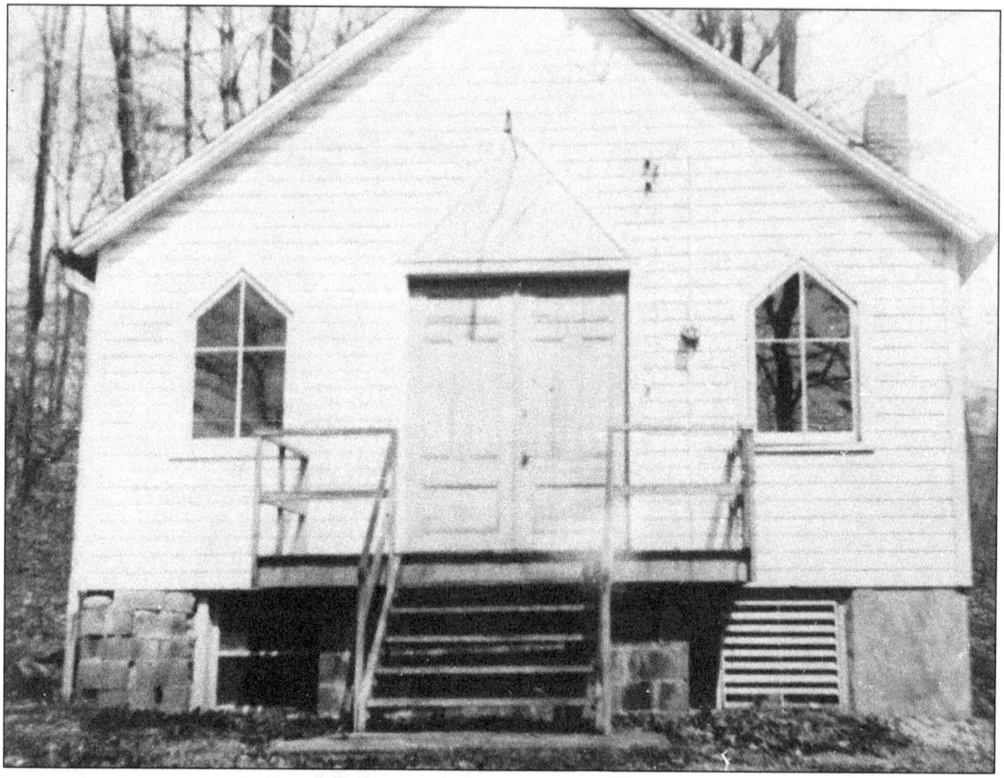

The South Stirling Chapel on Reinman Road was built in 1934 for $450 using second-hand lumber. The tiny building, now a private home, was home to the Ascension Lutheran Church, a congregation founded in 1932 by Reverend Joseph E. Bergquist.

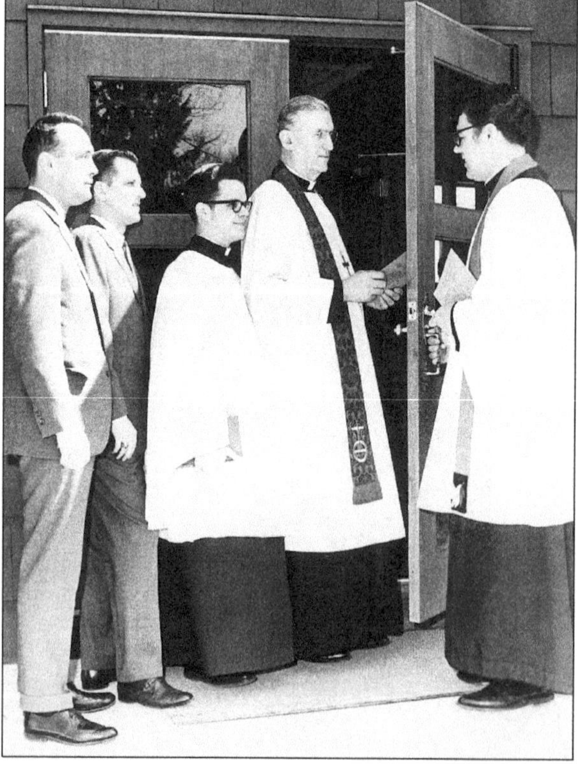

Ascension, by now known as Epiphany Lutheran, dedicated its new home on the corner of Mountain Avenue and Stirling Road on April 13, 1969. From left to right are: Walter Townsend, Charles Herman, Frederick Persiko, Dr. Edwin Knudten (president of the New Jersey Synod), and Nils Johnson (pastor). In 1996 the church was renamed Advent Lutheran when it merged with another congregation.

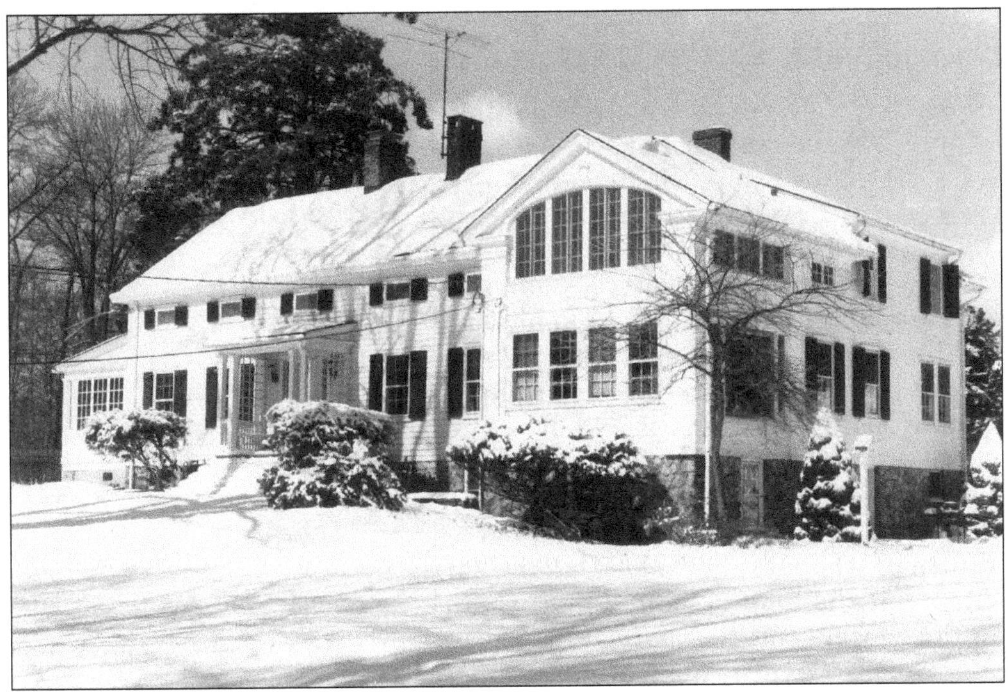

Jonathan and Sarah Ruckman lived in this fine house at the corner of Old Smalleytown and Stirling Roads built at the time of the Revolution in an area once known as Jenkinstown. Jonathan Ruckman died in 1835. The 100-acre farm was sold to the Moore family in 1850. The original part of the house is to the left.

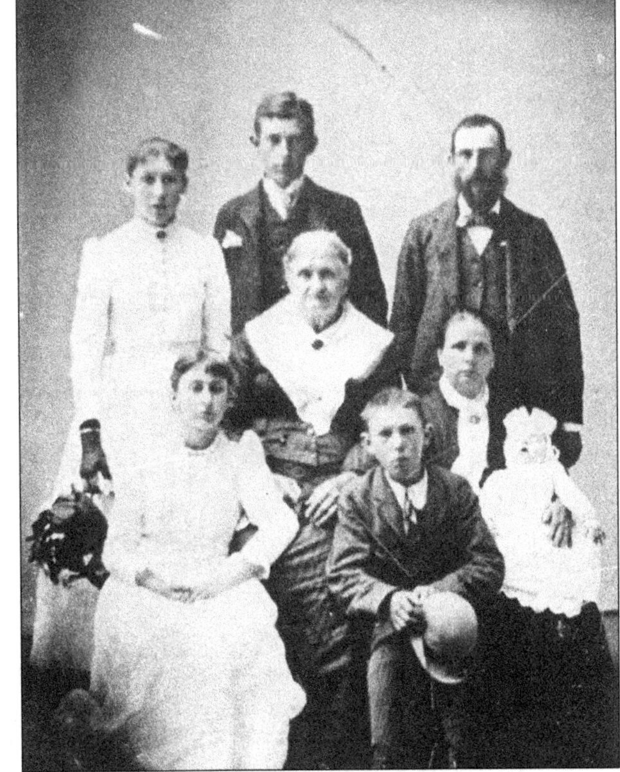

Isaac T. Moore and his wife, their son David, daughter Rhoda (who married Frank Stiles), daughter Belle, and son-in-law Frank Marsh pose proudly in this c. 1880 portrait. A well-to-do farmer, Moore lived in the old Ruckman house.

$20 Reward!

STOLEN from the stable of the subscriber, in Warren township, Somerset county, New-Jersey, on the night of the 15th inst. a deep BROWN MARE, nearly 4 years old, about 14 hands 3 inches high; had the mark of being galled by a saddle, another by the breeching of the harness, and on her rump a spot of white hair; she is a likely creature, with long switch tail, and carries herself well. The above reward will be given for the detection of the thief & return of the mare, or *Ten Dollars* for either, if the thief is lodged in any jail in the State, and the mare returned to Mr. Cory's Tavern, near Mount Bethel meeting-house.

WILLIAM RUCKMAN.

January 16, 1826. 3w*

Horse thievery was a major crime in the nineteenth century when such animals played a vital role in farming and transportation. The $20 reward William Ruckman offered in 1826 would be nearly $1,000 in today's economy.

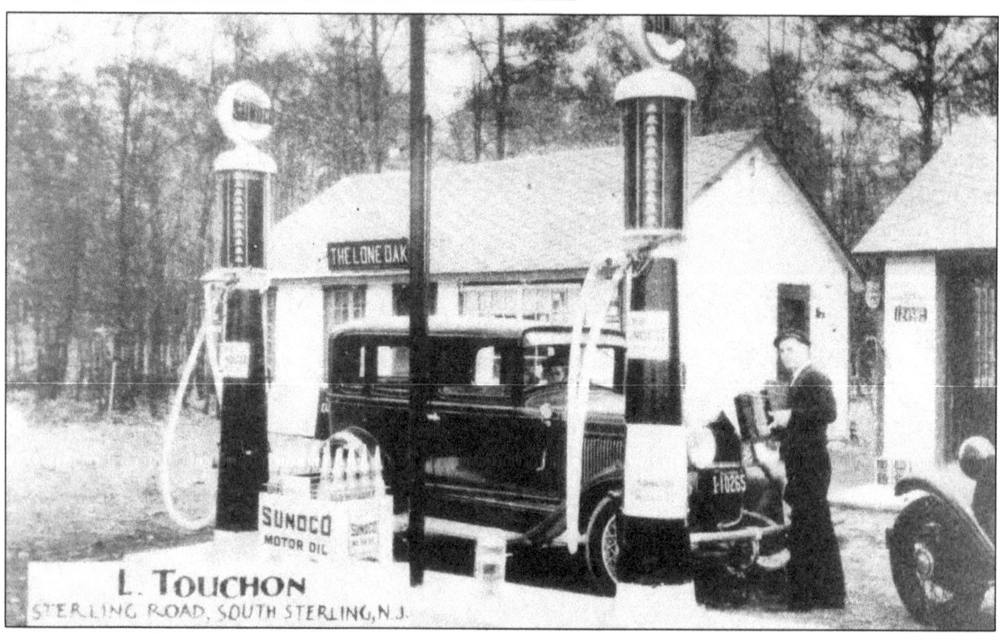

South on Stirling Road from the Ruckman house stood Leon Touchon's The Lone Oak, a general store and gas station he opened in the 1930s. The general store took on a second life in the 1940s when it became Touchon's Bar & Grill, a popular watering spot for many years. Rolf's Restaurant later occupied the site.

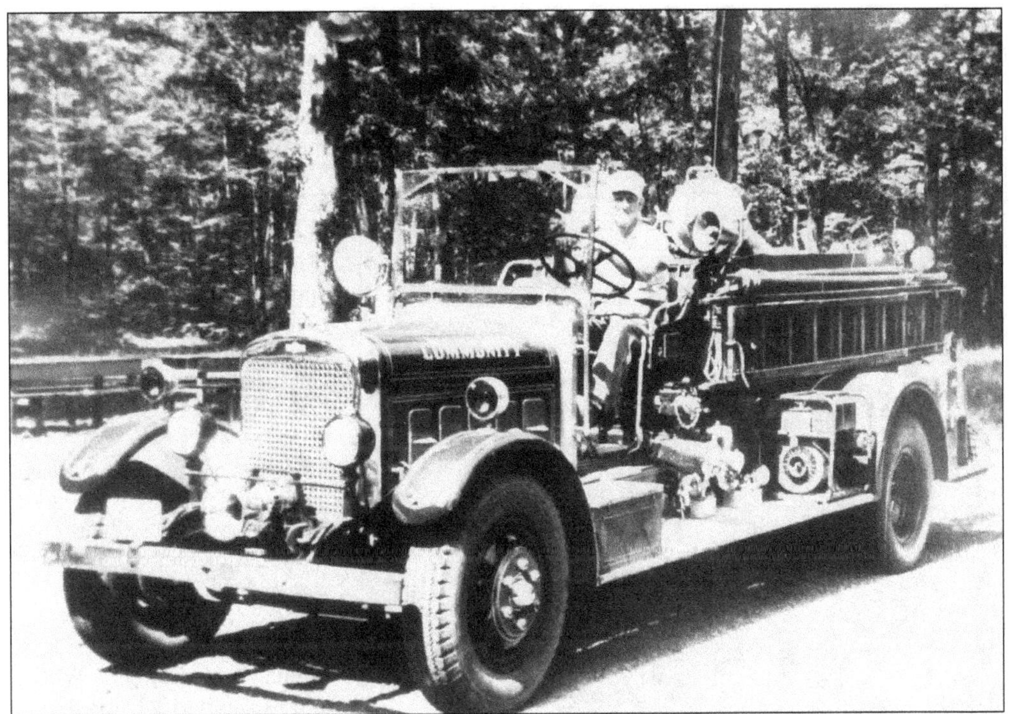

Community Volunteer Fire Company No. 3 was organized in 1940 with forty-nine charter members. In the early days, the volunteers fought mostly chicken-coop fires. The company's present firehouse on Community Place was built on land donated by Leon and Mary Touchon in 1945. Here, Chief Randy Phillips poses atop a 1930s Pirsch.

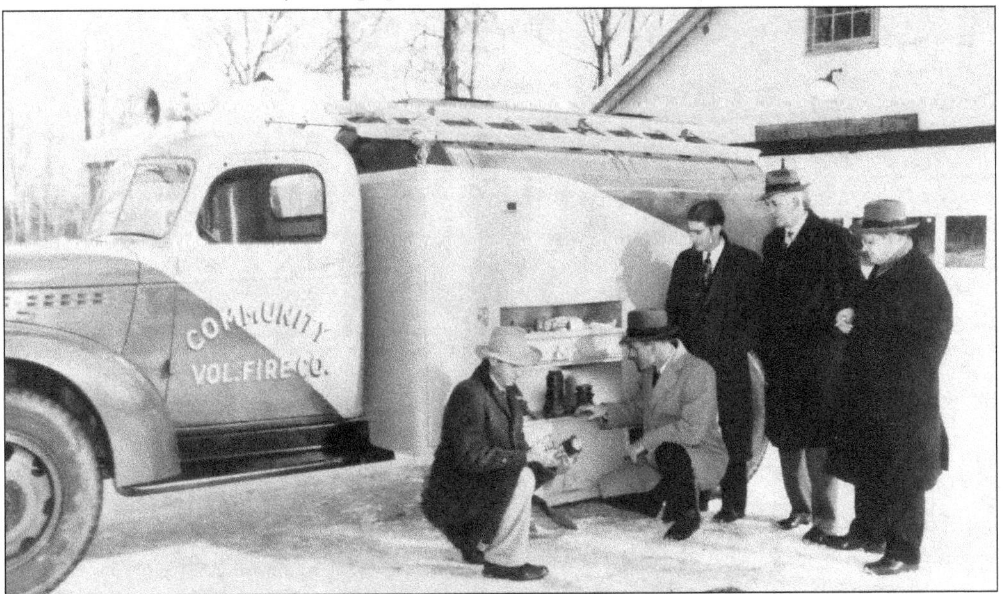

In June 1963 the Mount Bethel, Mount Horeb, and Community fire companies were consolidated into a township-wide fire department. The first township chief was Arthur Helmstetter of Community, serving from 1963-1977. His successor, also from Community, was Richard Streeton, chief for twelve years.

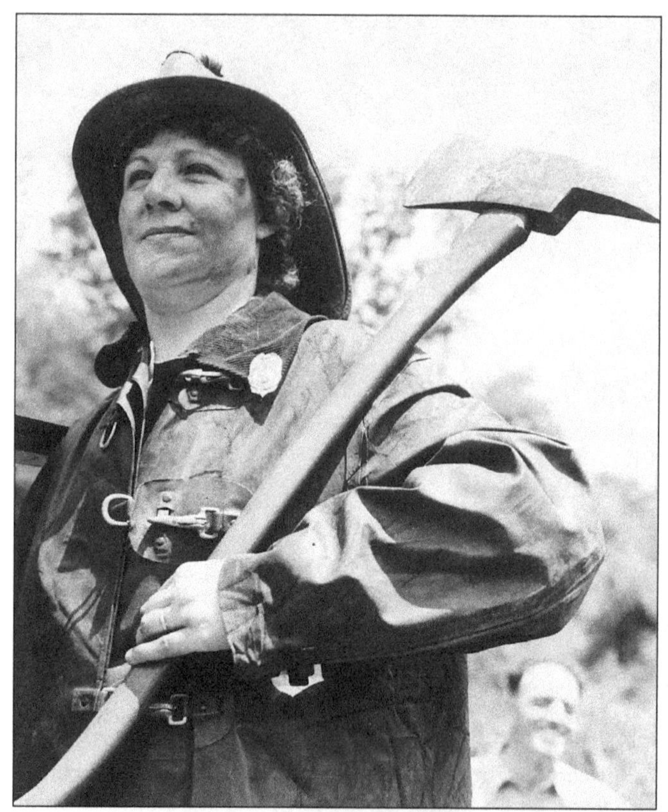

In the spring of 1943, twenty-seven women, all married and most the mothers of young children, became members of the Auxiliary Volunteer Fire Department. With many township men in military service, the women "cast off their aprons and house dresses" to help protect the township. Mrs. Raymond Zorn (pictured here) was chief.

Members of the Community auxiliary department included Mrs. Thomas Faust, Jean Quilty, Mrs. Henry Lawler, Betty McMurtry, Evelyn Agnew, Mary Touchon, Pearl Saffron, Sally Riker, Emma Baumann, Lena Wells, and Mrs. Charles Durlack. "Whenever a siren blows, everyone goes," Chief Zorn told inquiring reporters.

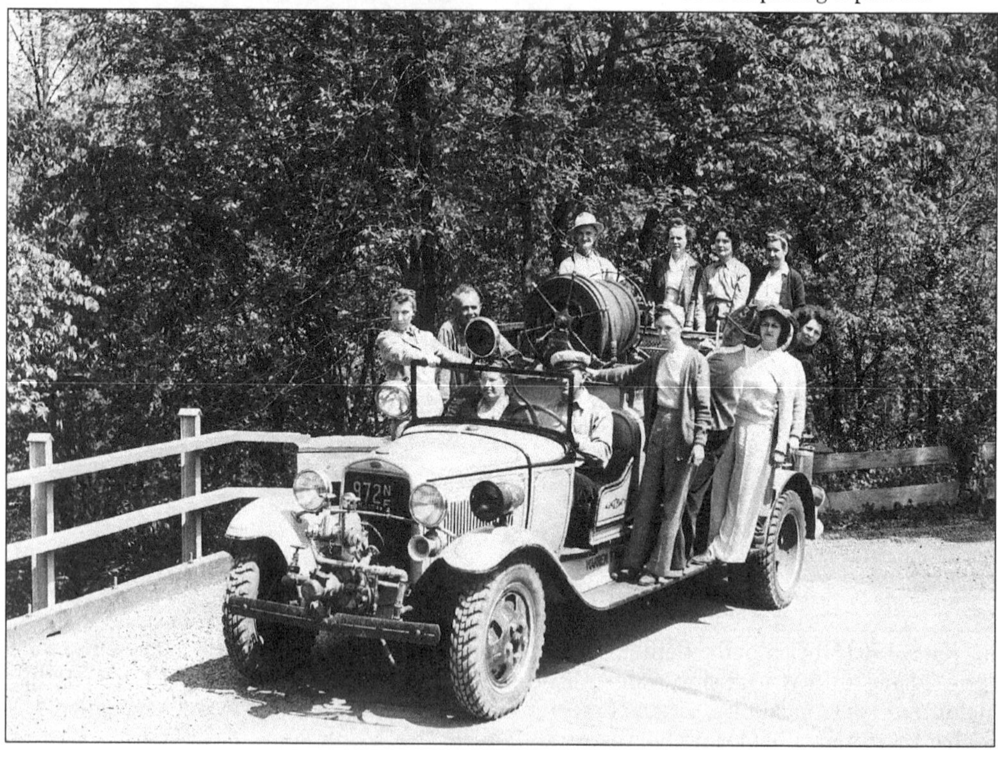

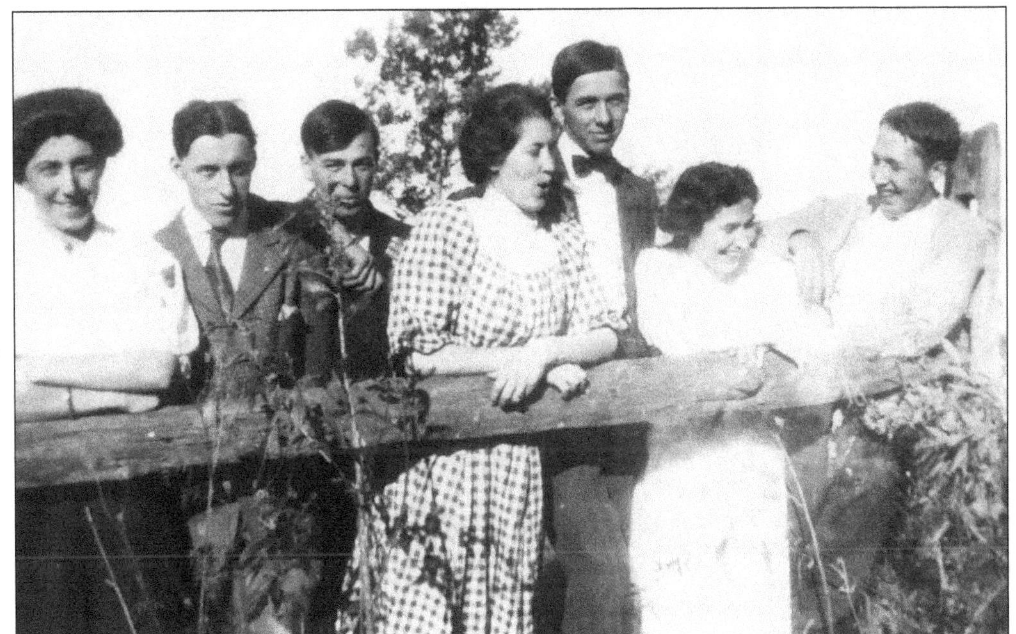

Life in Warren moved at a slower beat than it did in such places as Plainfield and Somerville. Many young people left the farms for the opportunities offered in nearby cities. Those that stayed found amusement in church socials, square dances held at the Grange or Junior Order Hall. Hayrides in summer—like this one *c.* 1917—and bobsledding in winter offered a chance to meet others of similar age.

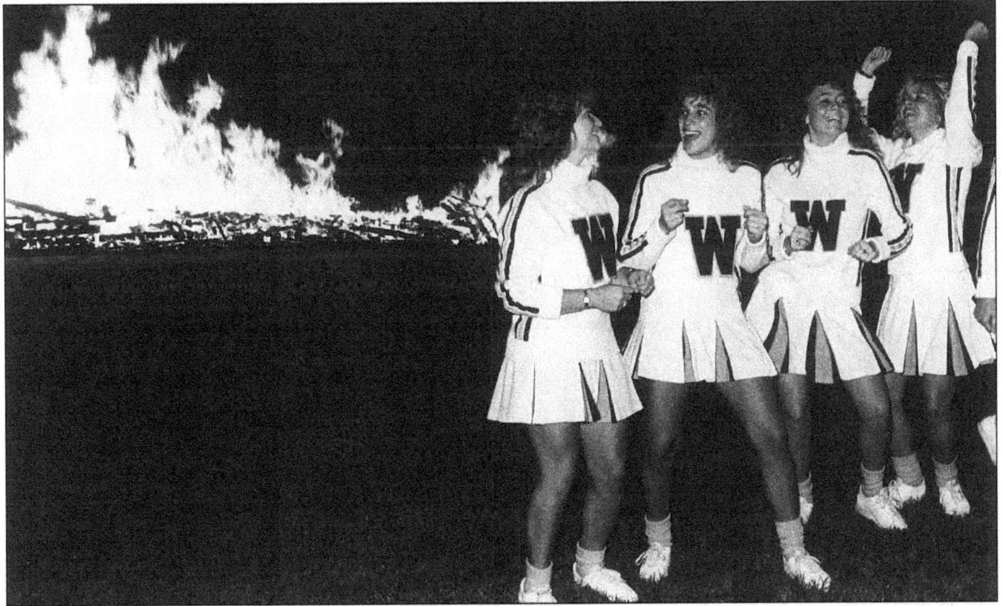

Until 1957, the year Watchung Hills Regional High School opened, Warren students attended North Plainfield or Bernards High School. The regional school's first principal, Dr. A. Gordon Peterkin, lost no time in announcing a dress code that prohibited slacks and shorts for girls and long shaggy hair on boys. In this 1987 photograph, Warrior cheerleaders lead the traditional fall pep rally.

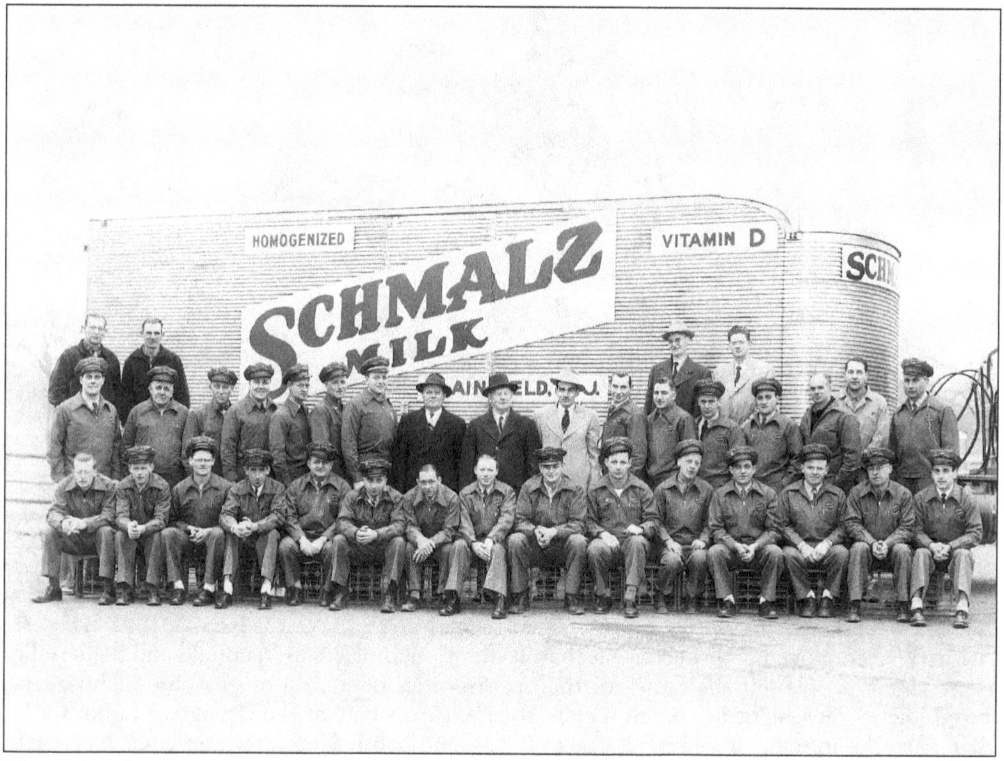

The Schmalz Dairy Farm occupied the northeast and southeast corners of Stirling Road and Mountain Avenue from 1916, when Edward, Henry, Frederick, and John Schmalz came here from Hoboken. A spectacular fire in 1950 destroyed the familiar red barns, but thirty-three cattle were herded to safety.

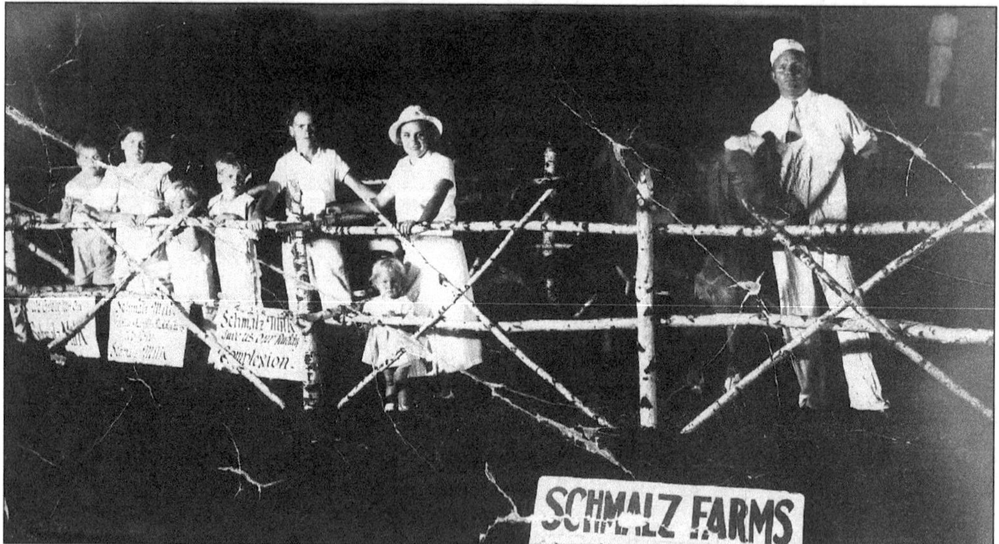

A nighttime parade in 1933/34 featured a Schmalz Farms float starring Farrell family members (as shown here from left to right) Richard, Doralu, William, John, Thomas, Margaret, and Mary. Henry Bell stands to the right of the cow. One of the signs proclaims: "Schmalz Milk Produces Healthy Ruddy Cheeks. We Love Schmalz Milk."

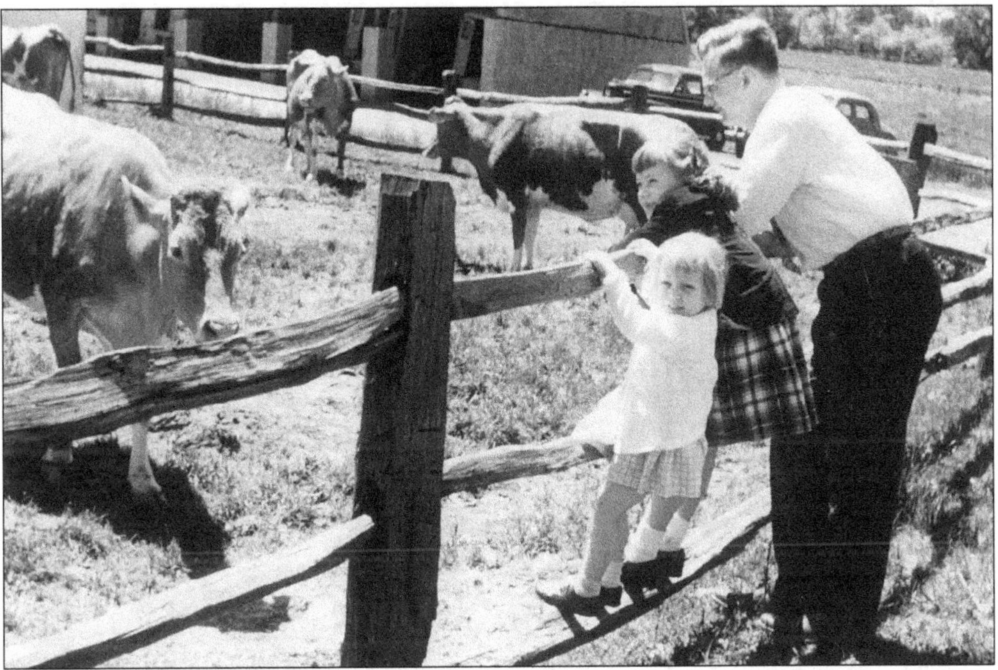

The Schmalz farm closed soon after the 1950 fire, making way for the regional high school. There were still a few cows left in 1956 when Carol, Beverly, and Warren Gerken, newcomers to Warren, paid a visit.

WARREN TOWNSHIP SCHOOL ELECTION

FEBRUARY 11, 1947

CENTRAL SCHOOL

5 - 9 P.M.

VOTE FOR THOSE THAT SPONSOR:

1. A BIGGER AND BETTER SCHOOL
Plans for new addition have been approved by the State.

2. A COMPETENT STAFF OF TEACHERS
During the most chaotic times in the history of American education an outstanding faculty has been retained.

3. AN ECONOMICAL ADMINISTRATION
Percentage increase in this year's BUDGET one of the lowest in Area. —VOTE FOR IT—

4. WHOLEHEARTED CO-OPERATION
Among Teachers, Principal, Parents and the Board.

VOTE FOR

PRESIDENT-WILLIAM B. J. REITZE
100% Attendance for 20 years.

ELLIOTT VAN DEUSEN
An outstanding Board Member with children in the School.

ORVILLE VOORHEES
A veteran Board Member with 6 years experience.

ZOIA HORN (MRS.)
Our Librarian and a very promising addition to the Board.

Paid for by Candidates.

After the South Stirling School closed, students from the area attended Central School on Mount Bethel Road. School centralization did much to rob Warren's villages of their unique characters.

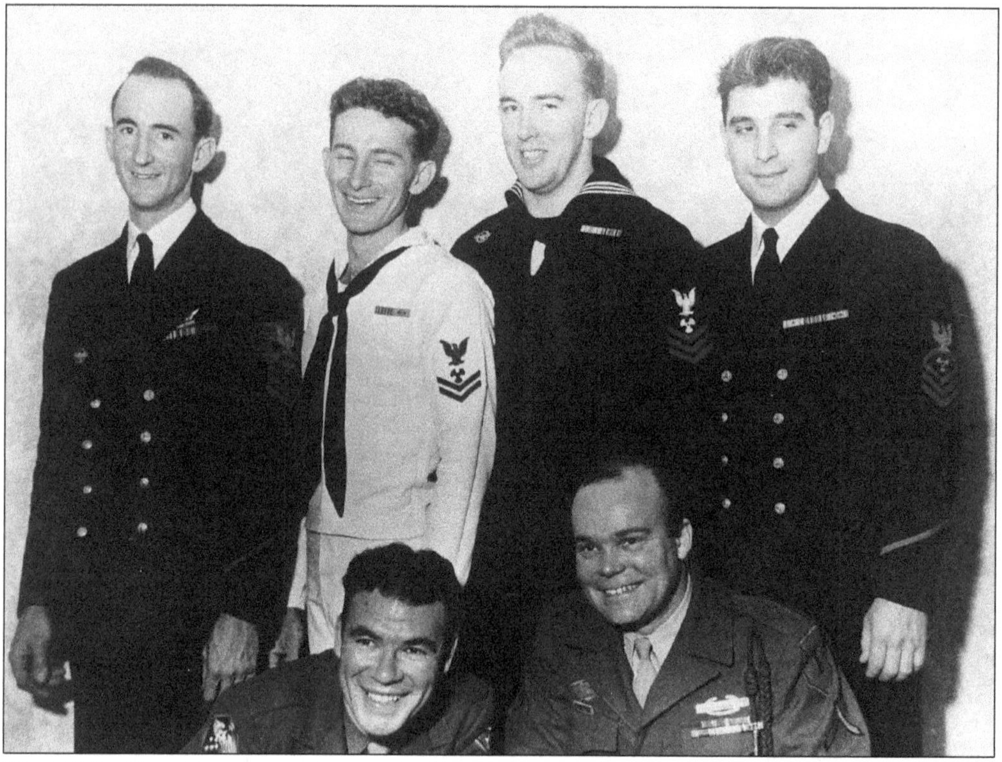

World War II and its aftermath created a burgeoning population in Warren as veterans returned home to start families and resume civilian life. In February 1949, six pals don their uniforms for a final reunion. From left to right are: (front row) Charles McConnell and William Bird; (back row) Wilbur Yarrington, Carl Jonas, Warren Yarrington, and Michael Ferrovecchio. Bird and Jonas were from North Plainfield.

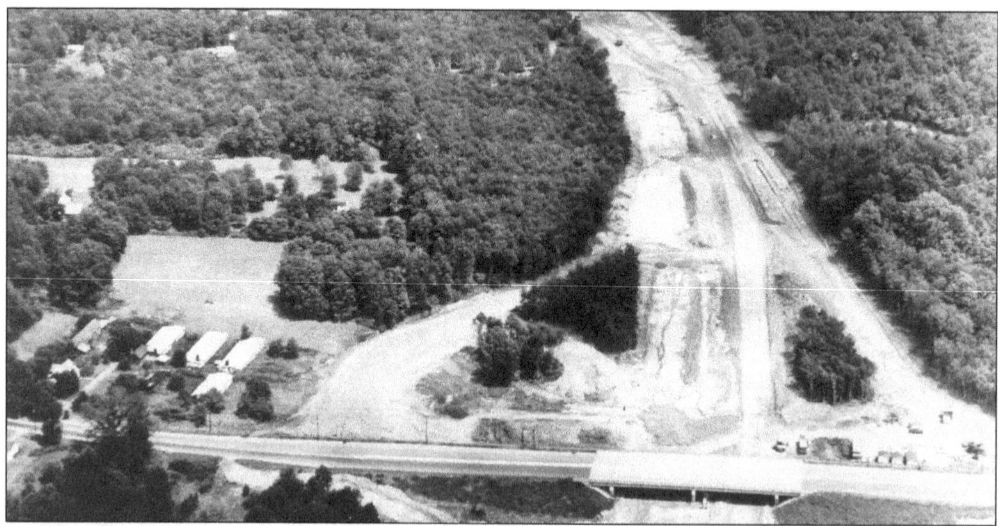

The construction of Route 78 (seen here looking east from Hillcrest Road) heralded the end of Warren's village life. Land purchases began in 1963. In 1968, clearance began on a 300-foot-wide strip that was 7 miles long. Said the local newspaper: "The changes are coming and we should be prepared."

Three

Mount Bethel

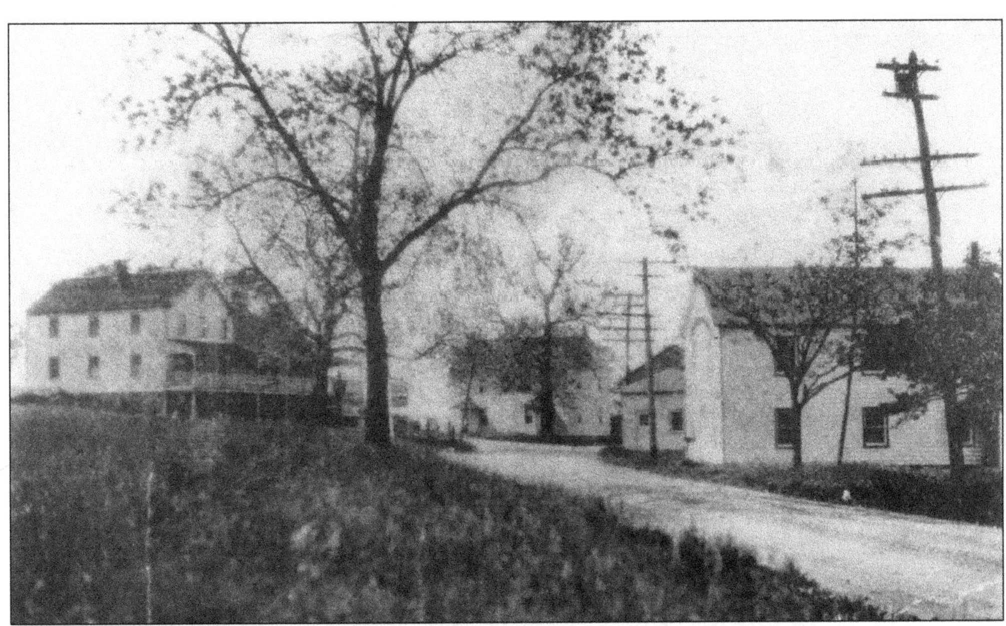

Settled before the American Revolution, Mount Bethel was the most densely-populated village in the township. This 1930s postcard shows, from left to right, the Villa Calosso, the Mount Bethel Baptist Meeting House, Mount Bethel Volunteer Fire Company's firehouse, and Fairview Hall, the home of Fairview Council No. 248, Junior Order, United American Mechanics. The general store is hidden behind the firehouse.

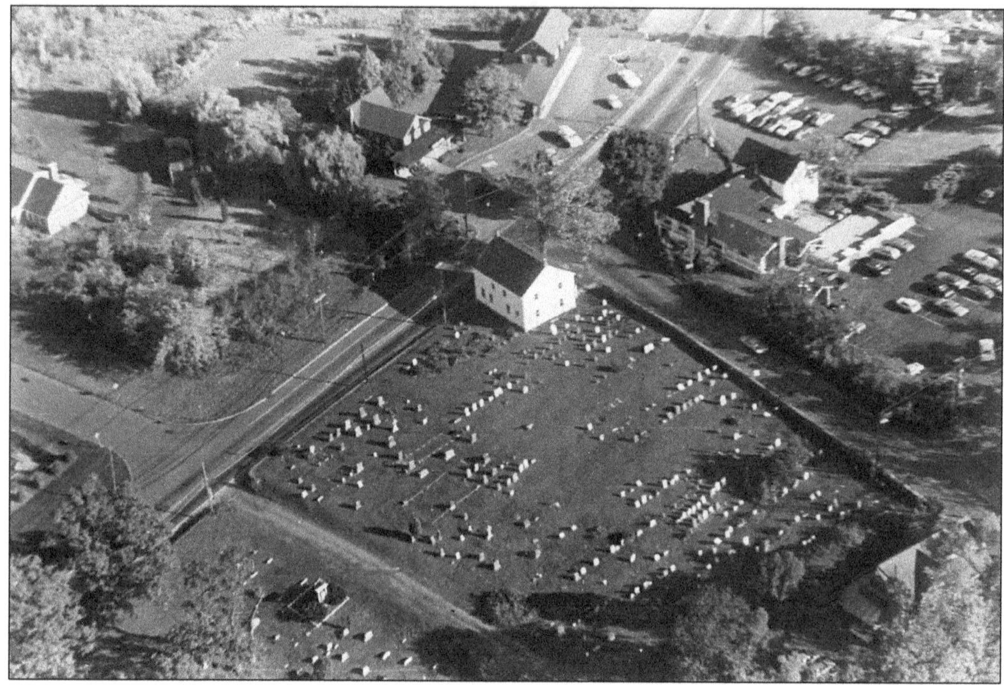

A 1982 aerial view of Mount Bethel shows the church, inn, general store, and Fairview Hall (both the store and the hall are now part of Mount Bethel Village, a shopping area), and the Baptist cemetery. At least six veterans of the Revolution are buried there.

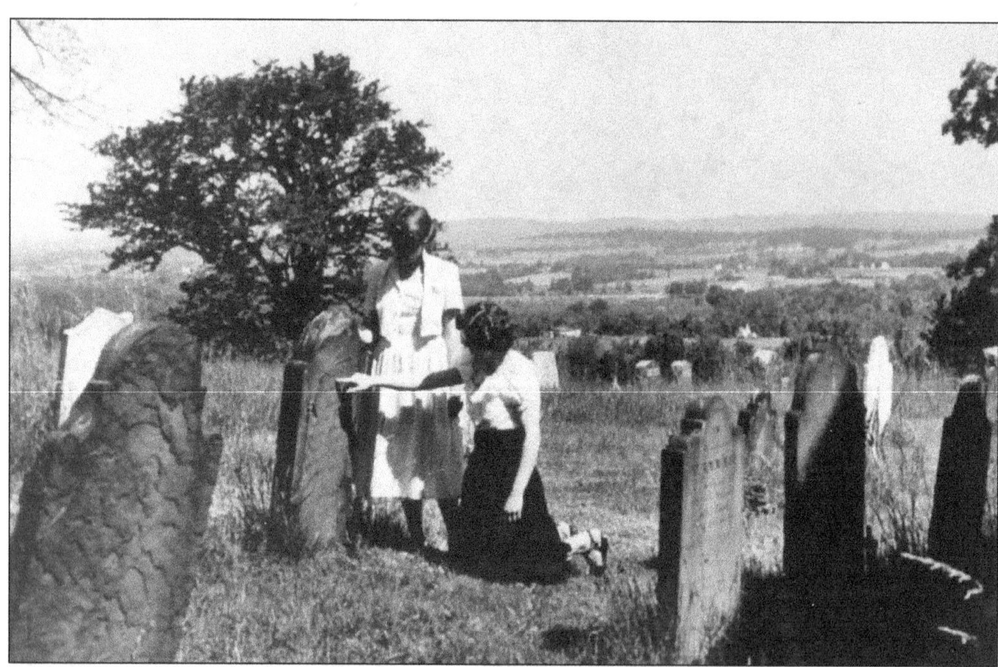

On Stony Hill overlooking the Passaic River valley, the cemetery has seen more than a thousand burials since Reverend Abner Sutton, Baptist pastor, was laid to rest in 1791. In 1950 when this photograph was taken, a newspaper reporter called Warren "the greenest place in New Jersey."

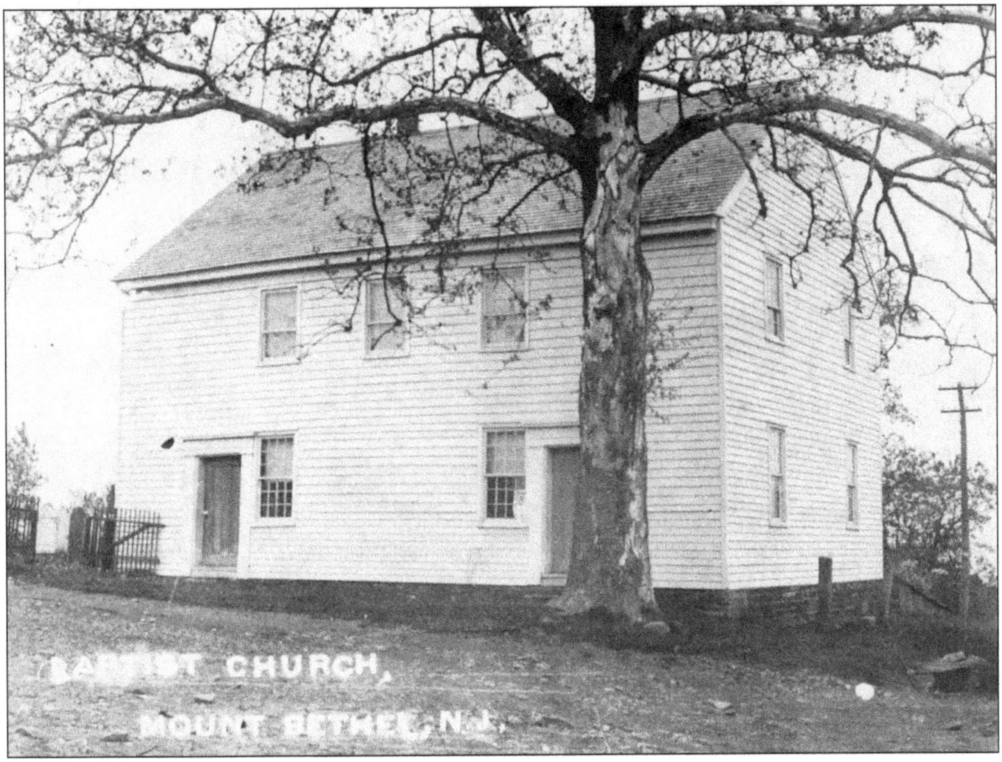

The Baptist Meeting House was built *c.* 1761 on the old Quibbletown Gap Road (now Old Church Road), then disassembled and moved to its present site in 1785. It is listed on the National Register of Historic Places.

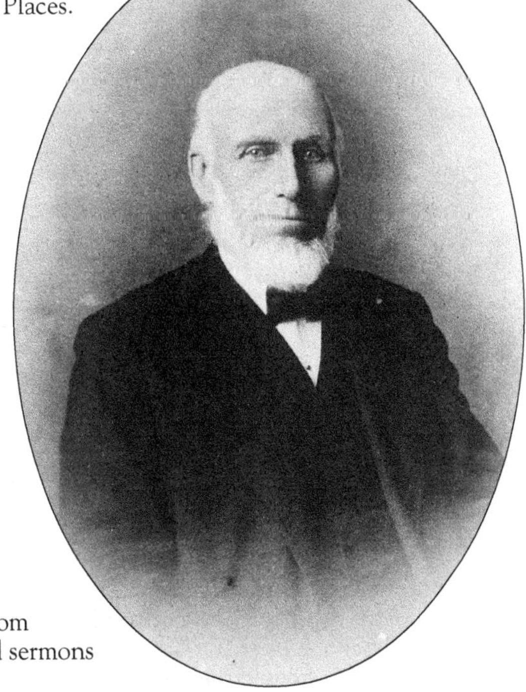

Reverend Peter Gibb (1835-1912), pastor from 1871 to 1911, preached nearly two thousand sermons during his years at Mount Bethel.

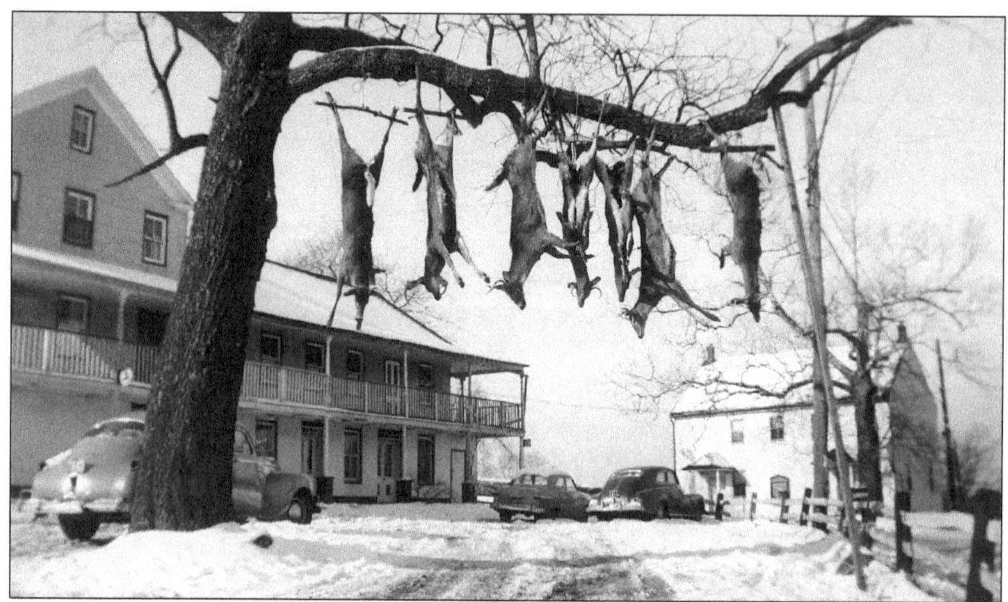

In the fall of 1947, township deer hunters strung up their game in front of Fred Zimmerman's Sans Souci. A raccoon and venison dinner at the Mount Bethel firehouse followed, cooked by Eddie DeFilippis.

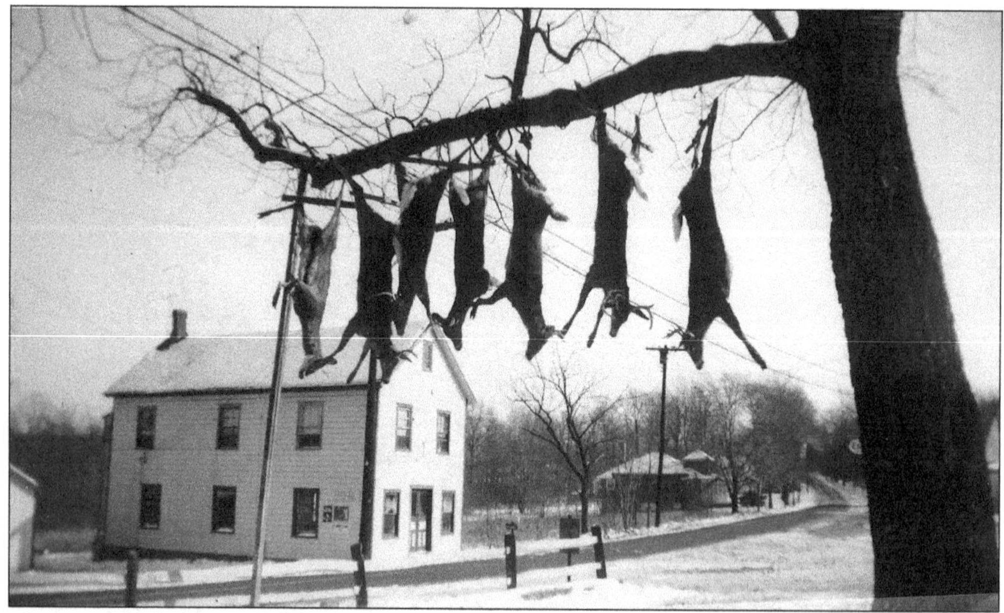

This companion snapshot looks south on Mount Bethel Road toward Fairview Hall and the old Mount Bethel School, by then Our Lady of the Mount's recreation building. At bottom left is the wagon shed that housed the fire company's Model T.

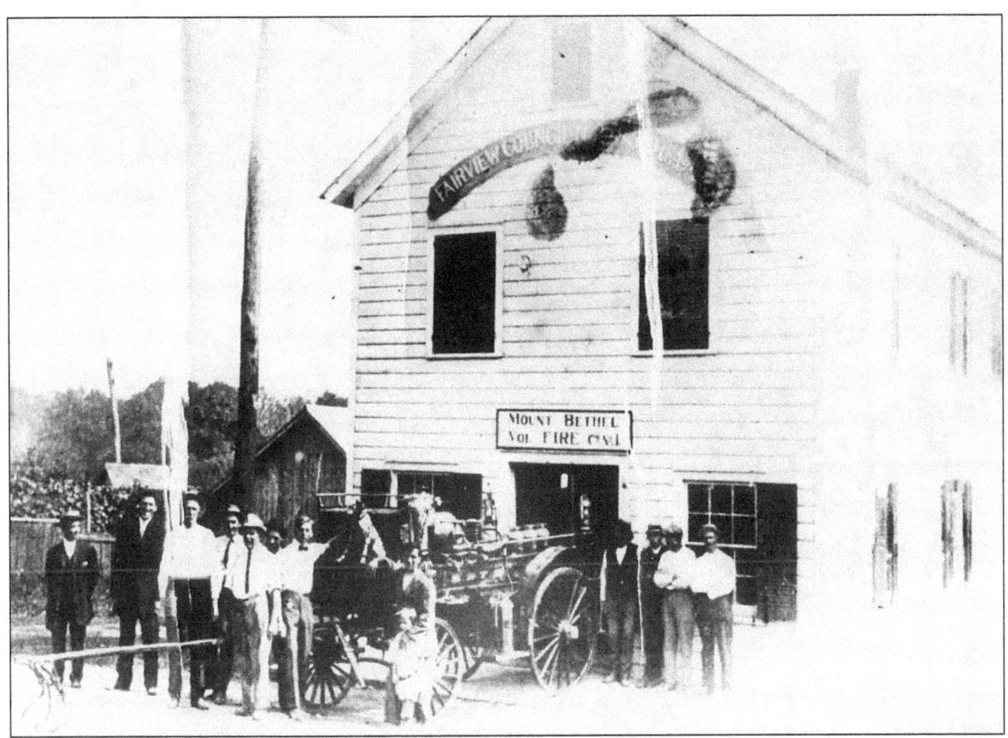

Members of the Mount Bethel Volunteer Fire Company, the township's first, stand beside their new horse-drawn chemical fire apparatus in this 1912 picture. The firehouse is the small shed to the left. The fire engine rolled as soon as the first farmer arrived with a team of horses.

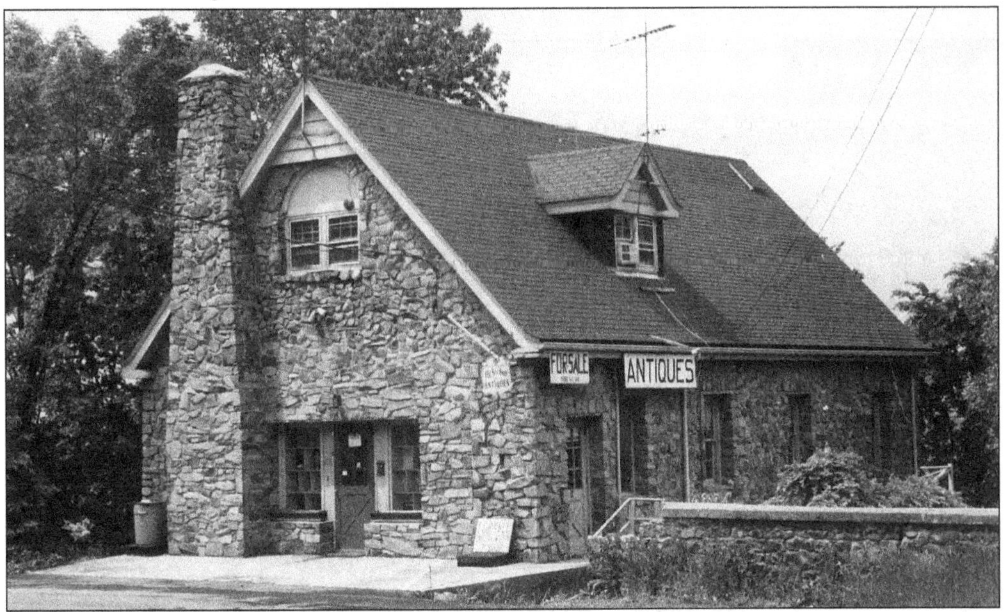

Mount Bethel firemen established their third home when they built this fieldstone building next to the cemetery entirely by volunteer labor in 1930-32. After the fire company moved to new headquarters further down Mount Bethel Road, the building became an antique shop and later a dress store.

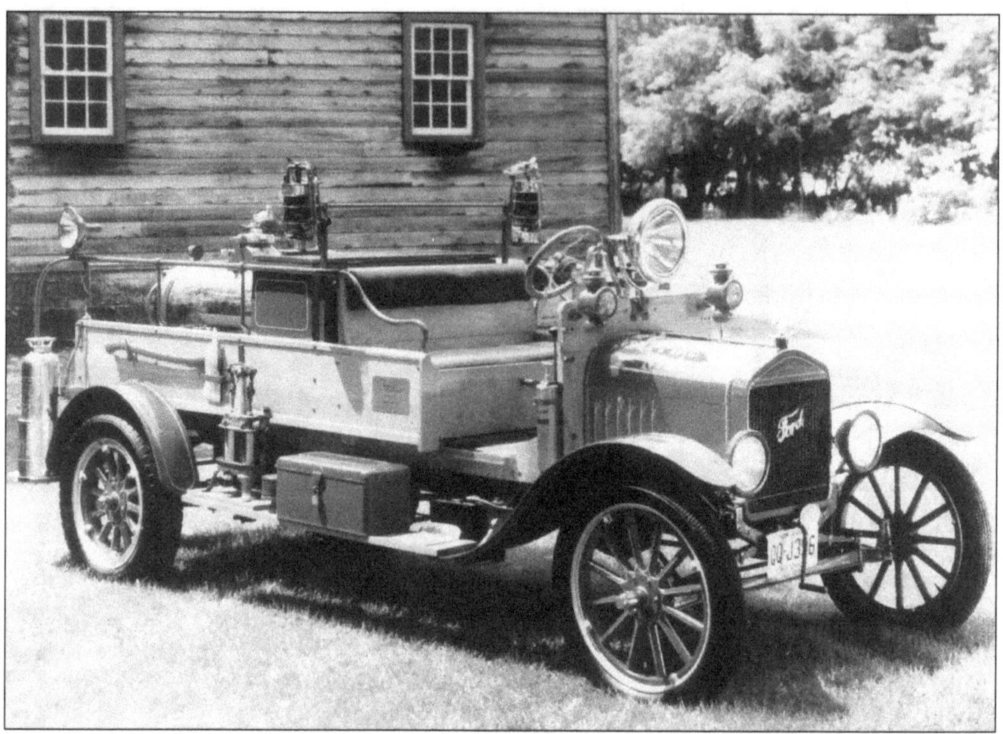

Mount Bethel's first motorized apparatus was this 1921 Model T chemical truck. Members bought the chassis and built the fire engine themselves. Donald Christie, a retired member, has restored the vehicle to pristine condition.

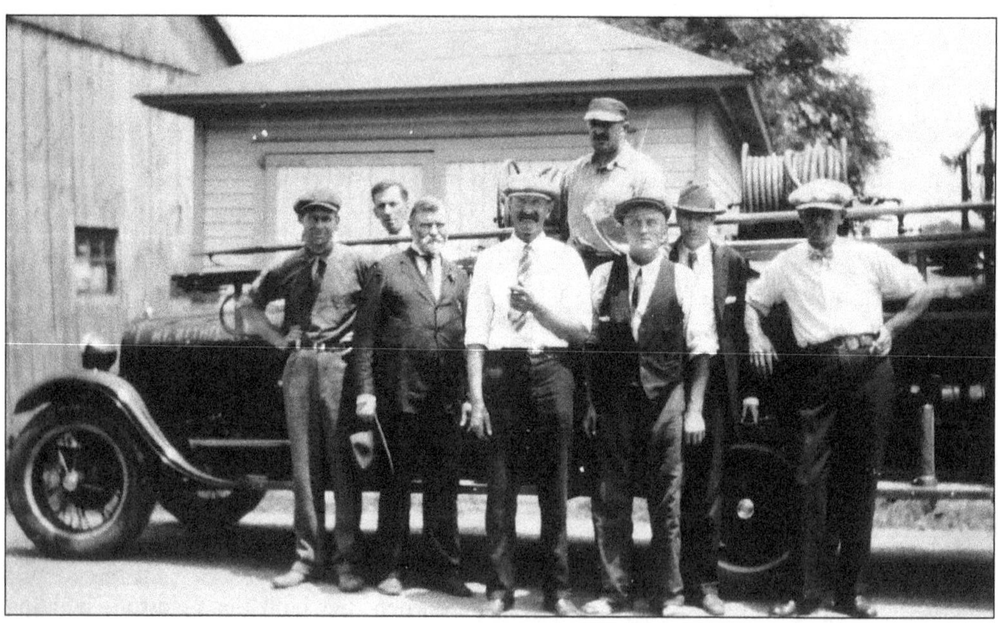

Henry Bell, Philip J. Freehauf Sr., Edward A. Shult Sr., Peter Williams, Andre Calosso, Otto Duderstadt, Edward A. Shult Jr., and Eugene Possien pose in front of Mount Bethel's second motorized apparatus, a modified Model A Ford.

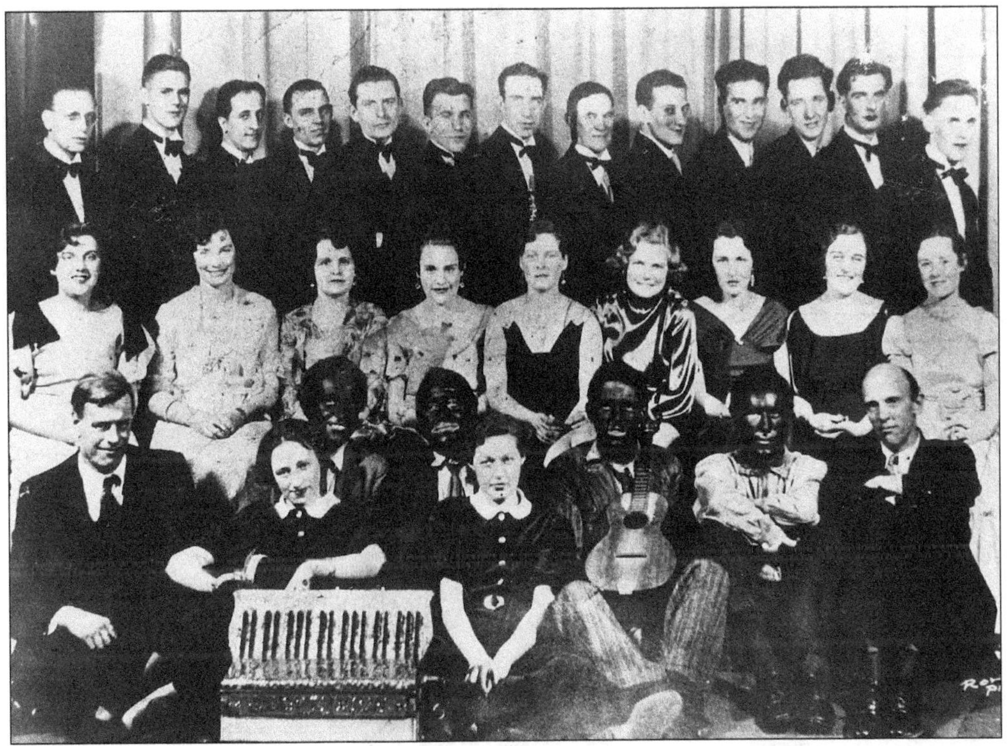

Hoping to raise sorely-needed funds during the Depression, the Mount Bethel Volunteer Fire Company put on its first minstrel show in February 1931. An immediate hit, the shows continued until the early sixties when they were held at the high school. Sandwiches, cake, and soda water were served after the 1932 performance.

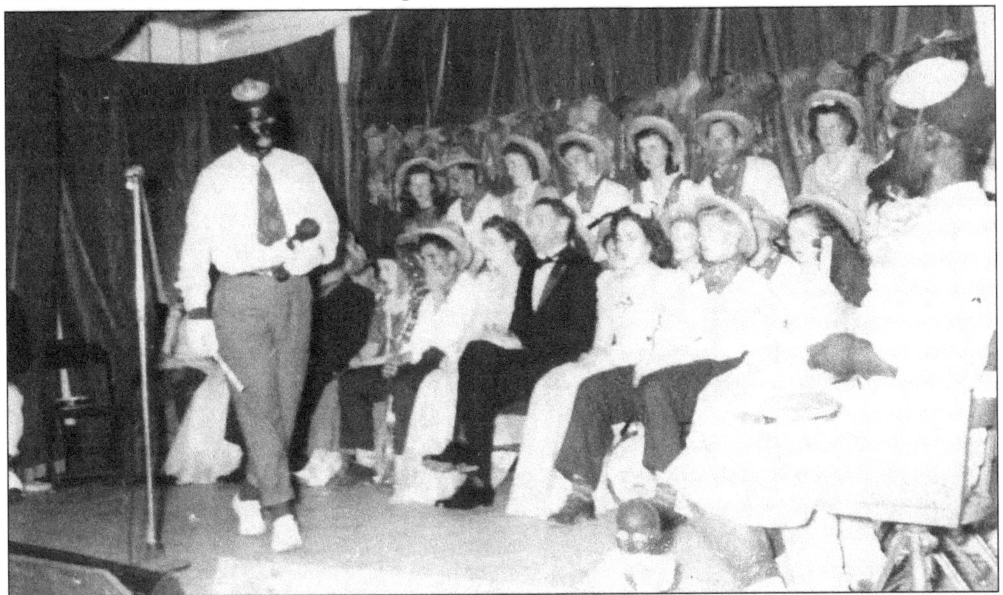

The 1945 show featured banjo, guitar, and harmonica music and end men Sassafras Duderstadt, Pork Chop Farrell, Egg Head Possien, and January Burness singing such popular tunes as "Are You From Dixie?" and "Down Where the Watermelons Grow."

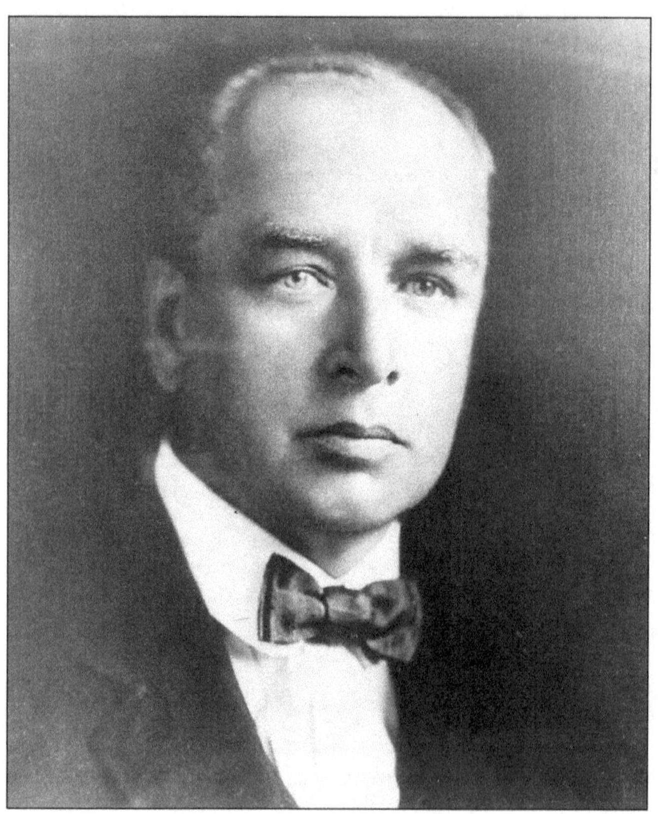

Reverend William H. Mount was pastor of Mount Bethel Baptist Church from 1913 to 1931.

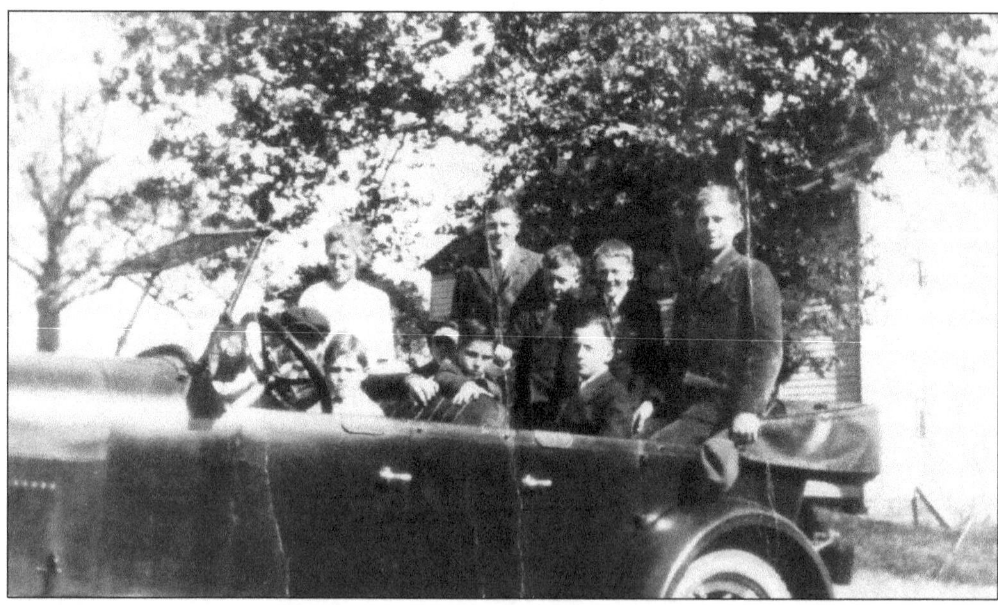

Pastor Mount's open touring car is all gassed up and ready to head for the Jersey shore in this 1923 photograph, taken in front of the Meeting House. Regis, William, Leslie, and Walter Ralph, and Henry Bell pose for the camera.

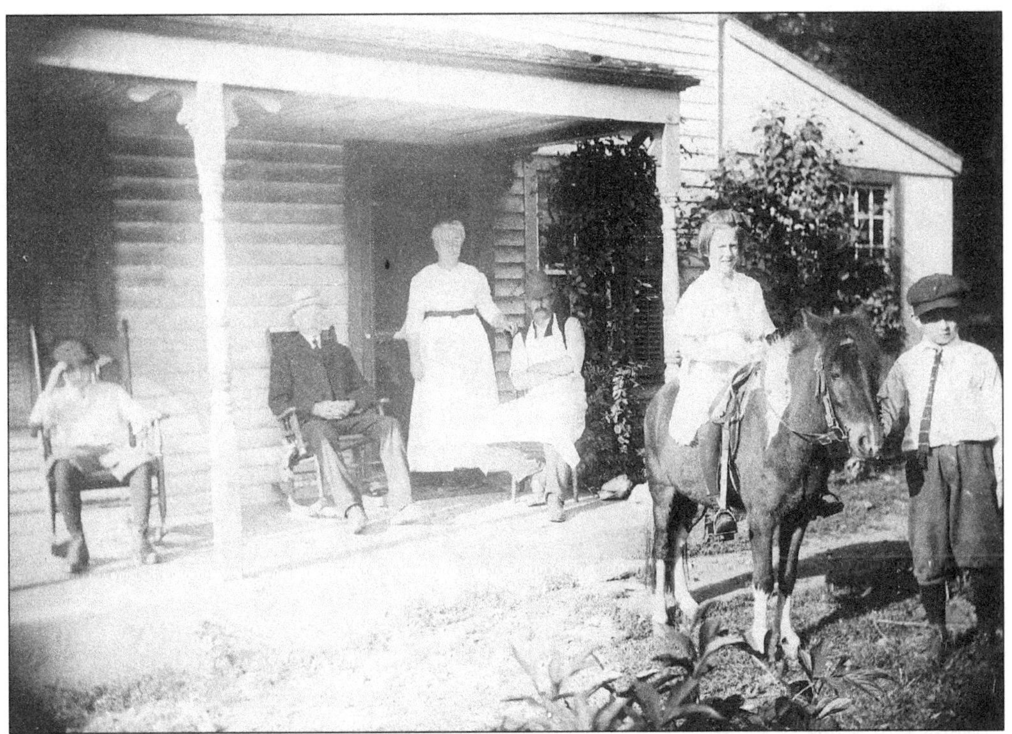

Members of the Ralph family were among Mount Bethel's earliest residents. Their home, recently demolished, stood opposite and somewhat north of the cemetery. In this 1908 view, Regis, William, Mary Jane, Frank W. Sr., Arline, and Frank W. Ralph Jr. pose with their pony, Goldenrod Feature.

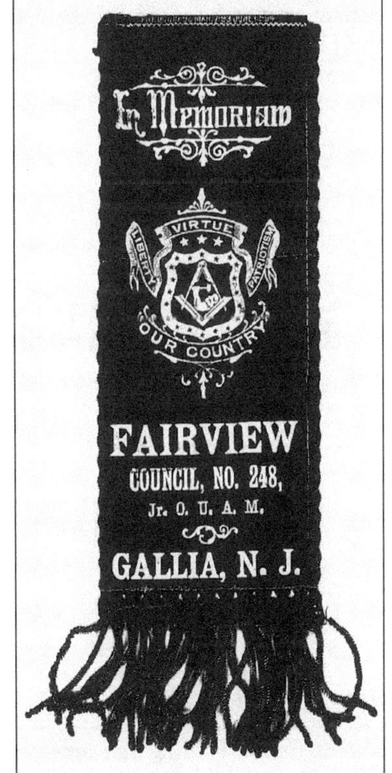

Gallia was the name of Mount Bethel's post office from 1895 to 1904. The Junior Order held its first meeting in 1897 in the upstairs parlor over N.H. Heidelhoff's grocery store.

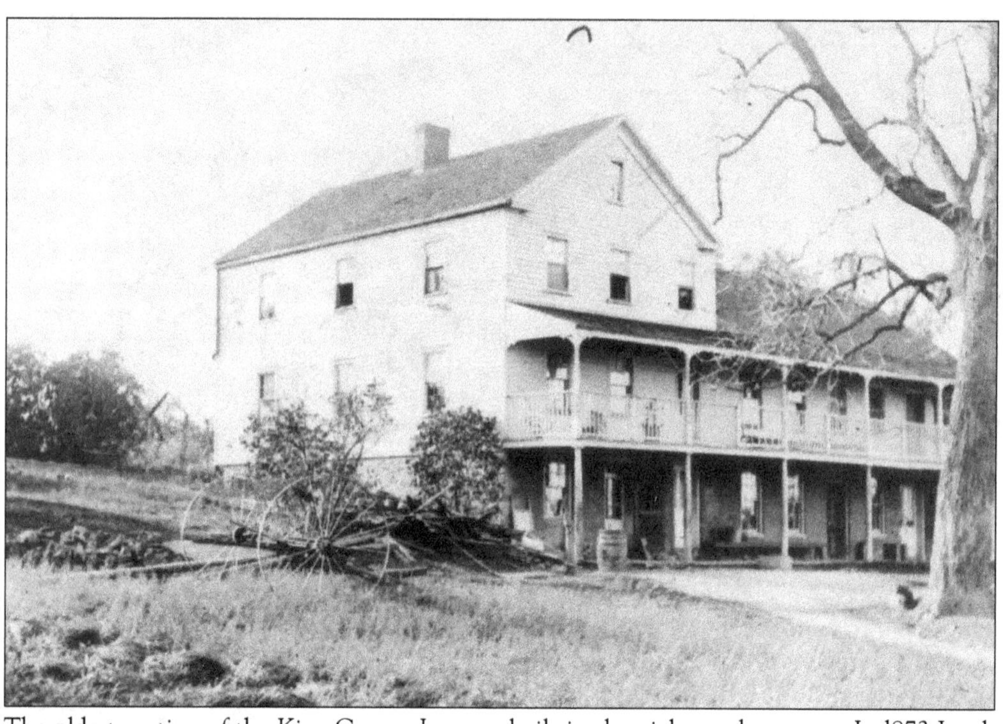

The oldest portion of the King George Inn was built in the eighteenth century. In 1873 Jacob Blimm, then the proprietor, advertised a stage line from Plainfield to Mount Bethel. Josephine Schaeffer, who later sang at the Metropolitan Opera, lived here in the 1880s. In 1909, the year this photograph was taken, the inn was frequented by city folk who came to enjoy the healthful country air.

SECOND ANNUAL MASQUERADE BALL

—OF THE—

MILLINGTON SOCIAL CLUB,

AT MT. BETHEL HALL,

THANKSGIVING EVE, NOV. 27, 1889.

MUSIC BY PROF. O'REILLY,

Mount Bethel Hall, as the inn was known in the late nineteenth century, was the center of Warren's social life.

The inn was also known as the Mountain House. Palmer's Picture Dances featured a hand-tinted slide show coordinated with music.

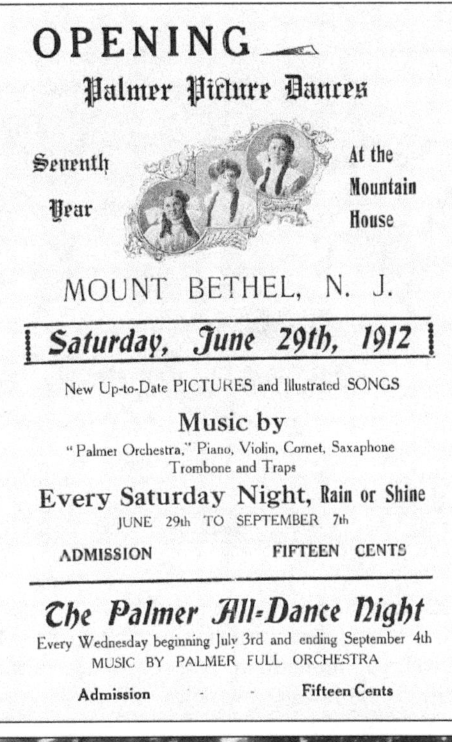

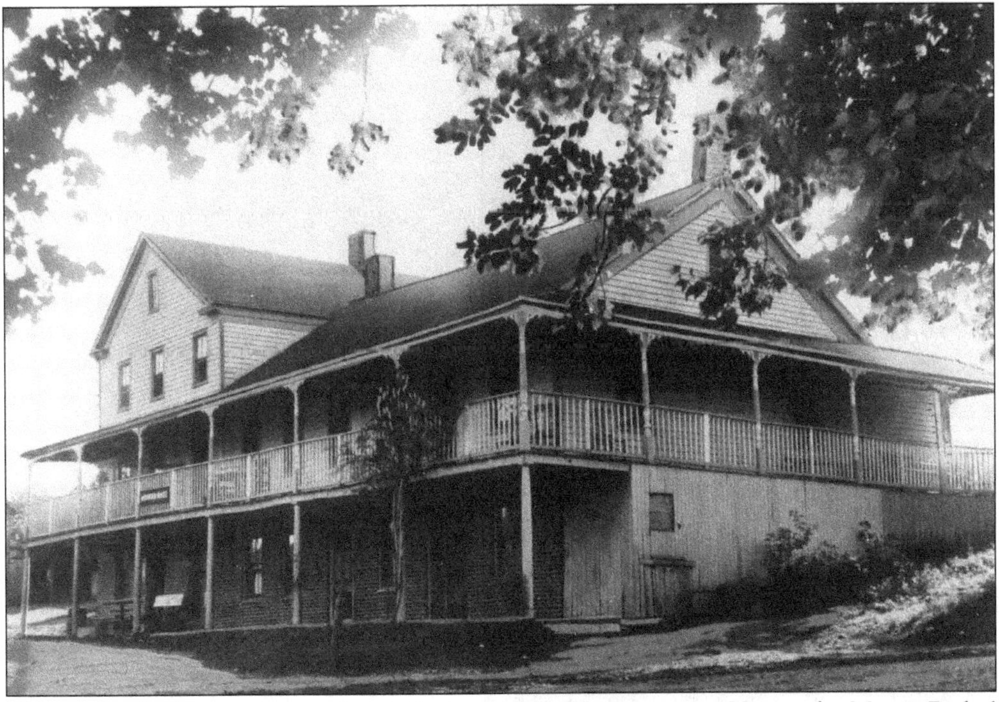

The inn has had many names since it first opened—The Mountain House, the Mount Bethel Inn, the Villa Calosso, the Sans Souci, and the King George Inn (after 1953 when Max and Dorothy Hayden turned it into a first-class country restaurant). During the nineteenth century the three floors above the tap room were used to house guests.

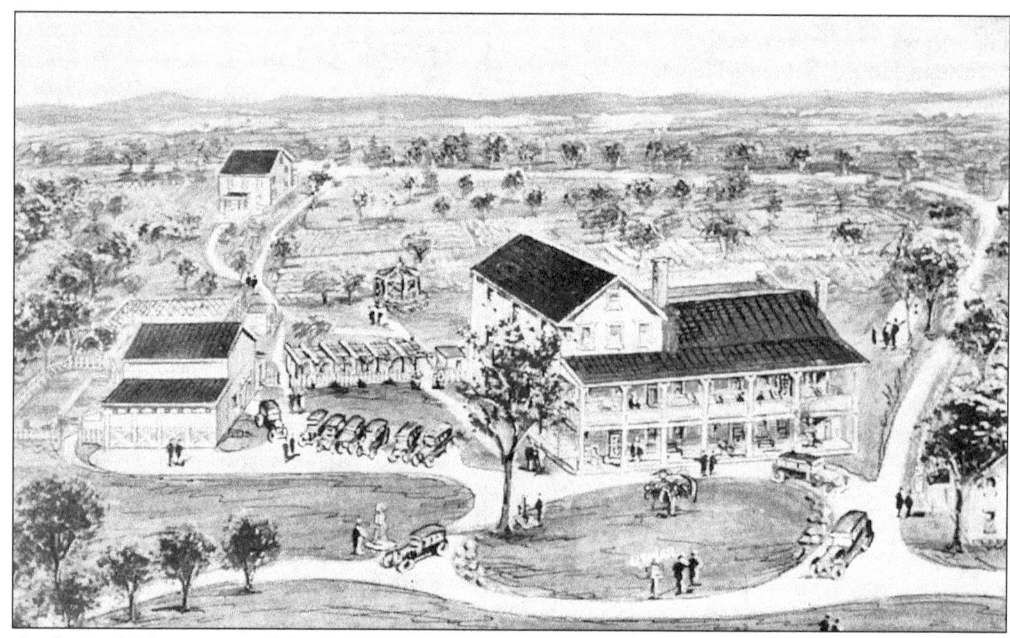

Andre and Clementine Calosso bought the inn in 1913 and owned it until 1940 when they sold it to Fred Zimmerman. A spring is said to run under the tap room, whose hand-hewn beams are still visible.

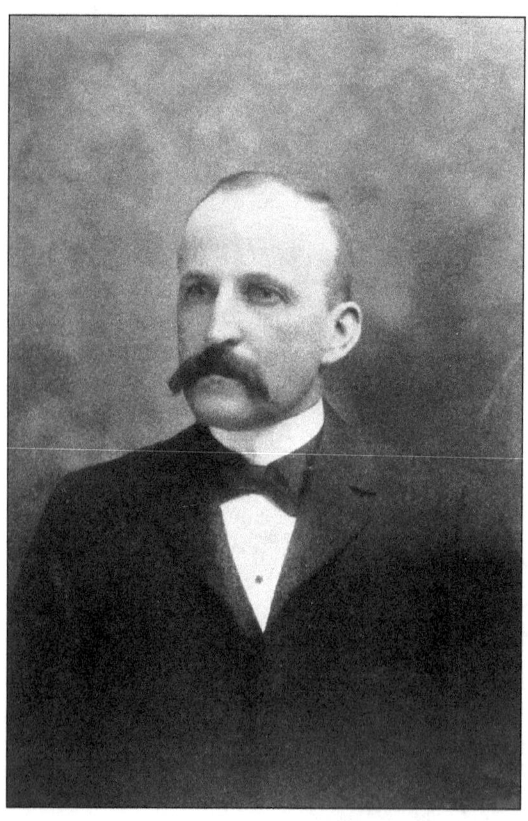

Dr. Peter J. Zeglio (1860-1935) was Mount Bethel's first doctor. Carved on his tomb in Mount Bethel Cemetery are the words, "He Lived for Others."

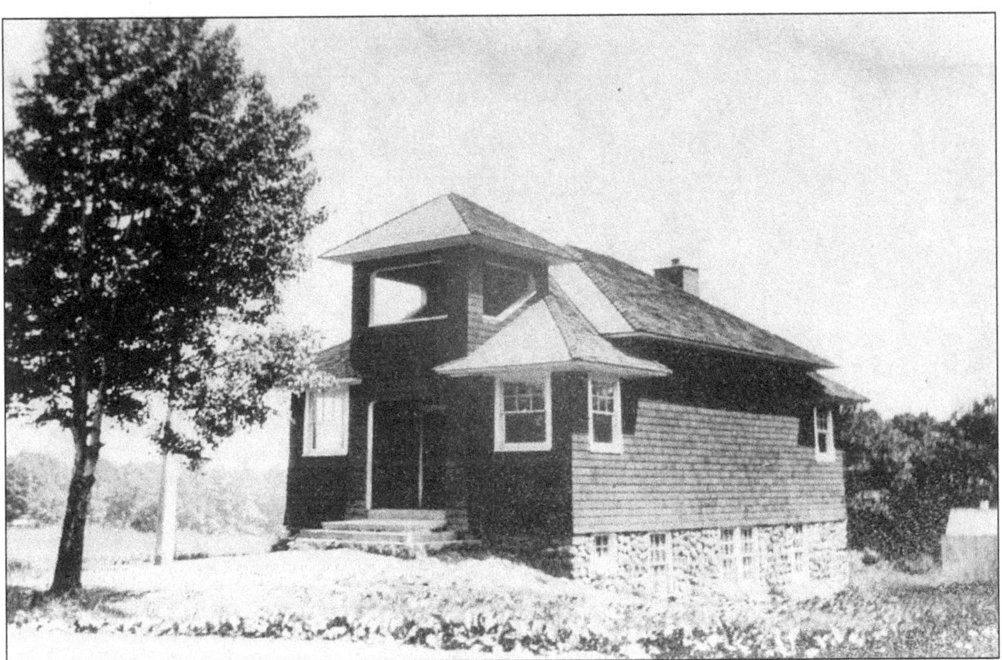

The Mount Bethel School was in use from 1914, when it replaced an old stone building, until 1933, when Central School opened. Our Lady of the Mount Roman Catholic Church acquired the building (which stood opposite the rectory) in 1936 for use as a recreation hall.

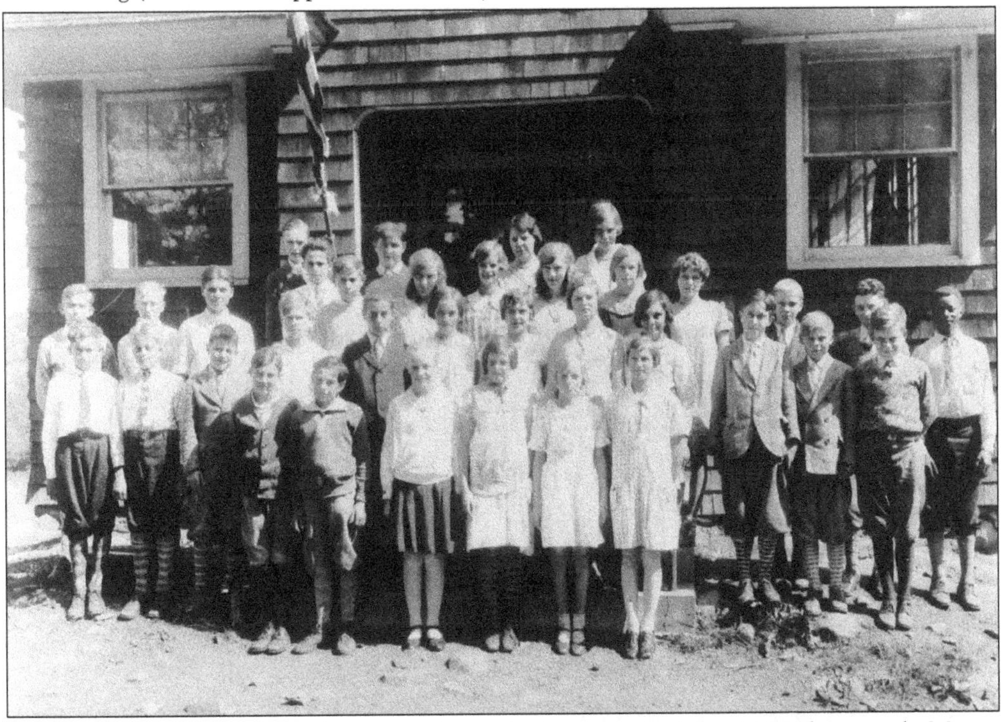

Helen Smalley stands second from the right in the back row in this *c.* 1930 photograph. Mount Bethel School's last teacher—she taught all eight grades—she went on to become Central School's first principal.

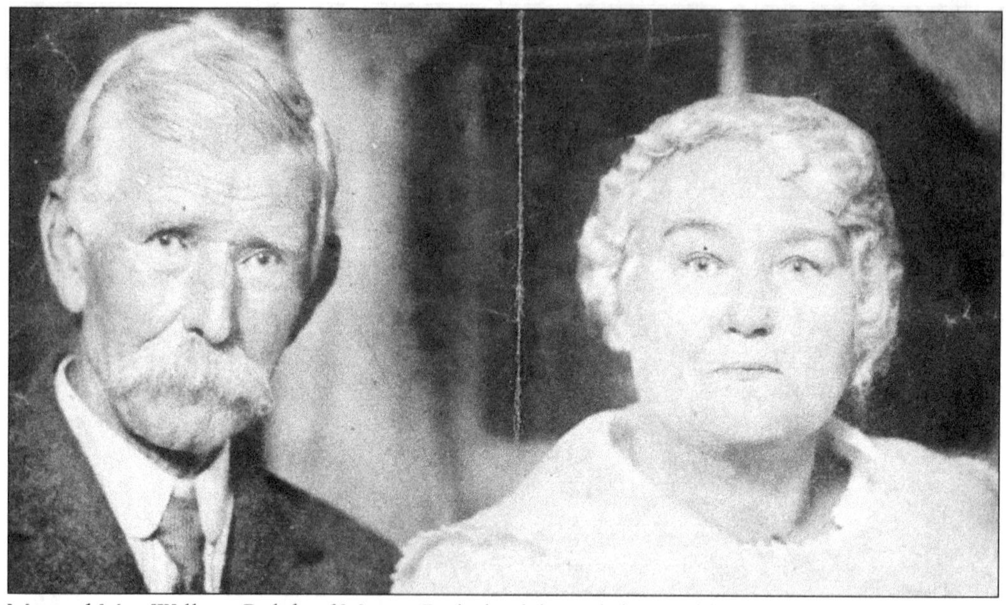

Mr. and Mrs. William Ralph of Mount Bethel celebrated their golden wedding anniversary on January 1, 1921. Ralph, who served in the 30th New Jersey Volunteers during the Civil War, died in 1922. His wife, the former Mary Jane Sharkey, "a fine reader, known among her friends for her excellent memory," died in 1938.

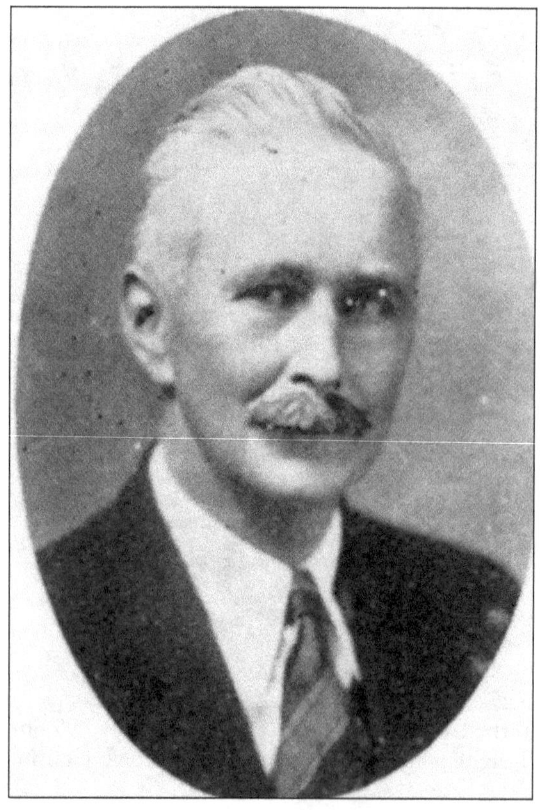

Frank W. Ralph (1874–1961), a prominent Democrat, ran unsuccessfully for county freeholder in 1929.

On August 5, 1930, Frank Ralph's grandchildren, Philip J. Jr., Frank R., and Arline B., posed in their play clothes in front of the old homestead on King George Road

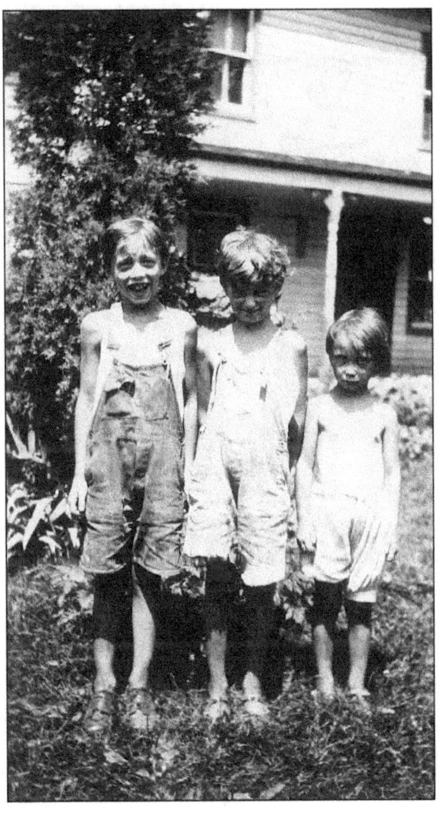

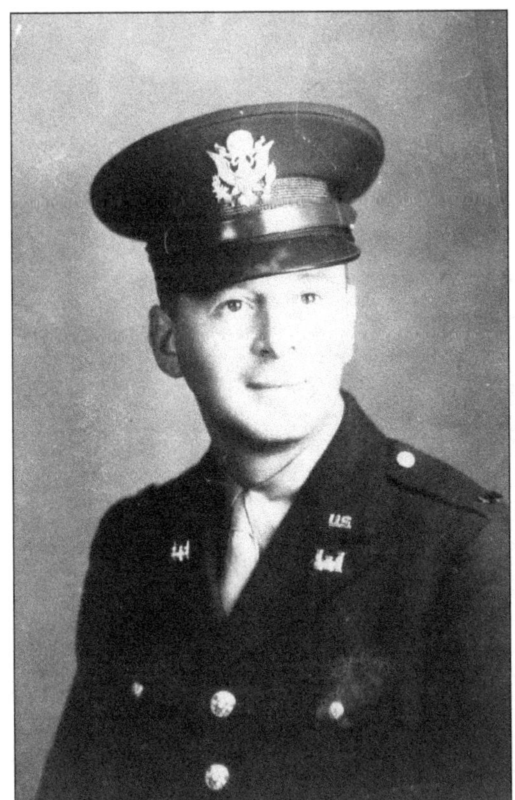

First Lieutenant William D. Ralph (1911–1944), one of three soldiers from Warren to die in World War II, lost his life on the Anzio beachhead.

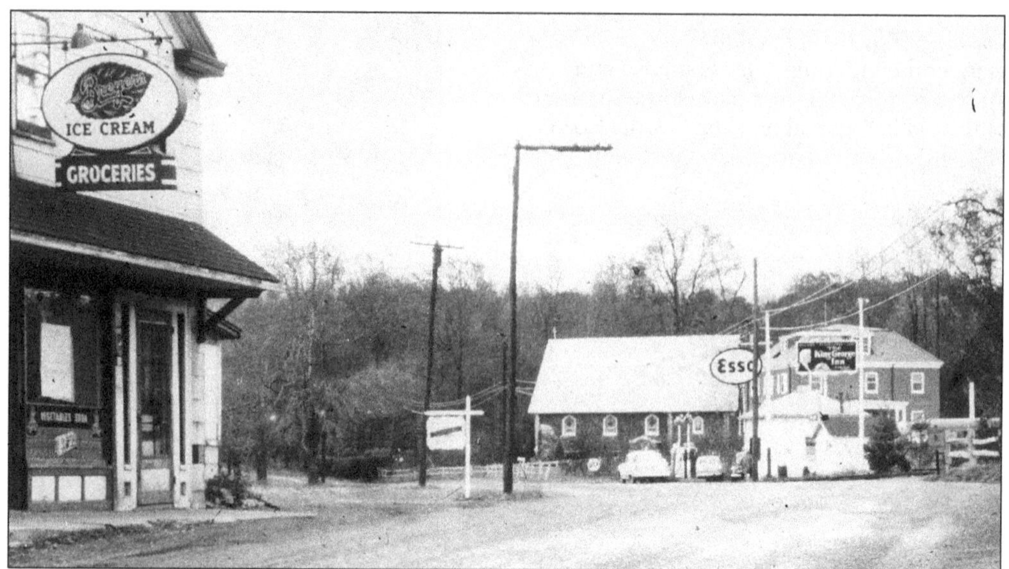

This view shows Mount Bethel looking south toward Our Lady of the Mount Church, *c.* 1960. To the left is the general store before it was moved back from the road in the 1960s. To the right is Philip J. Freehauf's Esso station and the sign for the King George Inn.

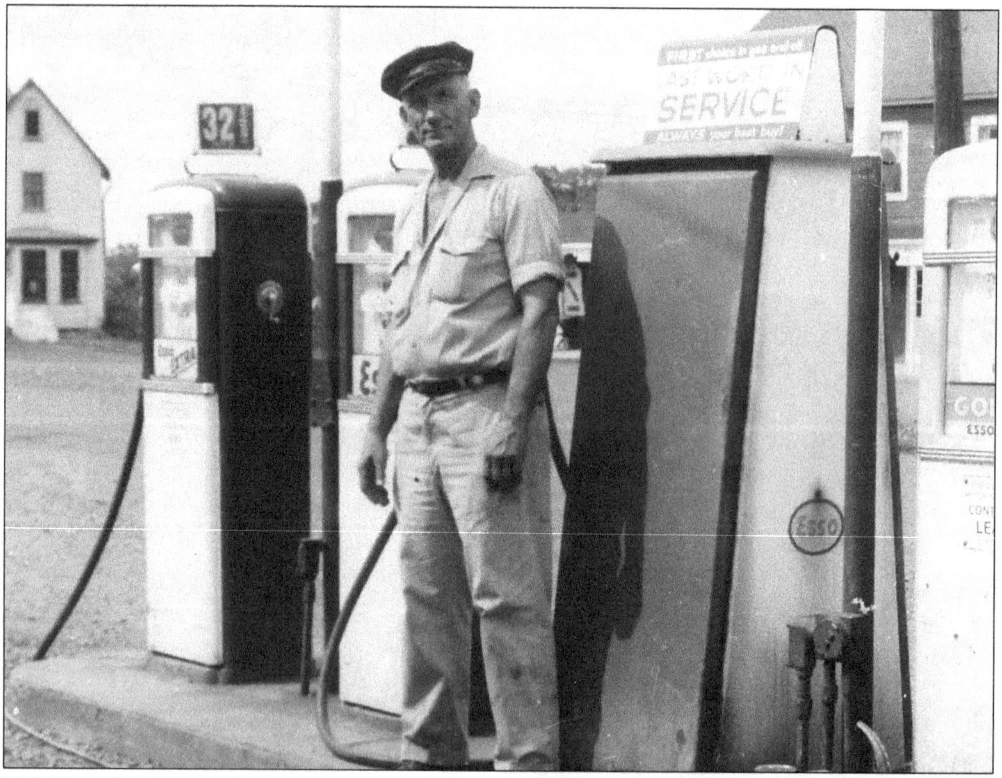

"P.J." Freehauf opened his gas station in 1932 after buying the site from the Calosso family. He acquired the old firehouse and moved it across the street to use as his garage. In 1948 P.J., who held the township's school bus contract, began an annual Christmas tradition of giving ice cream to Warren's school children. It cost him $13 that year.

Our Lady of the Mount Roman Catholic Church, organized in 1911, celebrated its first mass in this building built of native stone on December 22, 1912.

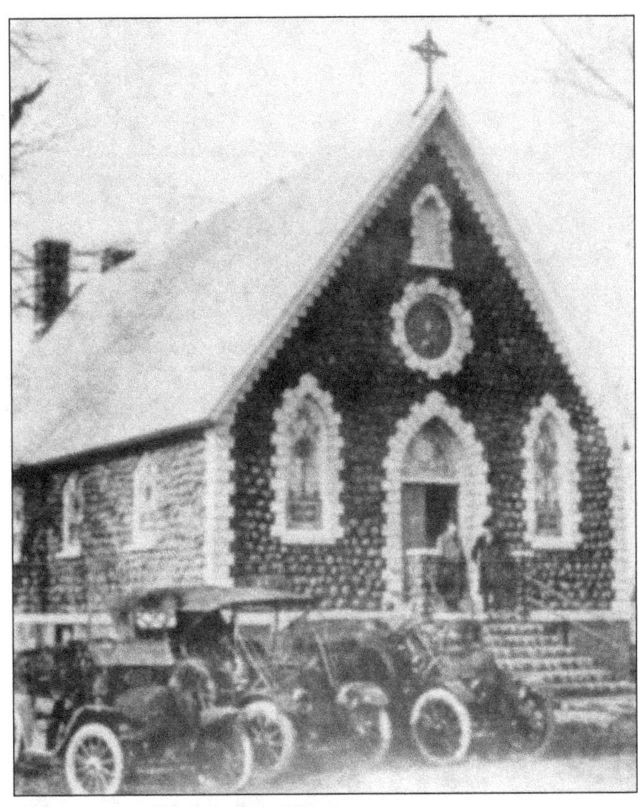

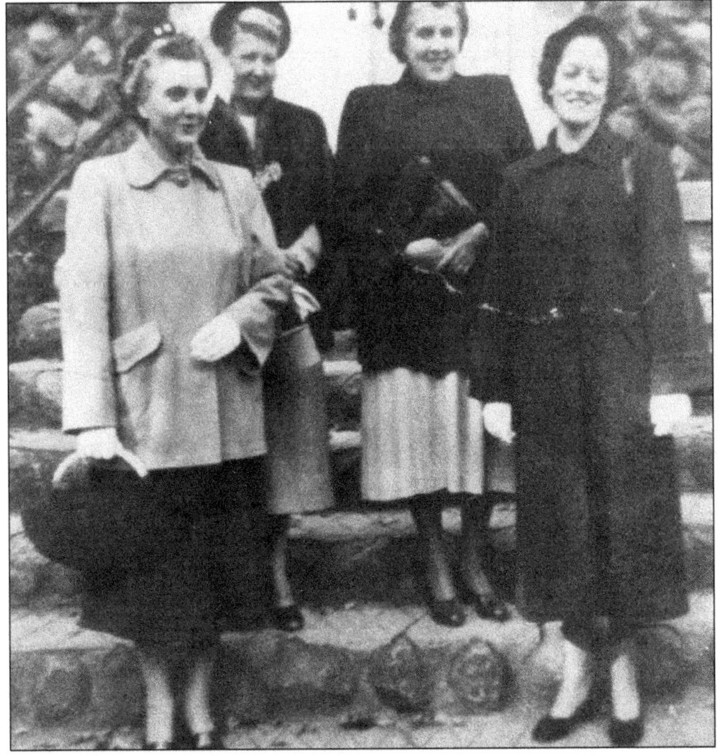

The Altar Rosary Society was organized in 1948. Officers were, from left to right: Helen Renzanka, Marie Wojnar, Sarah Arrighi, and Eileen McAvoy.

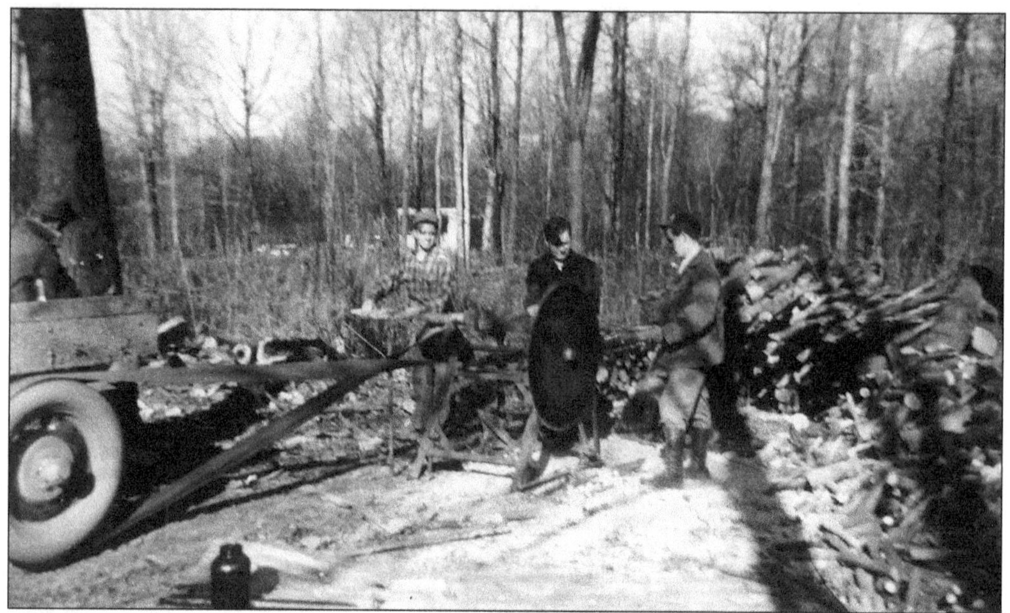

The Farrells lived near Mount Bethel School during the Depression years. In this 1939 photograph, brothers William, Richard, and Jack Farrell cut cord wood with an enormous buzz saw powered by a belt connected to the truck's rear tire.

HILLCREST LODGE

24 ACRES HIDDEN AMONG THE TREES AND HILLS IN THE WATCHUNG MOUNTAINS OF NEW JERSEY

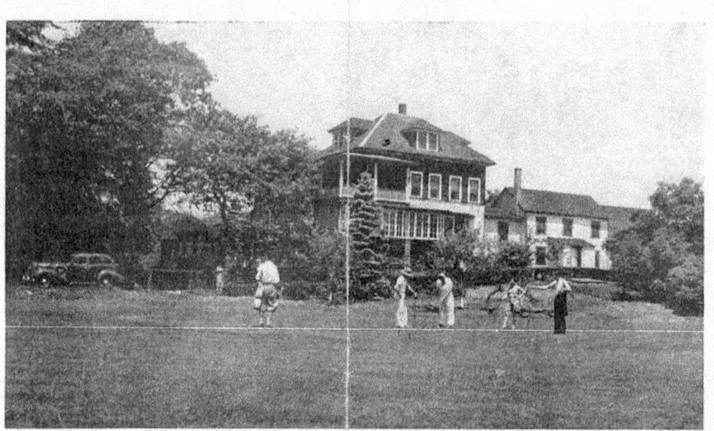

GOLF

AFTER A VIGOROUS WORKOUT
A COOL SWIM

During the twenties and thirties, Hillcrest Lodge, located on Mount Bethel Road just south of Reinman Road, offered lodging to Jews seeking escape from the city's summer heat. "Your Country Home" offered spacious bedrooms, a cheerful dining room, a golf course, tennis and handball courts, Ping-Pong, shuffleboard, mahjong, musicales, and cozy reading nooks. The main house burned in 1938.

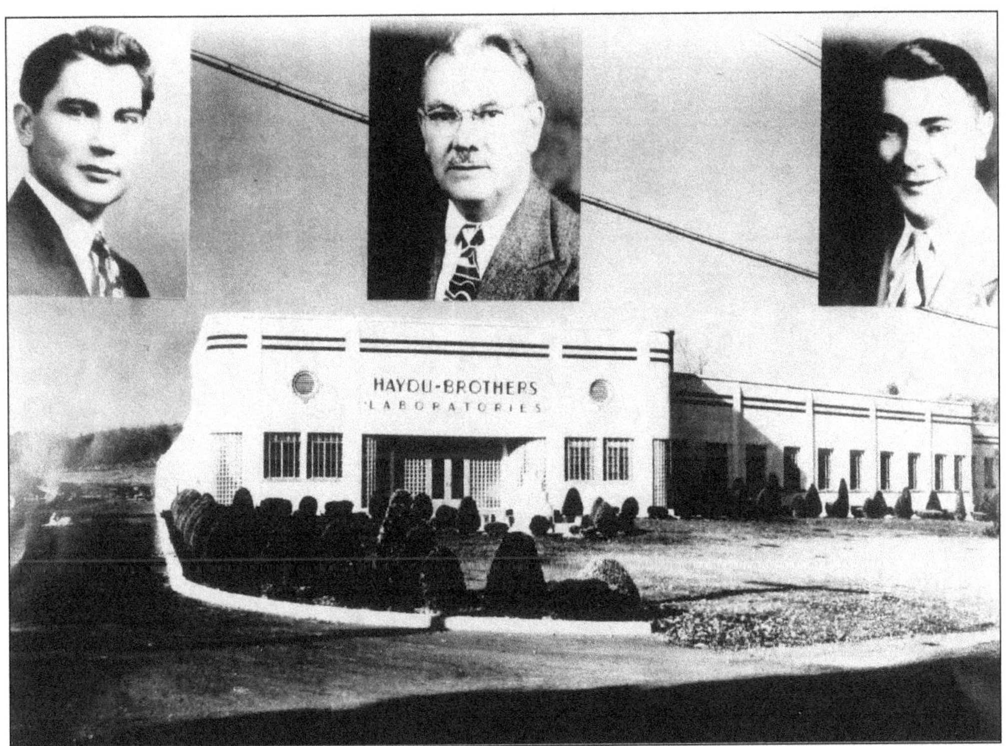

Less than a mile down Mount Bethel Road and across from Hillcrest Lodge was the Haydu Brothers factory, established here just as World War II began. Zoltan, John, and George Haydu first set up shop in some old chicken coops, and then built this modern building when wartime demand for their electronic components skyrocketed. Burroughs Corporation acquired the business in 1954.

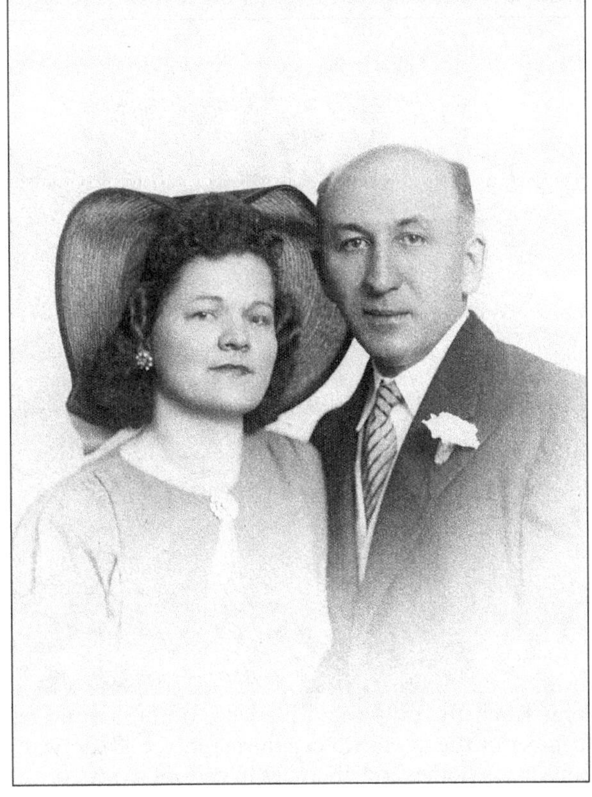

Frank and Stephanie Gebauer bought the Hillcrest Lodge property in 1946, establishing the Mount Bethel Knitting Mills on the site.

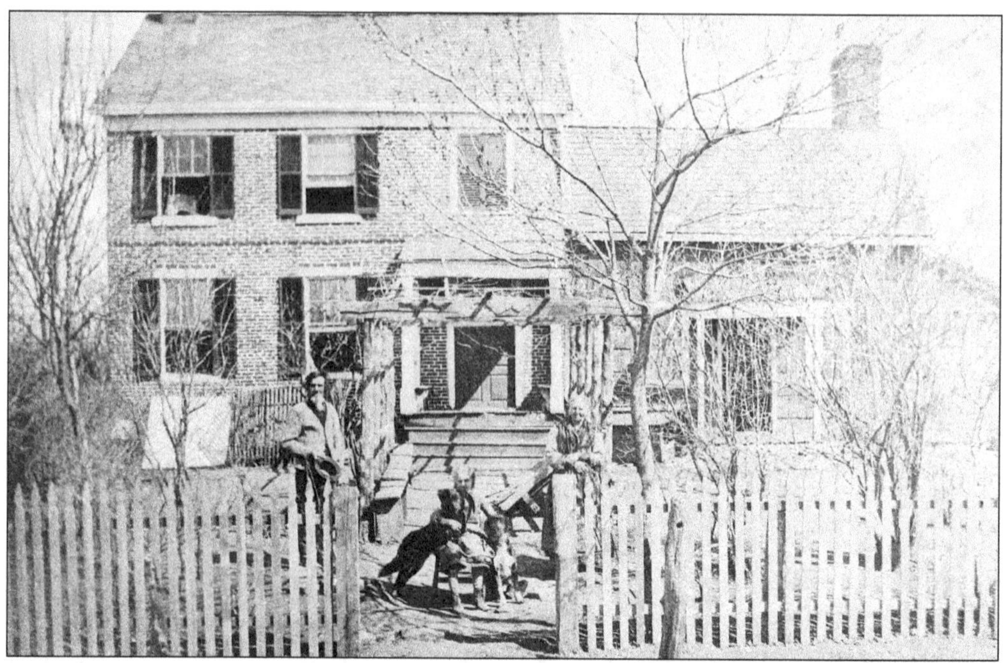

The original one-room section of the Kirch House on the corner of Mount Bethel and Reinman Roads was built about 1750, making it Warren's oldest standing building. The two-story section at left dates from *c.* 1800. Home of the Kirch family from 1857 to 1978, the township-owned house is on the National Register of Historic Places.

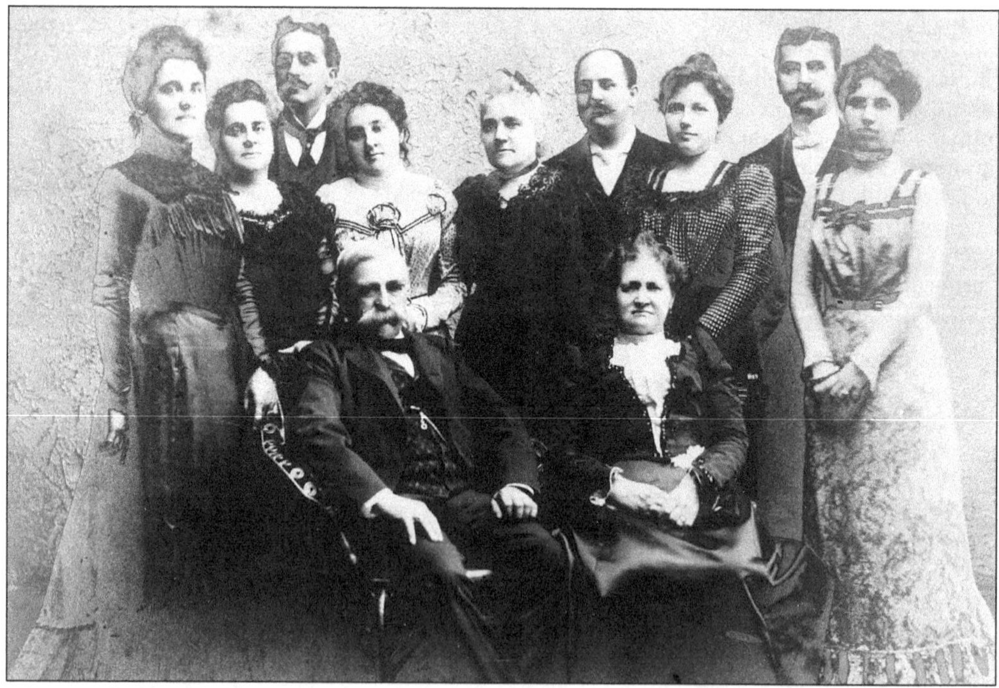

John Kirch (d. 1894), and his wife, Catherine, raised eight children in the house. Kirch, a member of the township committee in the 1870s, was a master carpenter and contractor who built many homes and churches in central Jersey.

Bertha Kirch, John's granddaughter, attended Mount Bethel School in 1909 when her teacher, Frederick H. Sage, commended her excellence in deportment.

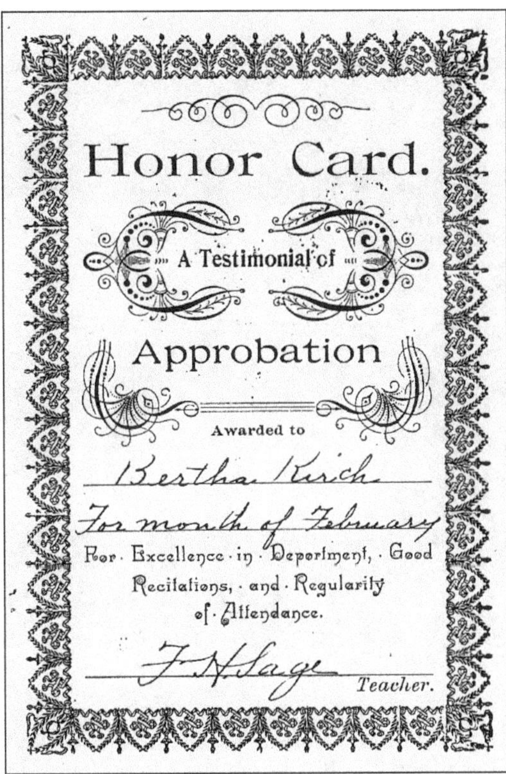

Honor Card.

A Testimonial of

Approbation

Awarded to

Bertha Kirch

For month of February

For Excellence in Deportment, Good Recitations, and Regularity of Attendance.

F. H. Sage Teacher.

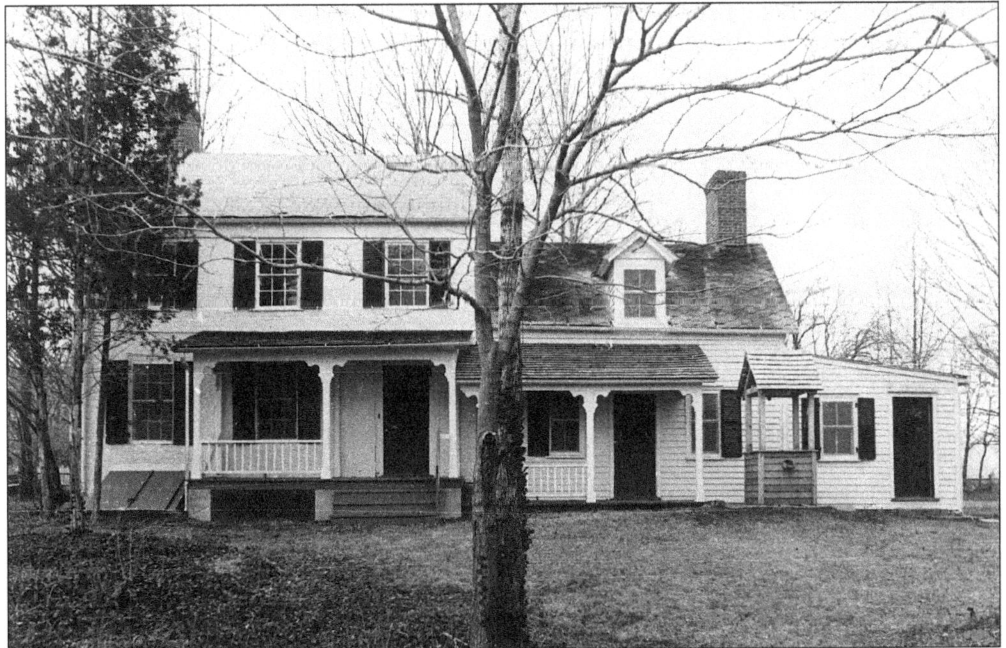

After the township acquired the Kirch House in 1980, volunteer members of the Historic Sites Committee saw to its restoration. A bee-hive oven, a walk-in fireplace, pine flooring, and a secret room that may have been a stopping-place on the pre-Civil War underground railroad are among its many features.

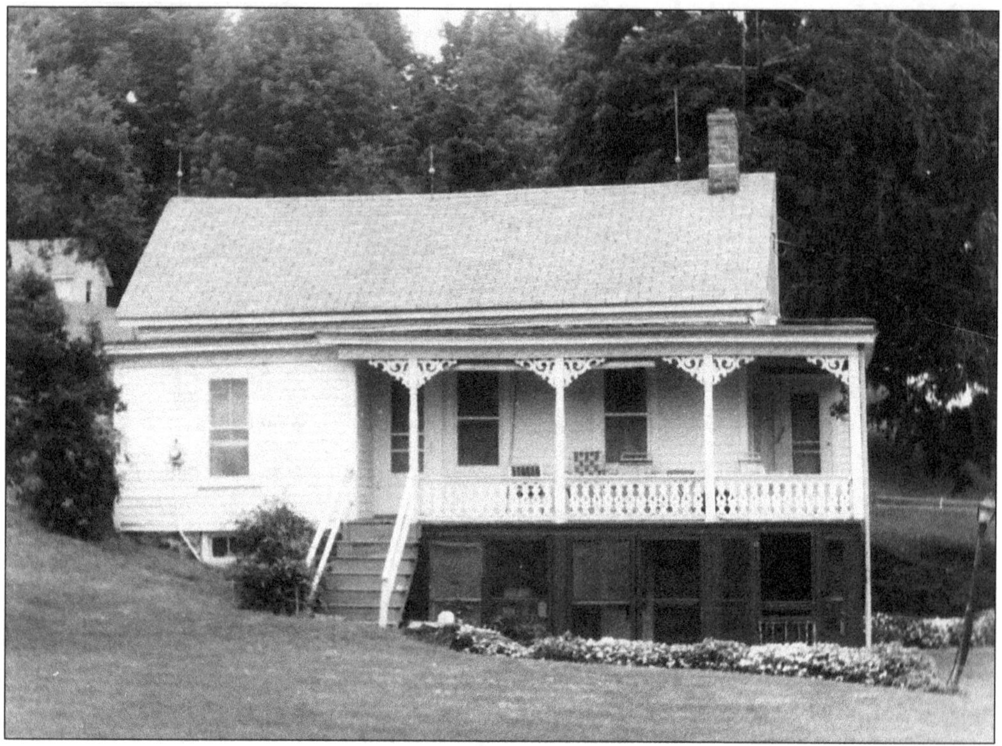

Down Reinman Road from the Kirch House is the Grossweiler House, a charming bank house tucked into the hillside. Built before 1800, probably by the Willet family, it was acquired by John G. Reinmann in 1861. The Grossweilers owned it from 1923 to 1993.

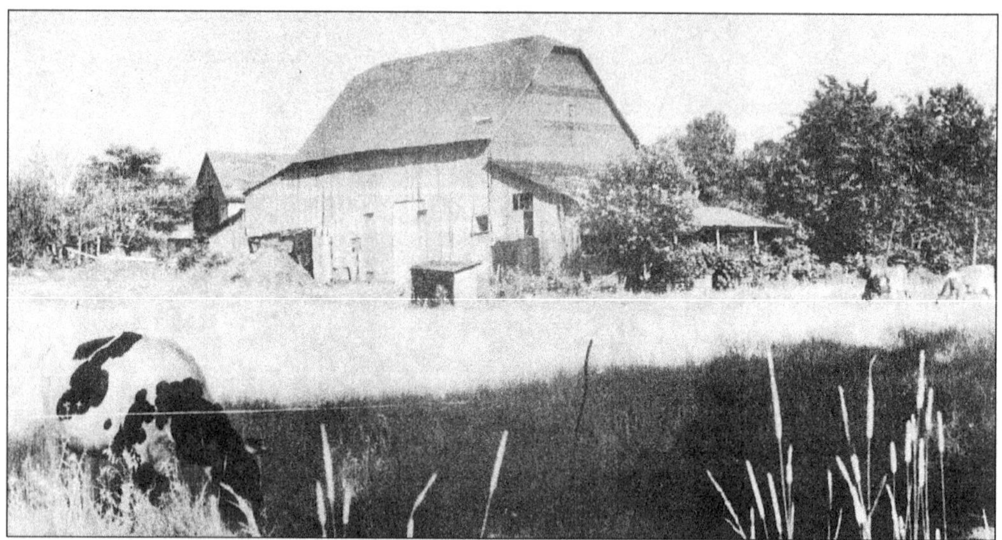

The Duderstadt barn on Dubois Road was built by George Baker *c.* 1847. Hugo Duderstadt (1846-1912), a cabinetmaker from Leipzig, bought the place in 1878. His grandchildren, Hugo, Henry, and Clarence, continued to farm the land as their father George had before them. Both George and Clarence Duderstadt served on the township committee.

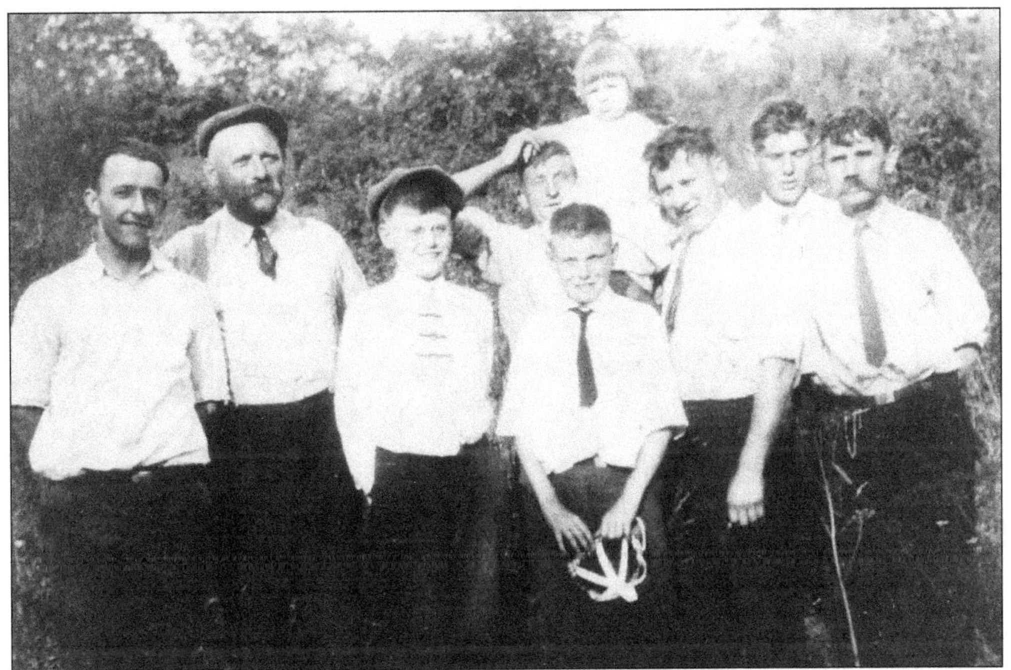

Friends and family gather for this 1926 photograph. From left to right are: Fred Nicaise, George Duderstadt, Hugo Duderstadt, Otto Duderstadt (with Joe Grossweiler on his shoulders), Henry Duderstadt, Joseph Grossweiler, Clarence Duderstadt (who served as mayor in 1956), and Philip Grossweiler.

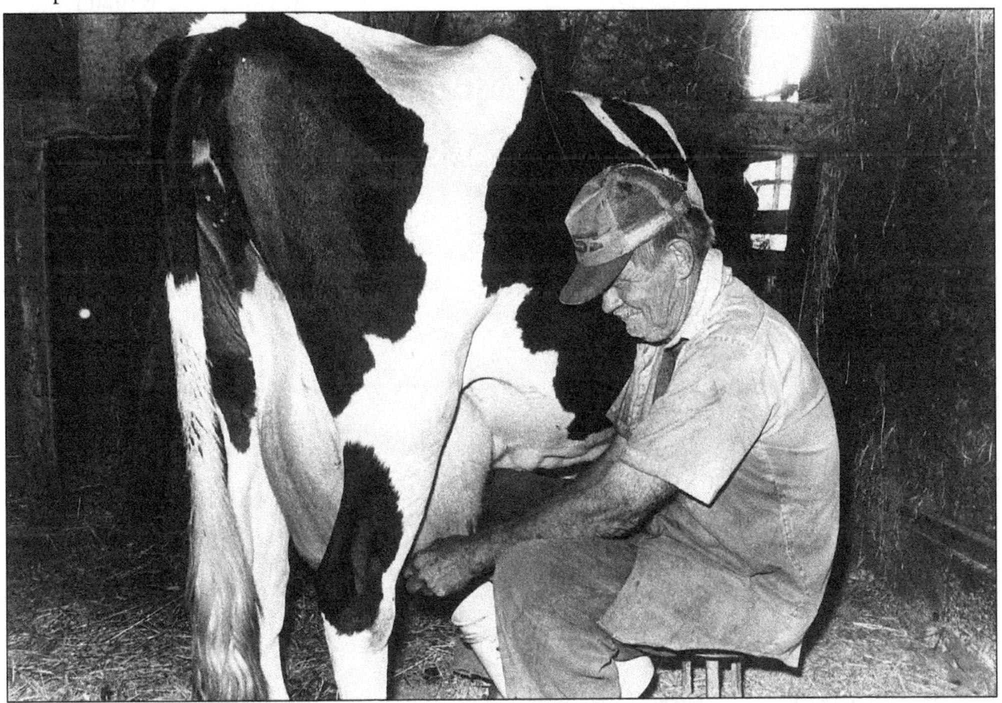

The Duderstadts own one of the last working farms in Warren. Hugo milks a cow in this 1985 snapshot.

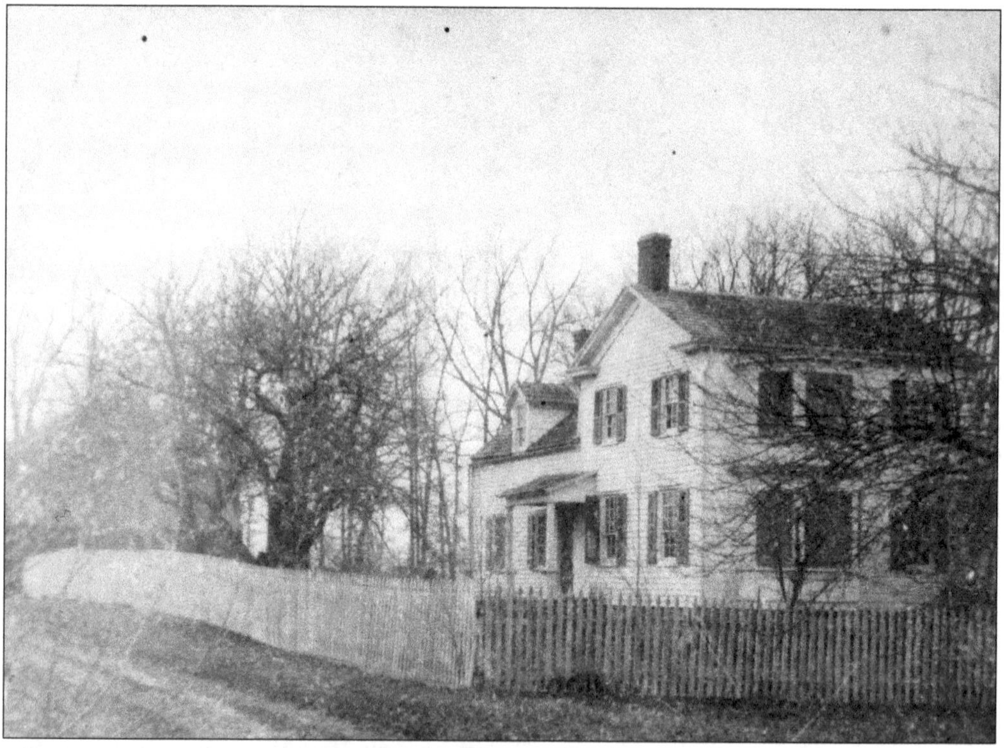

To the west of Mount Bethel, on Mountainview Road near William Penn Road, stood Patrick Sharkey's farm and home, pictured here *c.* 1890. Sharkey was born in Dublin on Saint Patrick's Day, March 17, 1826.

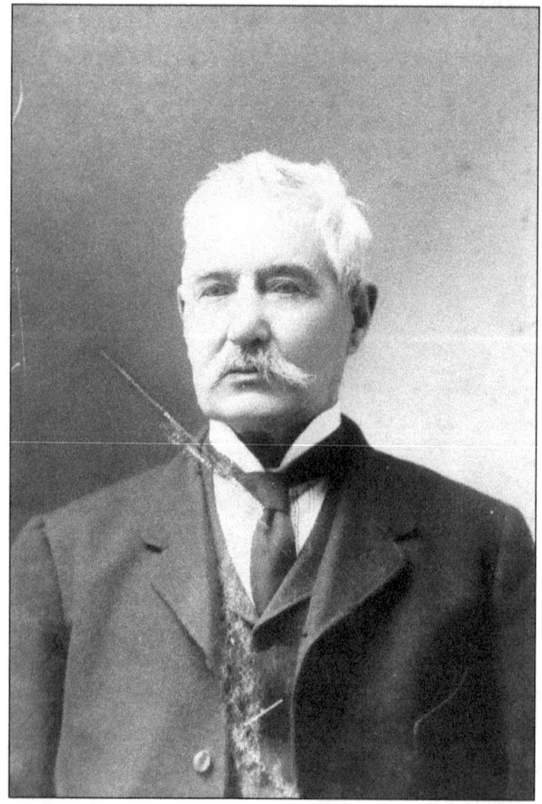

Sharkey, who died in 1909, served in the 35th New Jersey Volunteers, 1864-65.

Farmer George F. Dealaman (1880-1968) was the grandson of Morris Diehlmann, a shoemaker from Germany who settled here in the 1870s.

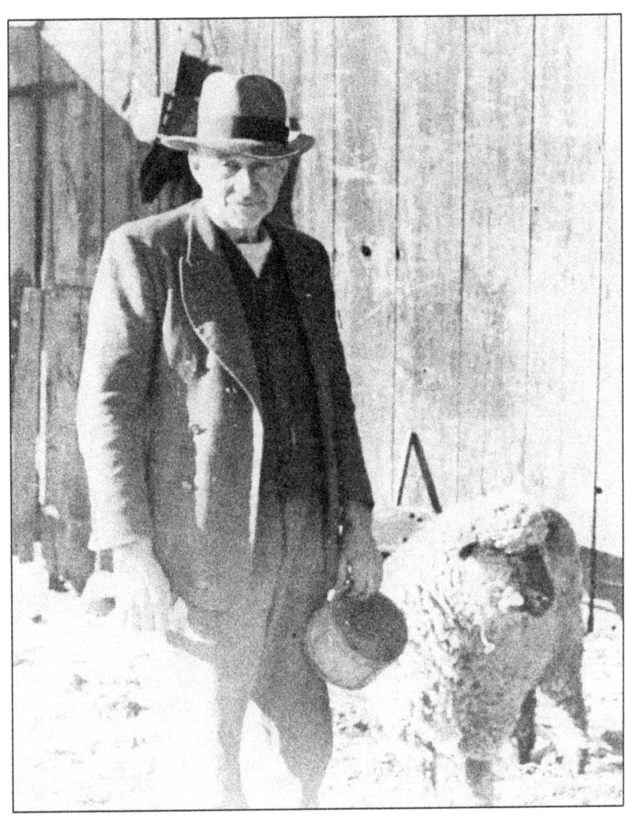

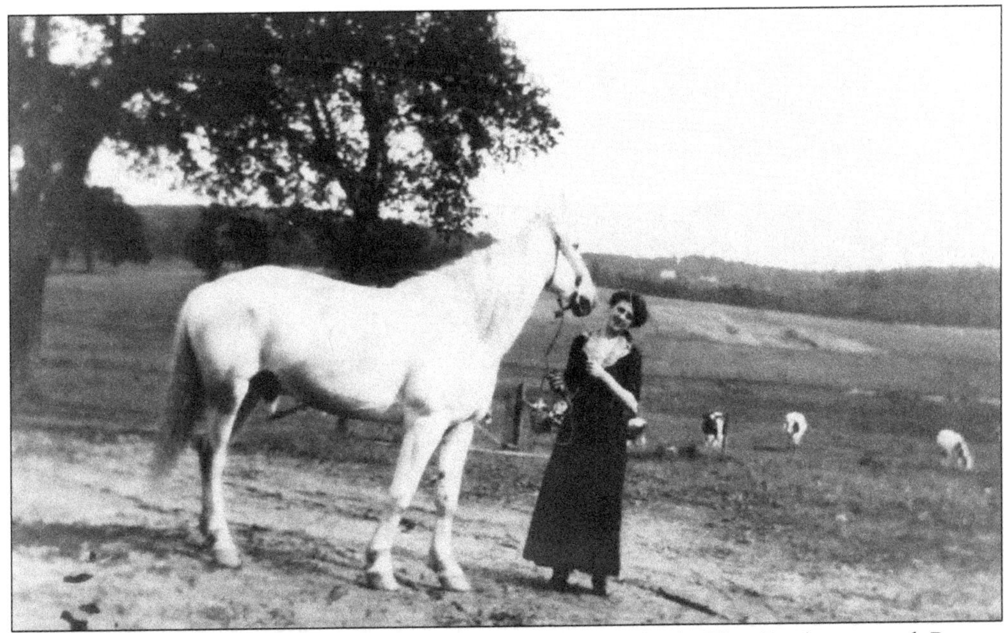

Shown here is Mary Elizabeth Williams Bowers (1885-1982). The Dealaman and Bowers families were neighbors on Mountainview Road. The Williams (originally Wilhelm) family had a farm on Mountain Boulevard, now the site of the Garden State Florist.

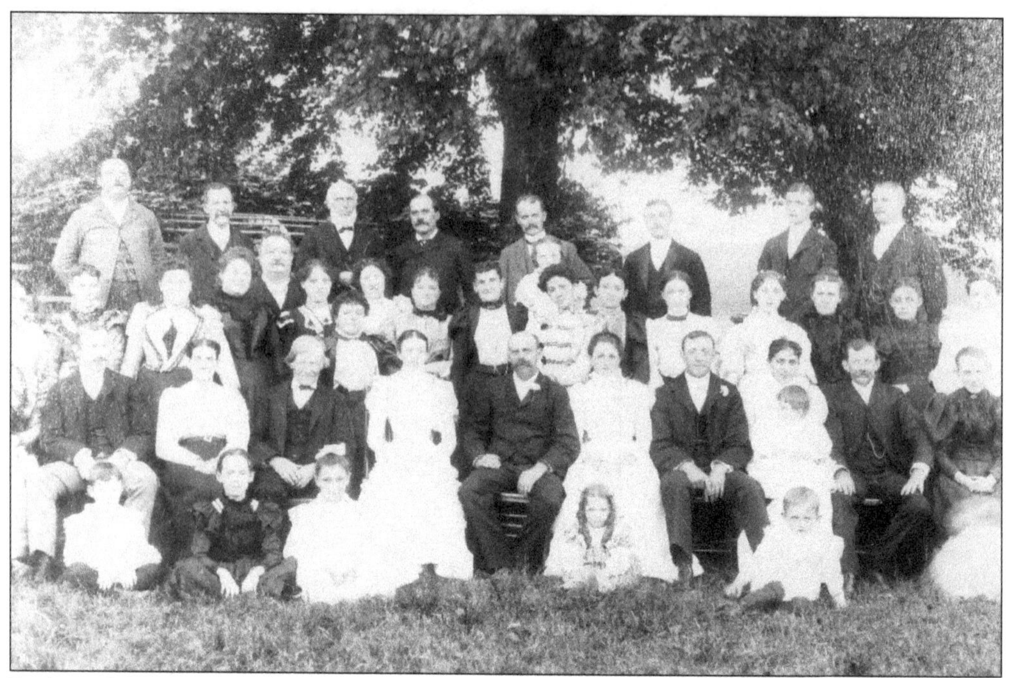

Bride and groom's families gather to celebrate the 1895 marriage of Katherine Williams and Robert Zergiebel. Zergiebel (1860-1912), who farmed 128 acres of Mountainview Road, served on the township committee and was a county freeholder, 1894-97. Eugene and Mary Bowers bought the Zergiebel place in 1913 with a $100 down payment.

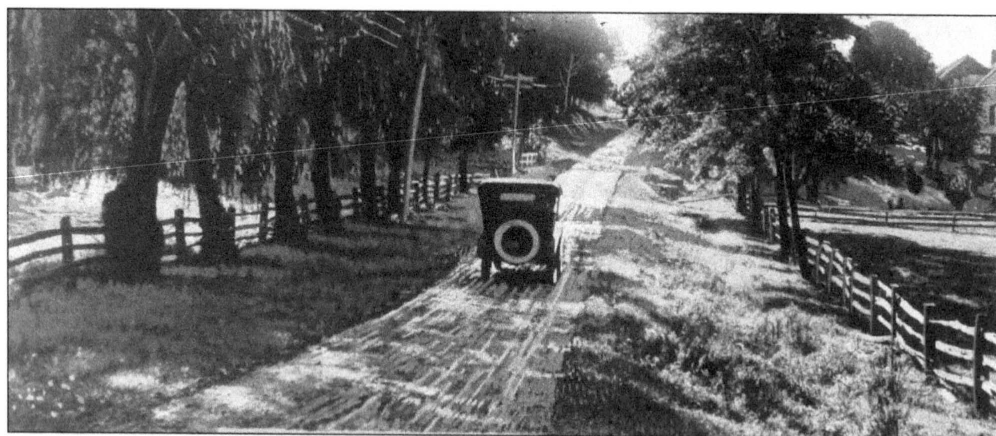

The Mount Bethel section of Warren extends as far east as Cory's Brook. A solitary car battles the rutted road as it heads west on Mountain Avenue toward the bridge over Cory's Brook in this 1925 view.

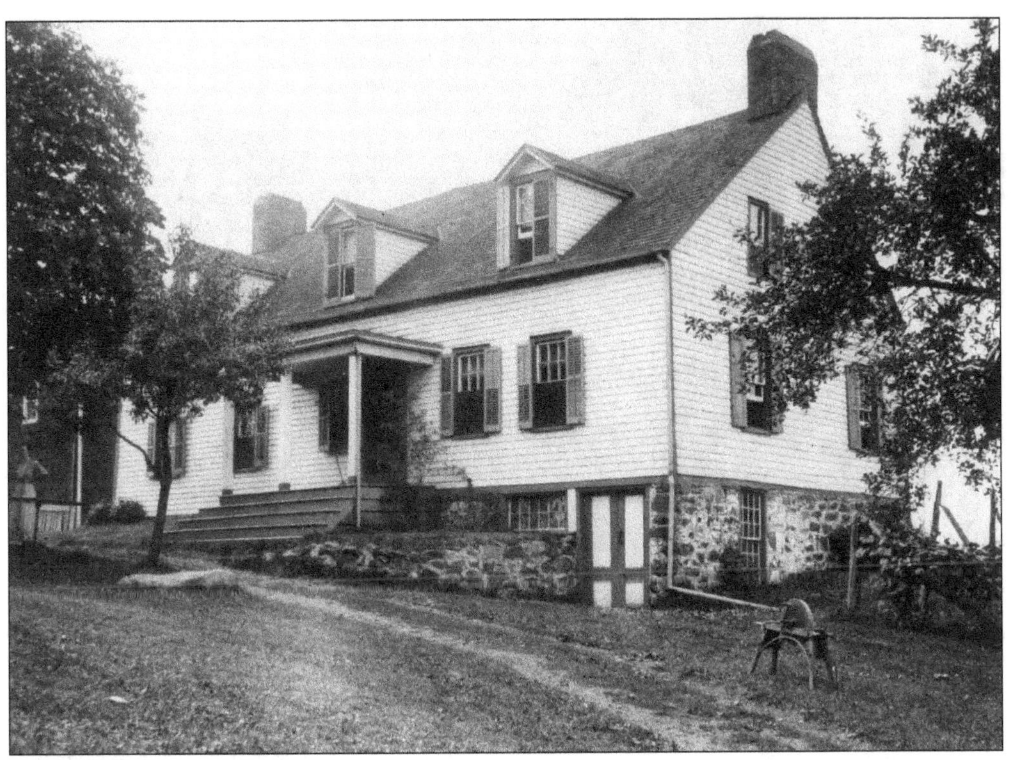

On Mountain Avenue just west of Cory's Brook stood the home and farm of John C. Cooper. A carpenter and farmer, Cooper bought 167 acres from the heirs of Alexander Kirkpatrick in 1858. Then as now, a green and fertile meadow stretches from Mountain Avenue to the banks of the Passaic River.

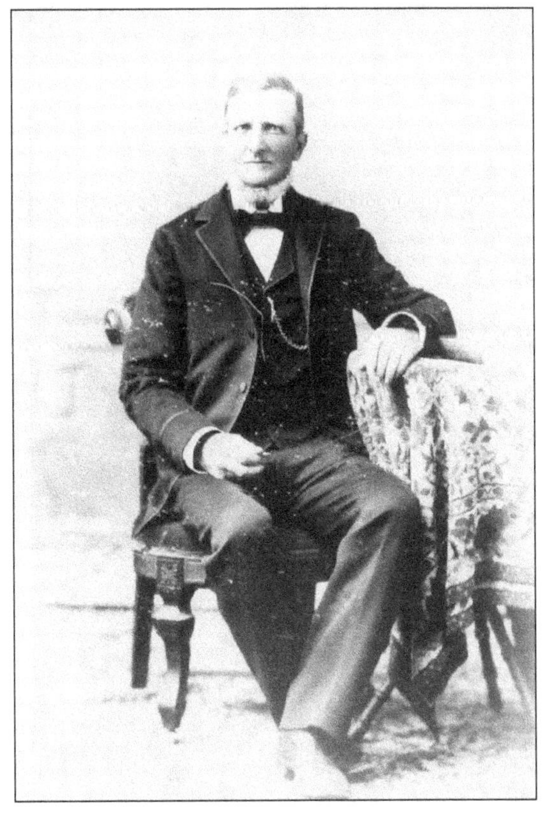

Hardworking John C. Cooper (1832-1898) poses here.

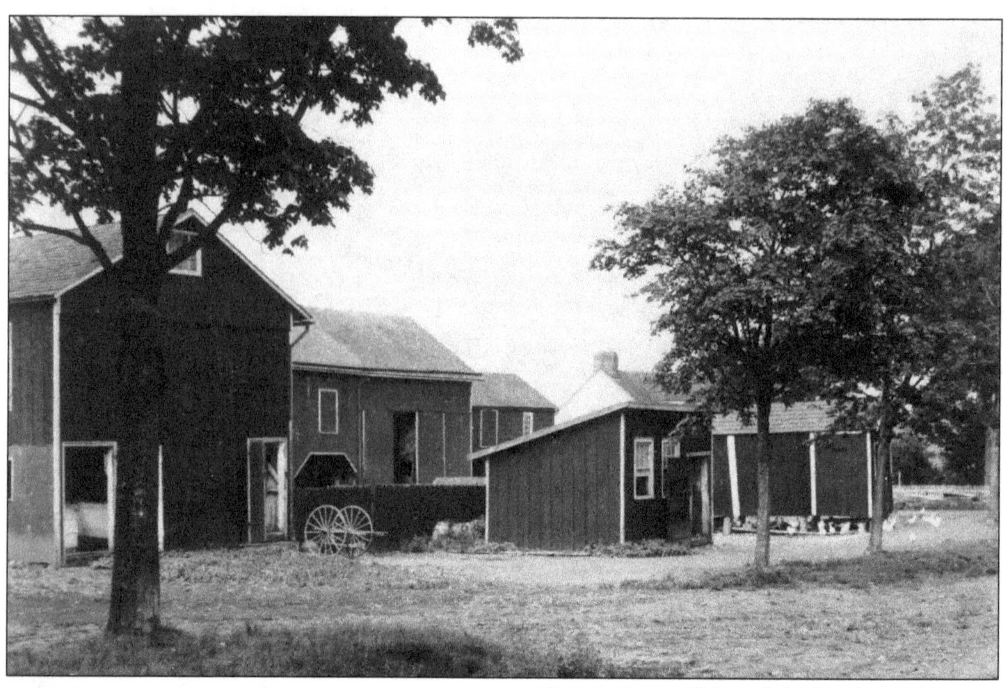

Cooper's son, Edward, "a farmer of the modern, progressive type," served as president of the Somerset County Board of Agriculture for thirty-five years. Cooper's barns were torn down in the 1960s to make way for the Glenhurst Golf Club, which in turn was replaced in the late 1980s by several modern homes. Hidden in the brush on the side of the road, Cooper's spring still runs clear and cold.

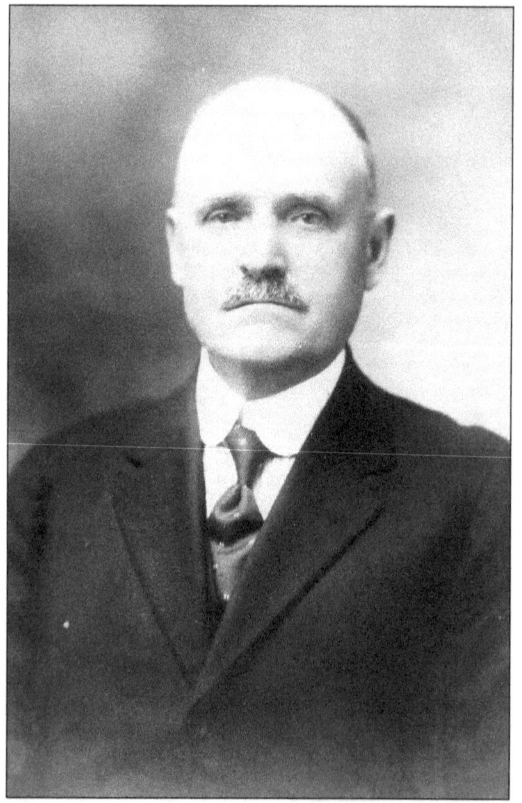

Edward E. Cooper (1865-1942), County Sheriff and Assemblyman, was a dealer in hardwood timber, loose hay, straw, and milk.

Cooper's daughter, Ida May, married George Wittmann in 1917.

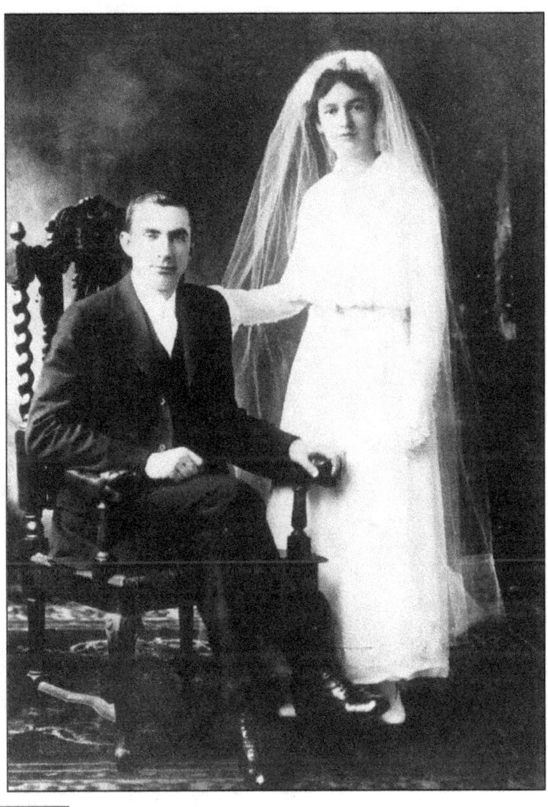

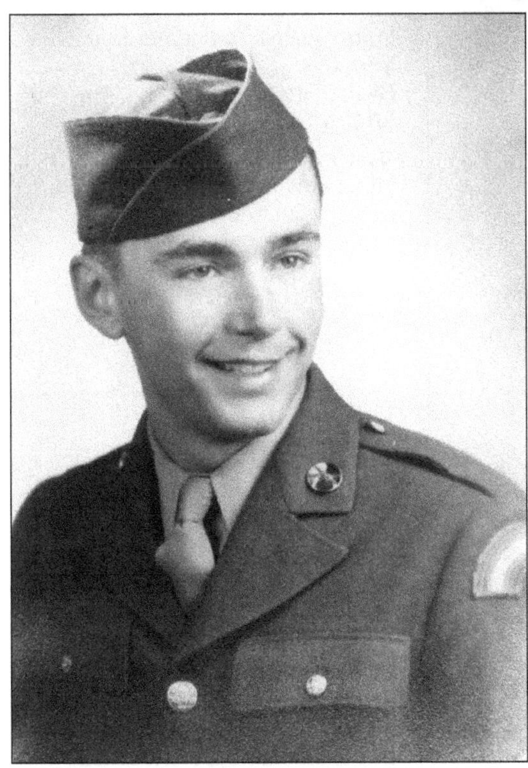

Their son, Everett E. Wittmann (b. 1925), a staff sergeant in the Army, was killed in the south of France in January 1945.

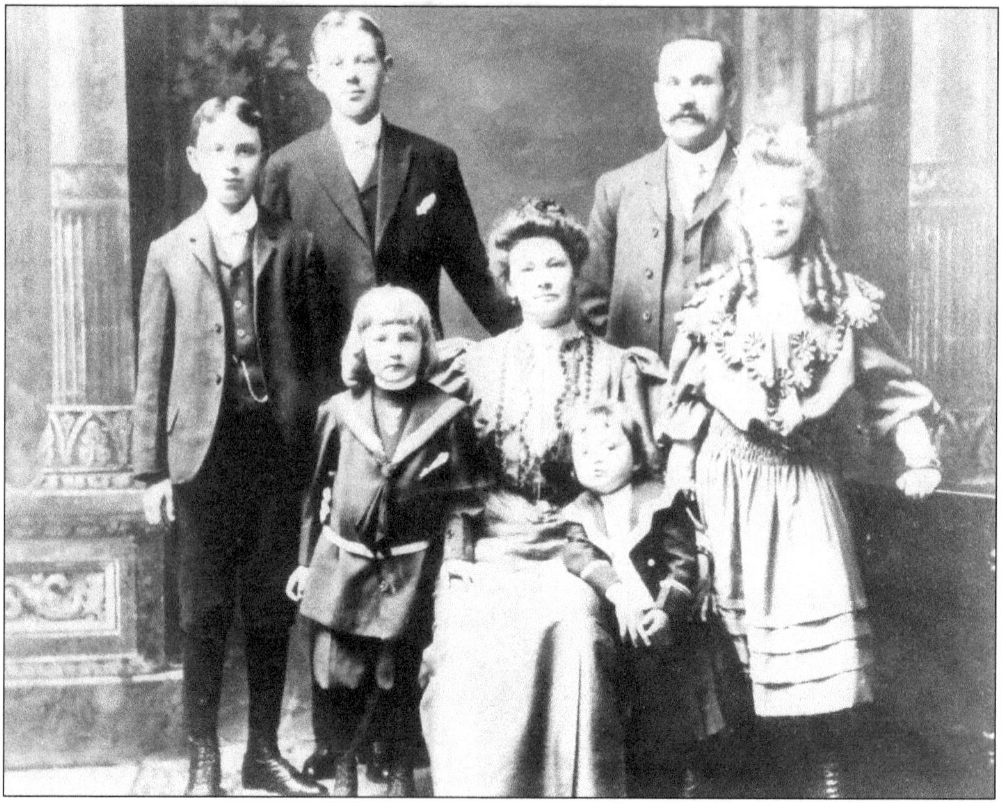

Louis Wagner, a butcher from New York City, bought the 100-acre farm west of Sheriff Cooper in 1917. It was a small operation at first, with chickens, horses, pigs, twelve cows, and some fruit trees, "just enough to get by on," remembers his granddaughter.

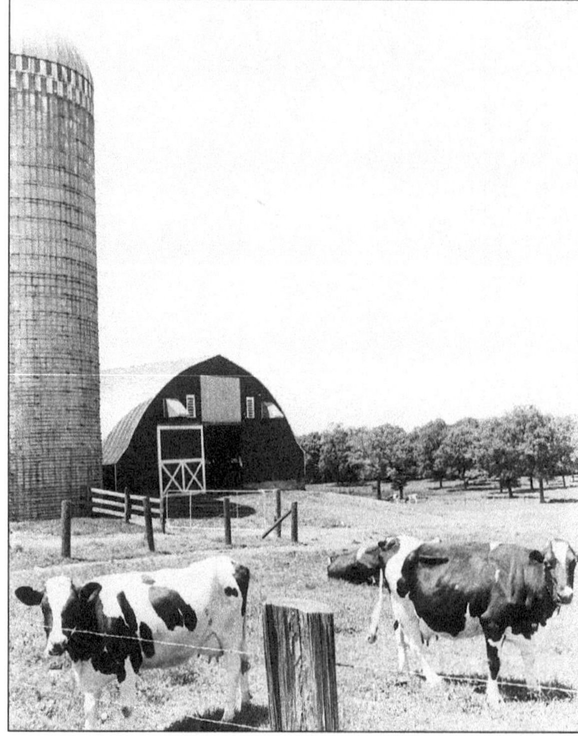

In the 1950s there were twelve working dairy farms in the township. When Charles Wagner closed the farm and store in 1987, it marked the end of an era in Warren's history.

Dina, Louis, and Charles Wagner and Rover pose here in 1945.

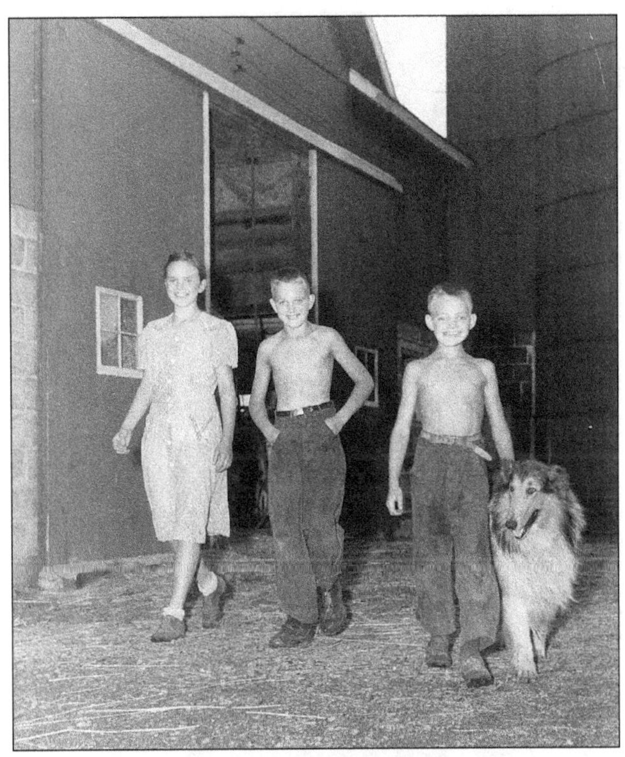

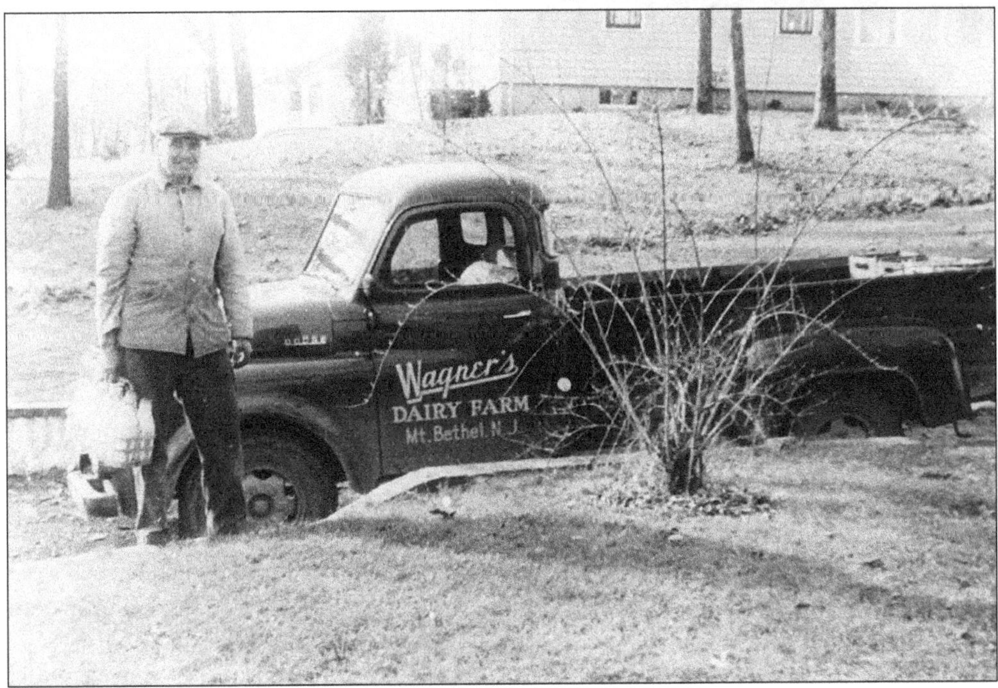

Milkman Charles Wagner, seen here in 1953, delivered milk and cream to more than a thousand families in Warren, Watchung, and nearby communities. One hundred and twenty Holstein cows contentedly chewed their way from one pasture to another. In 1975, the family gave up its milk route and opened the Wagner Dairy Farm store on Mountain Avenue

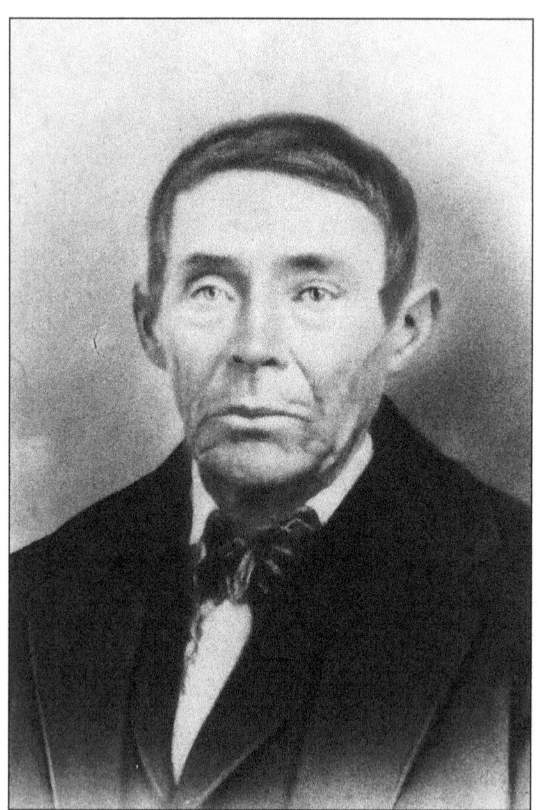

Israel Ralph (1796-1860), a shoemaker and soldier in the War of 1812, lived on King George Road north of the Baptist Meeting House.

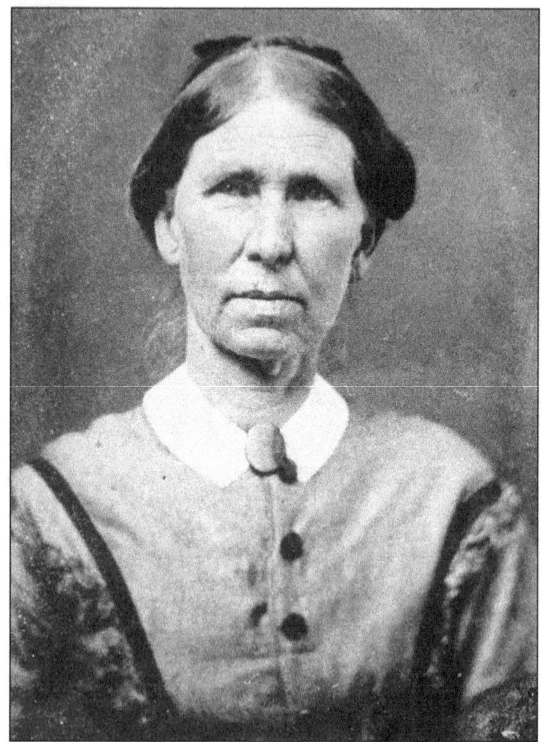

Rhoda Drake Ralph (1812-1879) was Israel's wife. In 1819, the township's overseers of the poor apprenticed her for a term of ten years.

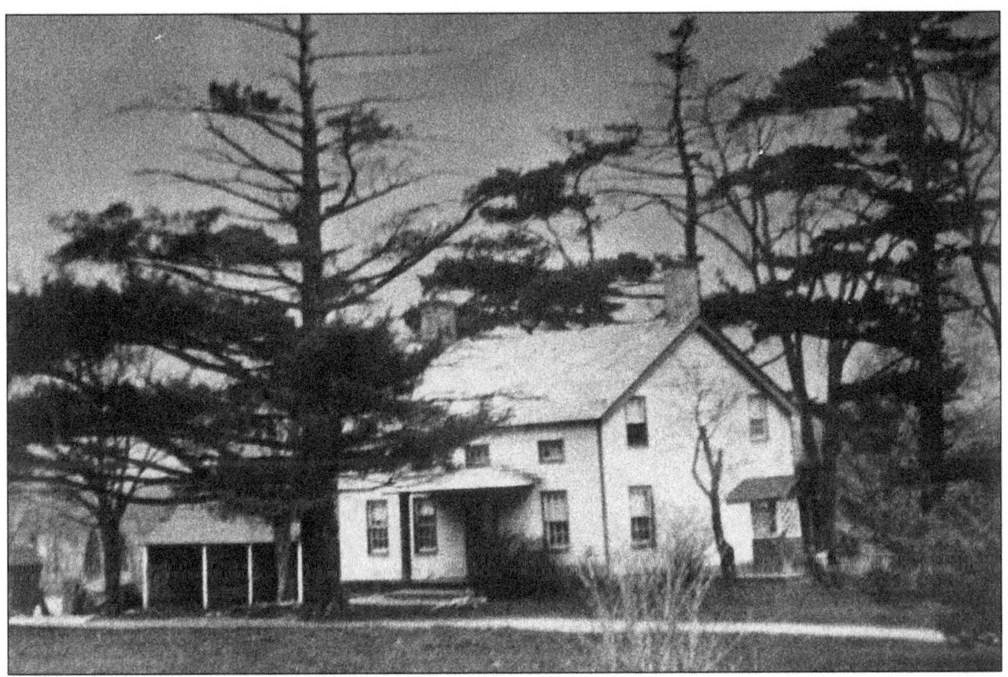

The home of Thomas Terrill, the first township clerk in 1806, stood on King George Road where AT&T is now completing its office complex. Built c. 1760, it was later home to the Ralph and Hayden families. One of the white pines pictured here still stands at the Route 78 exit.

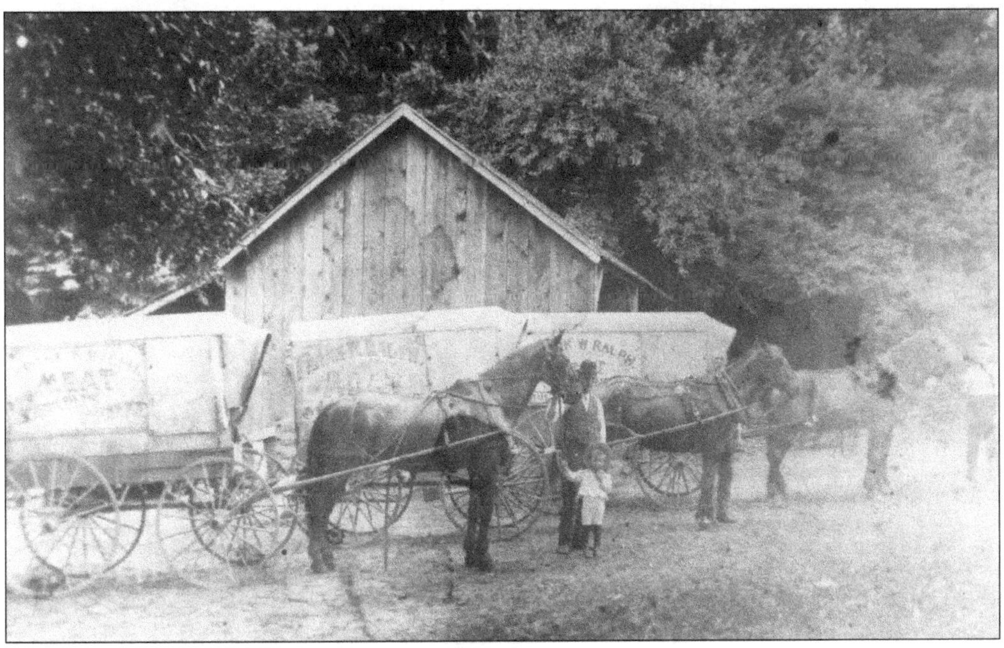

In this 1903 photograph, butcher Frank W. Ralph Sr. and his three meat wagons prepare for their day's round of deliveries. With Ralph are William (his father), Frank W. Jr., and Bert Van Fleet. Ralph started his butcher business when he was seventeen, working out of facilities on King George Road until 1928 when he moved his operation to Millington.

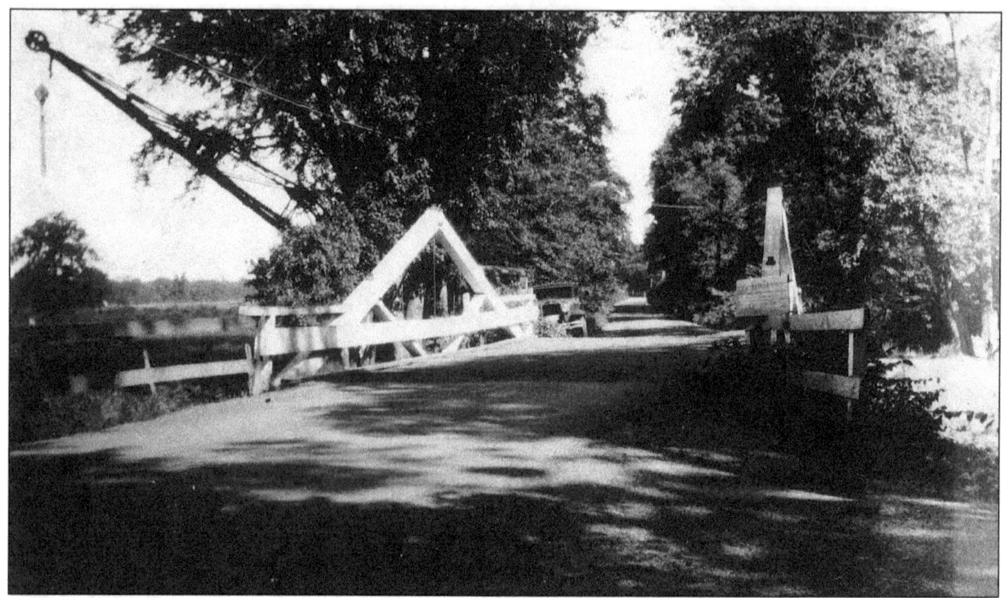

This A-frame bridge carried King George Road over the Dead River until 1932. Arline Freehauf, who took this picture just before the bridge was demolished, remembered that when the Dead and Passaic Rivers flooded, King George Road became a broad pond in which neighborhood children swam.

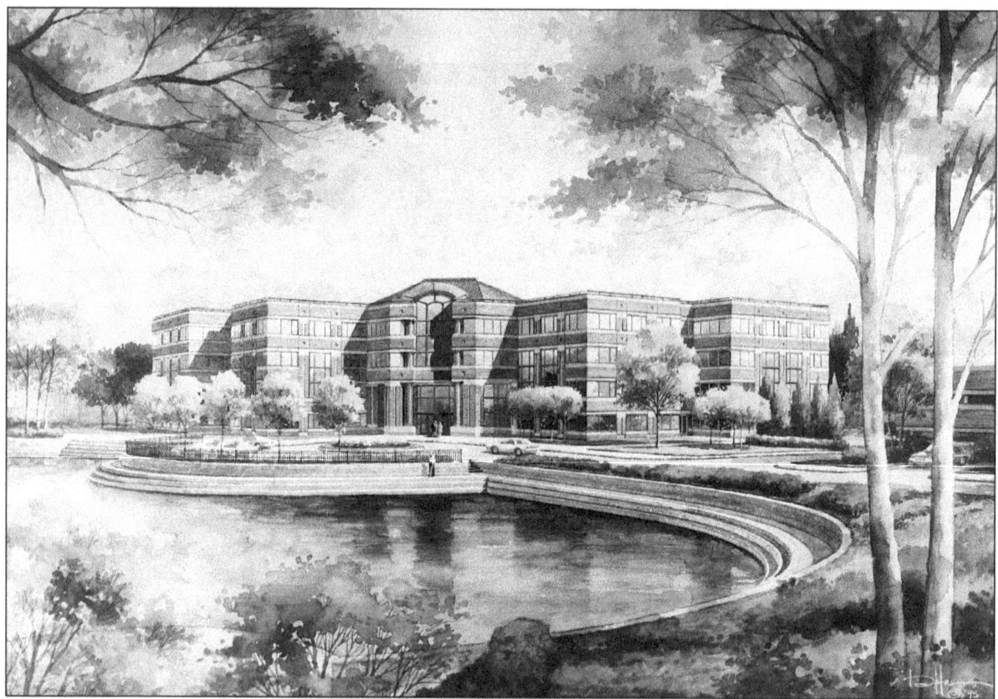

Studebaker-Worthington acquired a 192-acre site at the corner of King George Road and the future Route 78 in 1971, but it was not until 1992 that AT&T received permission to build five four-story office buildings. When completed this fall, the center will be home to Lucent Technologies and one of the largest such office complexes in central Jersey.

Four

Coontown

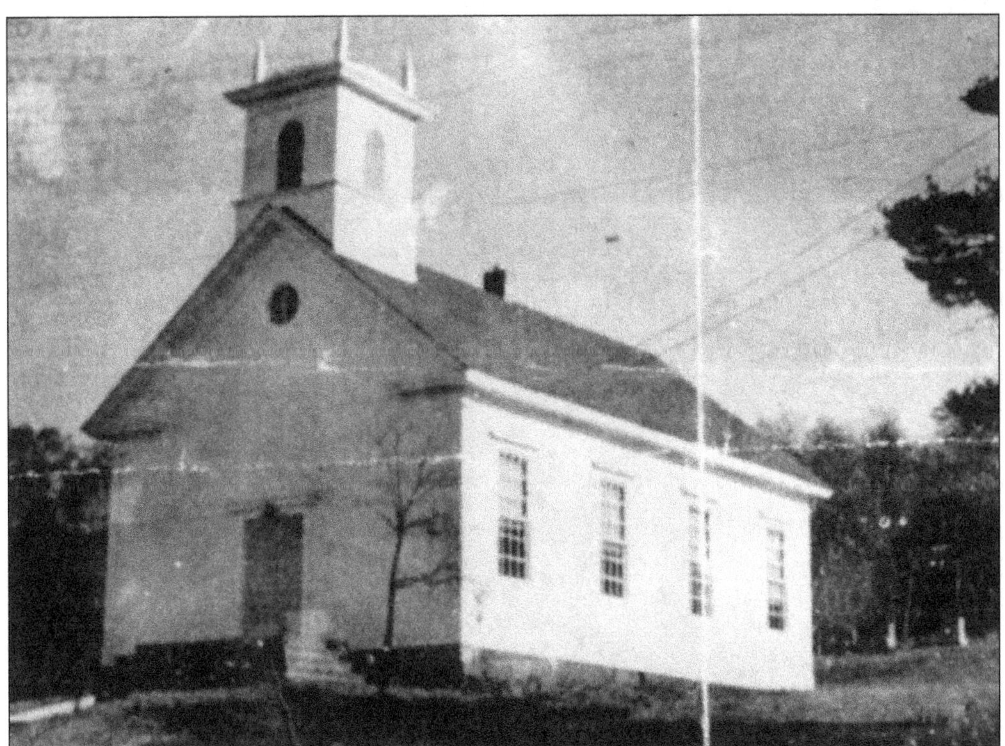

The area around the intersection of Mount Horeb and King George Roads was once known as Coontown, a name derived from the Coon family that farmed the area since the Revolution. Once the site of a distillery, cider mill, blacksmith shops, a hat factory, and two stores, by 1880 the area had reverted to farmland. German families that settled into Coontown in the 1840s founded a Lutheran church in 1846. In 1849 they raised their first building, replacing it in 1871 with this structure. In 1855 the congregation joined the Dutch Reformed Church, then the Congregational denomination in 1871.

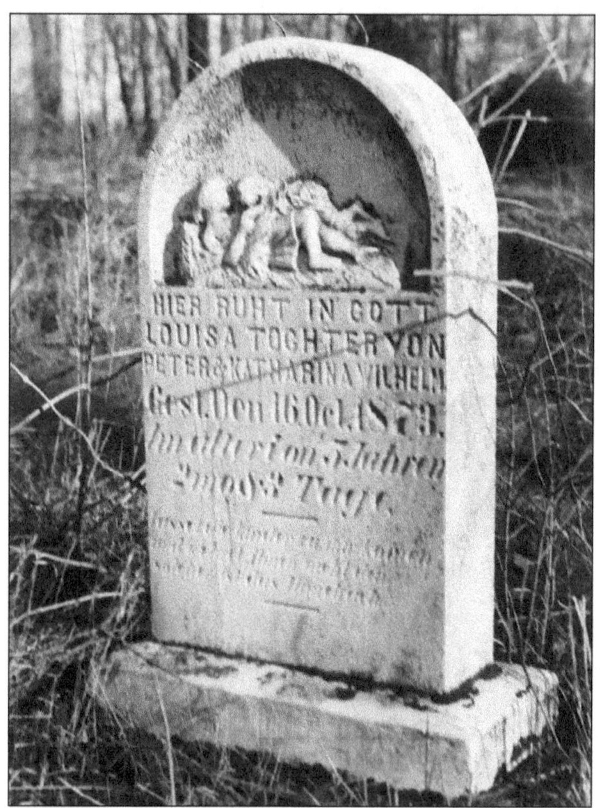

The "sturdy, frugal Germans" who settled Coontown in the 1840s retained their native language for several generations. The original records of the Coontown Church are in German, as are many tombstone inscriptions in the cemetery, including this one, dated 1879. Gradually, the old German names were Americanized: Wilhelm became Williams, Freitag became Freiday, and Bauer, Schmid, and Klein became Bowers, Smith, and Cline.

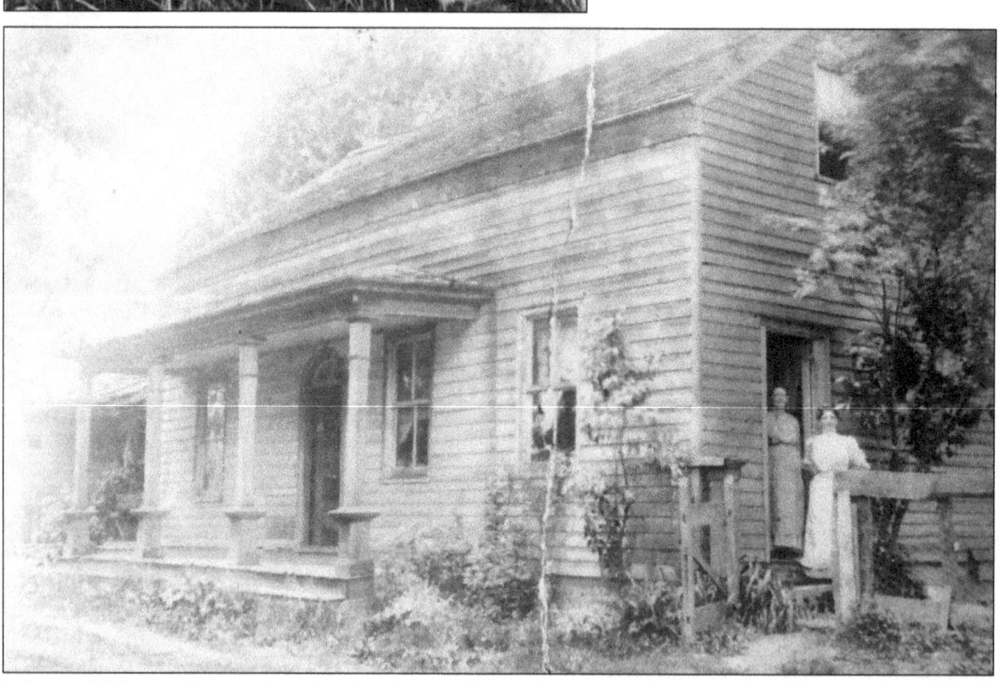

John and Nancy Bowers bought this late-eighteenth century house at 200 King George Road, once owned by John Coon, in 1846. Founding members of the Coontown Church, they were the parents of George Bowers, who later served as minister of the church.

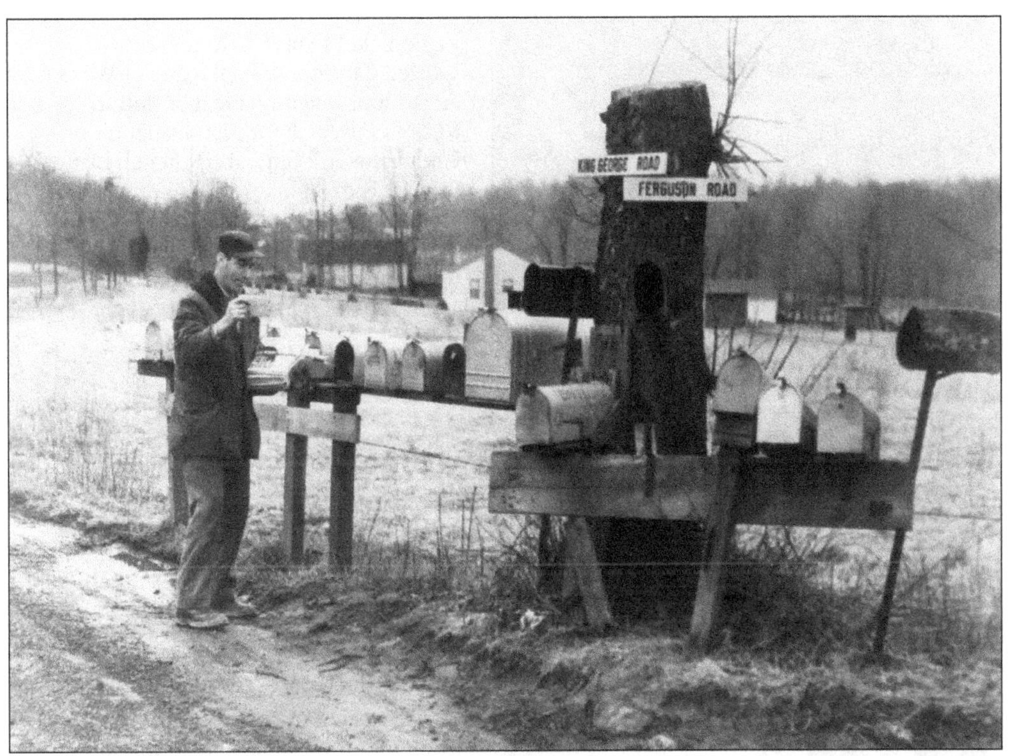

King George Road is one of the oldest in Warren, appearing on a 1761 map. The Fergusons lived here in the late nineteenth century. In this 1952 view, postman Bill Merighi sorts mail at one of Warren's "outdoor post offices," just one of many stops on RFD 2, a 29-mile route out of Plainfield.

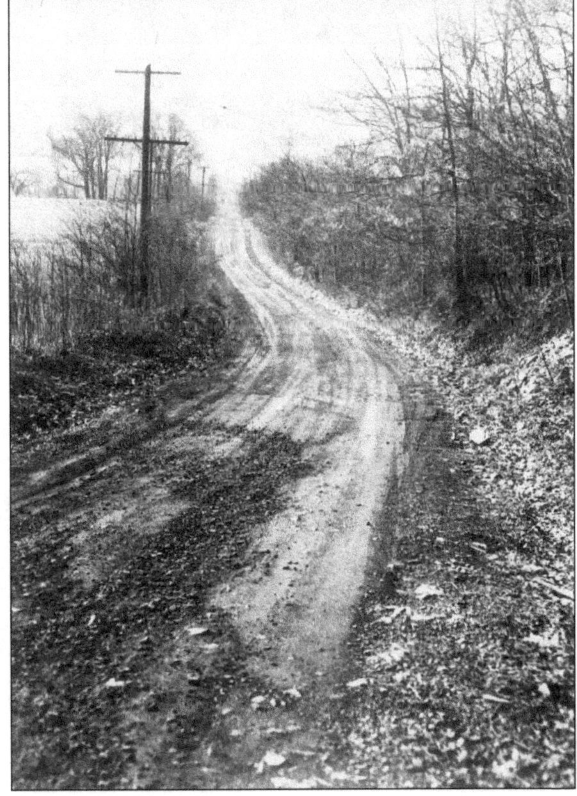

This is what upper King George Road looked like as recently as 1953. For generations road maintenance was the responsibility of adjacent landowners who received credit on their taxes for the work they did. After the turn of the century, the township assumed responsibility. In 1908 Charles Mundy charged the town $9 for six days labor working on the roads.

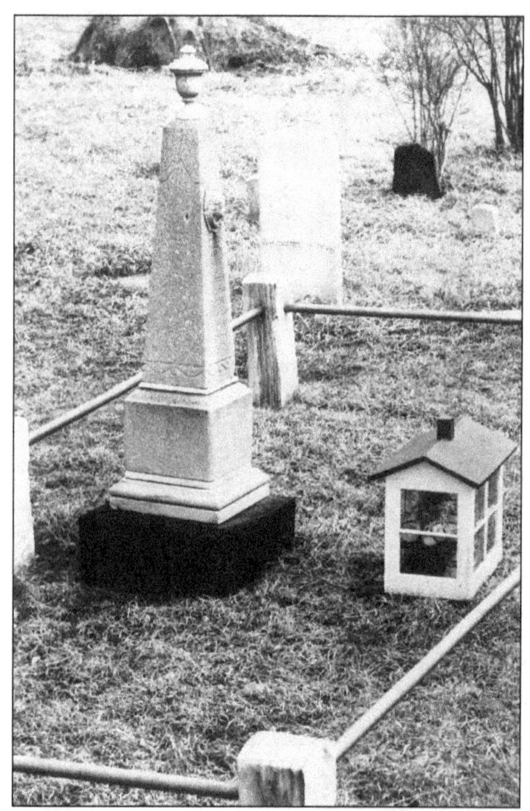

Lizzie Eckel's grave behind Trinity United Church was once one of Warren's attractions, even rating mention in *Ripley's Believe It Or Not*. Daughter of Catharine and Emmanuel Eckel, Lizzie died in 1882 at age 12. On her stone are these words: "She was lovely, she was fair, and for a while she was given; then an angel came and claimed her own and bore her home to heaven."

There was an elaborate doll house on her grave, with a set of child's party dishes on the table, a doll with a china head, and a book entitled *Little Pillow*. Lizzie's doll house, lovingly cared for by members of the congregation for nearly a century, was destroyed by vandals over twenty years ago.

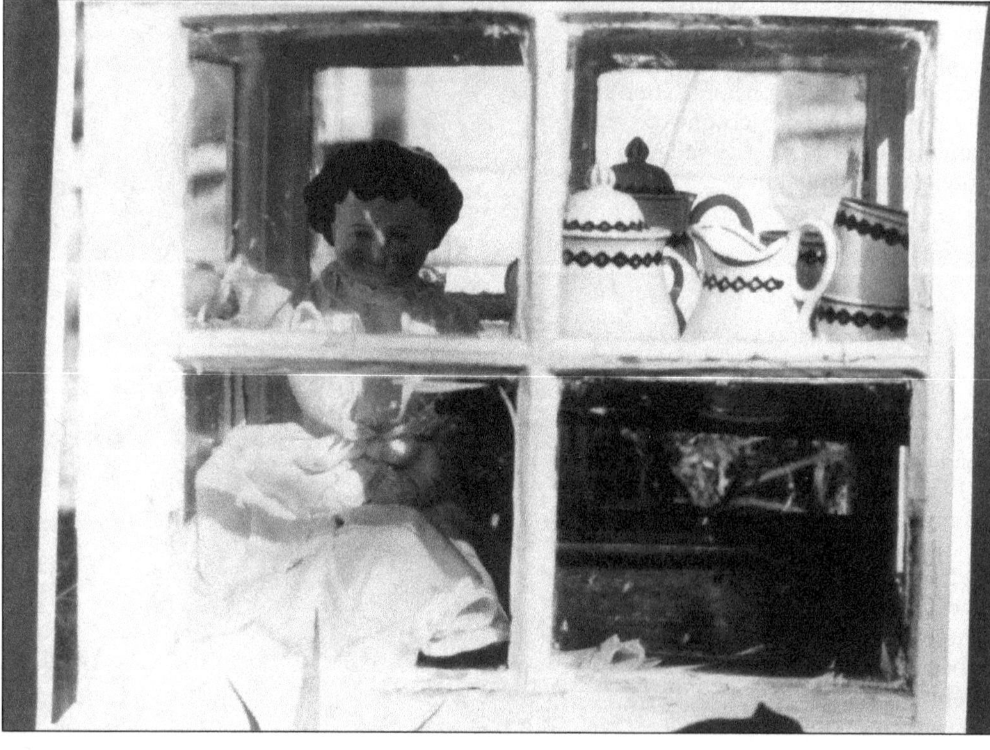

The experiences of Adam Herlich (1815-1890) were common to many Germans who settled in Coontown. Arriving here in 1853, Herlich married Catharina Goos and served as elder and church clerk of the Coontown Church.

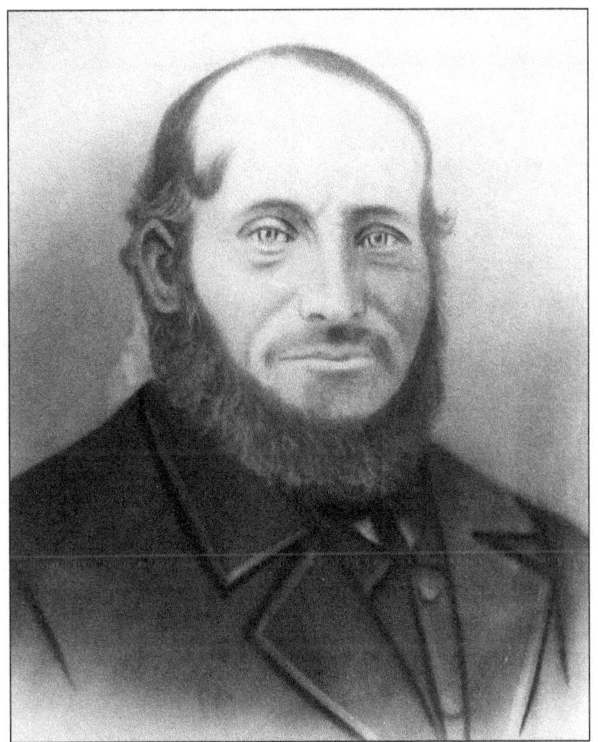

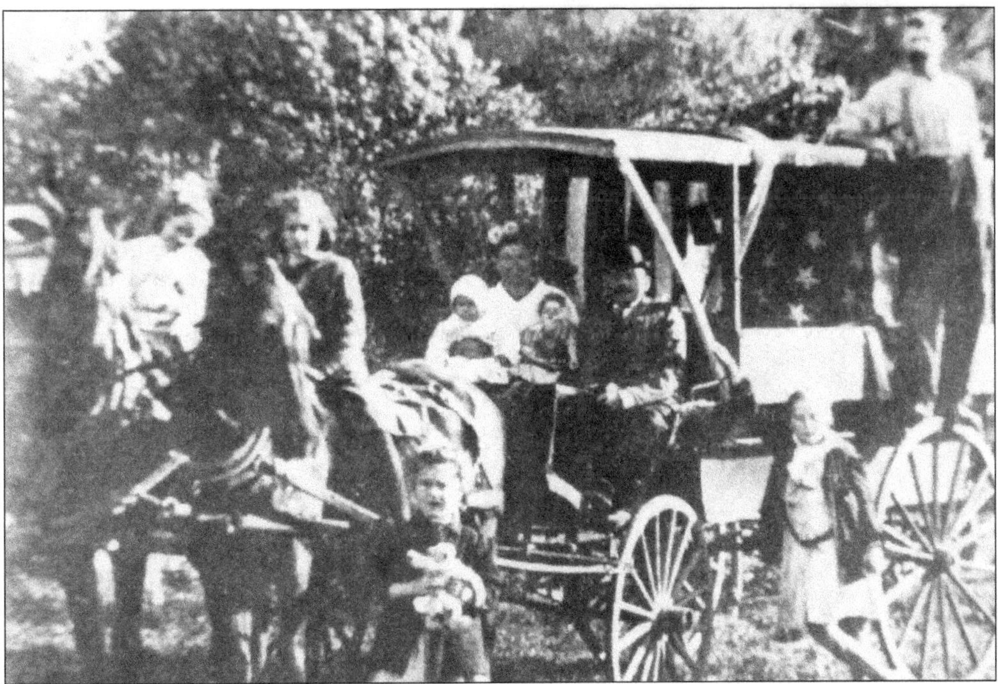

Life on Coontown's farms followed the seasons: sowing in the spring with harvesting in the fall, leaving little time for rest or pleasure. Church activities dominated the neighborhood, although as this *c.* 1900 picture shows, July 4th offered an excuse to decorate the family buggy and venture to Washington Rock for a picnic.

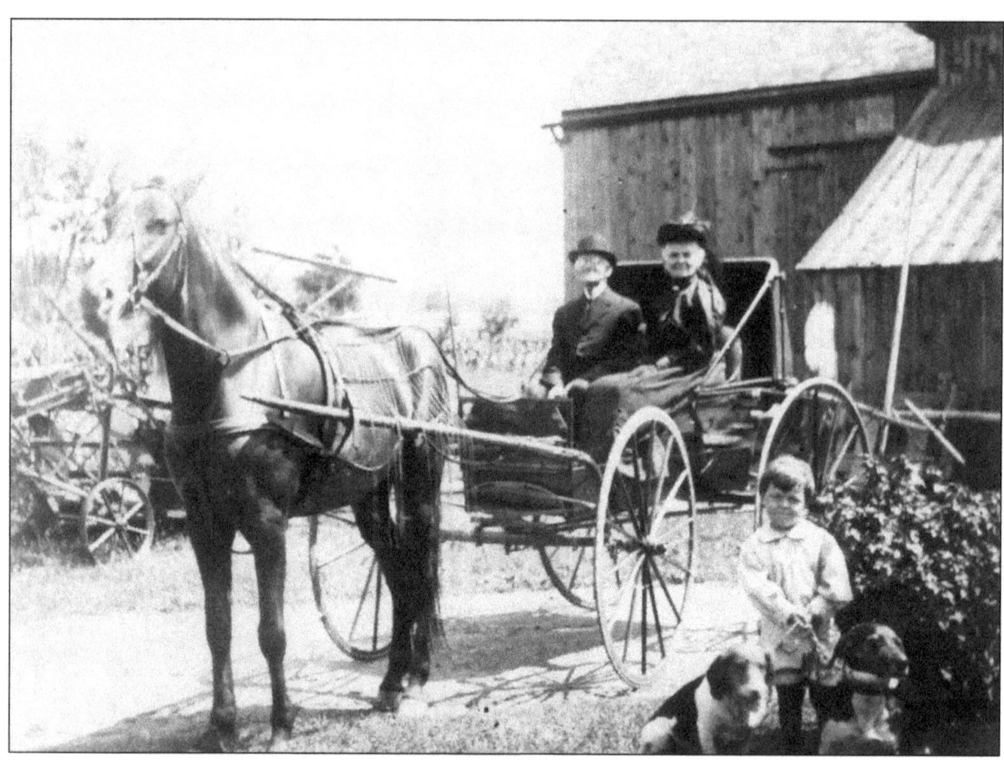

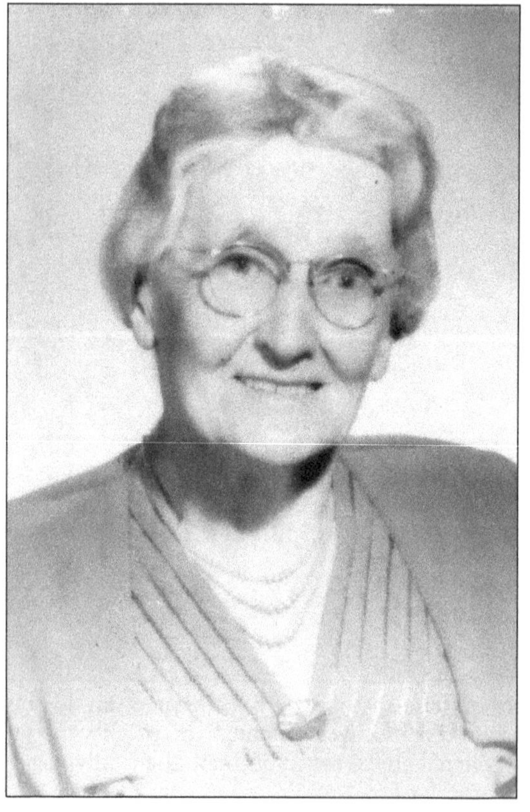

George Bowers, three years old when his family arrived in Warren, married Louisa Miller in 1867 and divided his life between farming and preaching. The Bowers family bought a 60-acre farm near where the town hall now stands in 1896, then sold it to Nathan Hofheimer in 1915. Pastor of the Coontown Church from 1872 to 1879 and again from 1894 to 1931, Reverend Bowers died in 1932. The Bowers are seen here in front of the barn with one of their grandchildren.

Mamie Bowers Miller (1870-1975), Reverend Bowers's daughter, taught at Mount Horeb and South Stirling Schools, wrote poetry, played the organ, and sang in the church choir. In her youth she took part in all the plays and social events her father planned for his small congregation.

George Freiday, born Johann Georg Freitag in Germany, came to America in 1839. His grandson, Peter (1888-1954), married Maude Bowers in 1915. A machinist in his younger days, Freiday turned to dairy farming, for many years selling milk to families in Warren and the Plainfields.

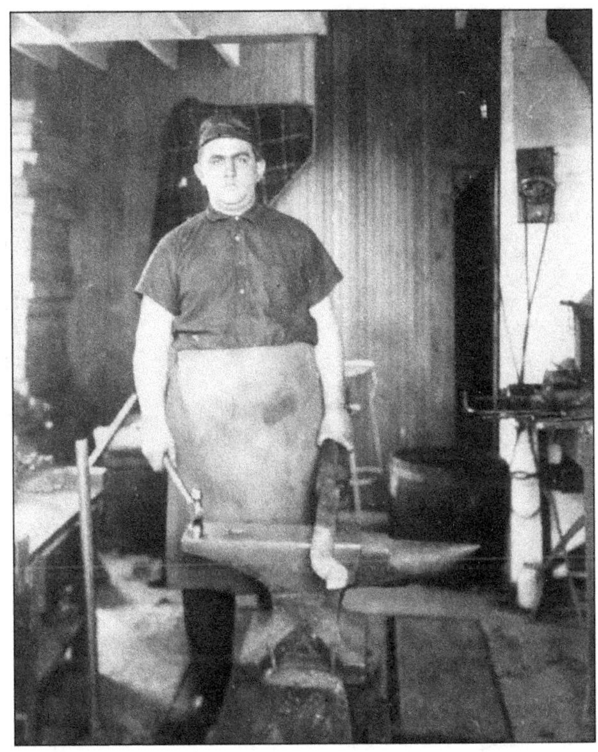

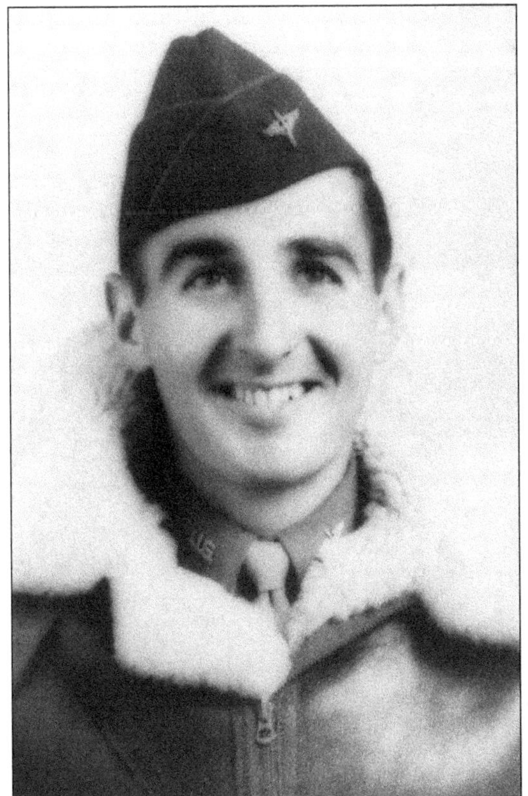

Nearly two hundred men and seven women from Warren served in World War II, representing roughly 9 percent of the township's population. Milton Freiday (b. 1917), Peter's son, was a bombardier with the United States Army Air Force.

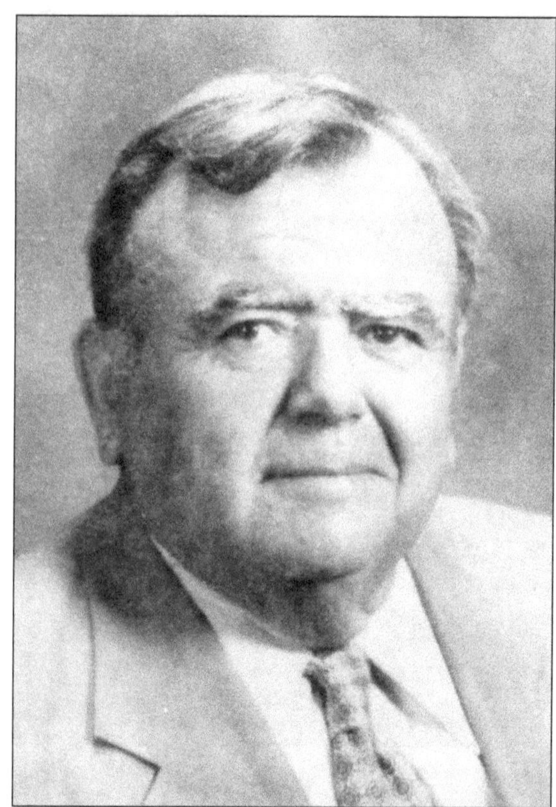

Angelo L. Tomaso (1929-1992), who lived next to Trinity United Church, retired in 1990 after serving thirty-one years as superintendent of schools. Joining the system as a teacher at Central School in 1953, he became superintendent six years later, overseeing the rapid growth of the school system. During his term, Mount Horeb, Washington Valley, and the Middle School were built. In 1990 a grateful town renamed the Washington Valley School in his honor.

Perhaps Coontown's most unusual building is this "castle" at 107 King George Road. Another unique structure is the Alliance Bible Church at 52 Mount Horeb Road, which consists of two geodesic domes constructed in the 1980s after a design pioneered by R. Buckminster Fuller.

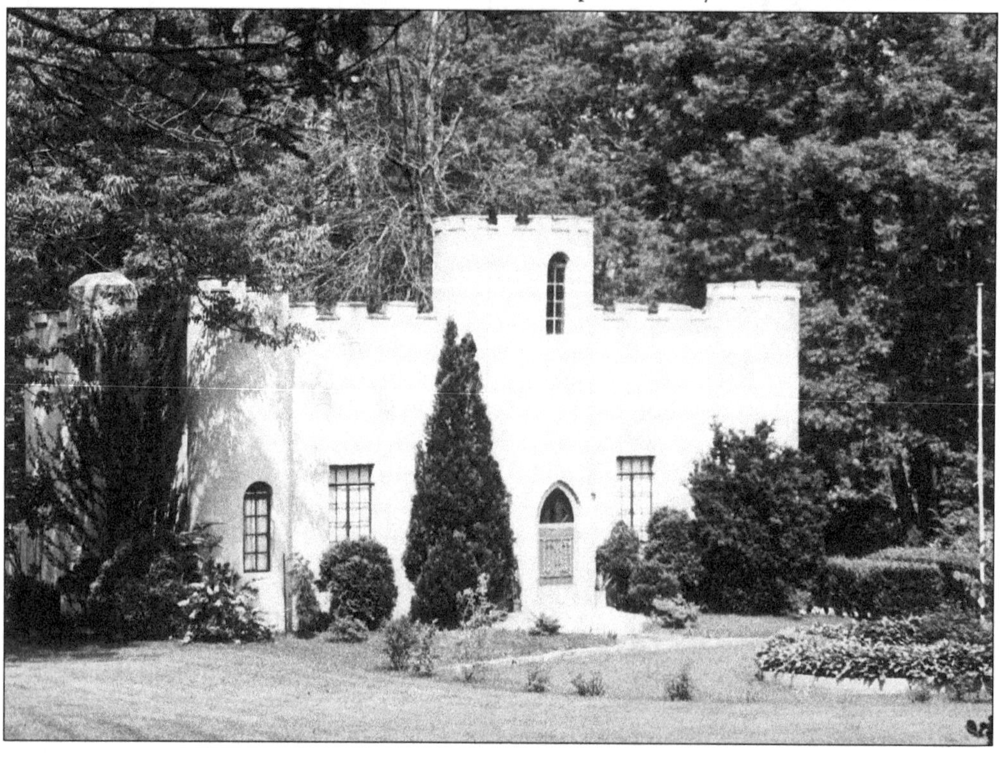

Waylande Gregory (1905-1971), a virtuoso in ceramics, built his studio at 16 Mountain Trail in the Aztec style after moving here in 1938. A nationally-recognized artist, he created such enormous works as the *Fountain of the Atoms* (displayed at the main entrance to the 1939 World's Fair) as well as busts of such well-known figures as Henry Fonda, Einstein, and Hildegarde.

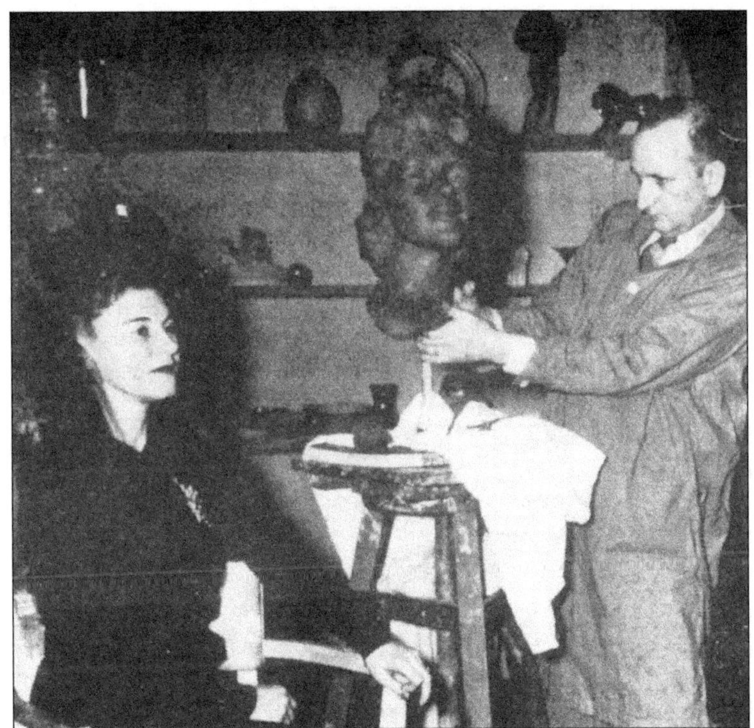

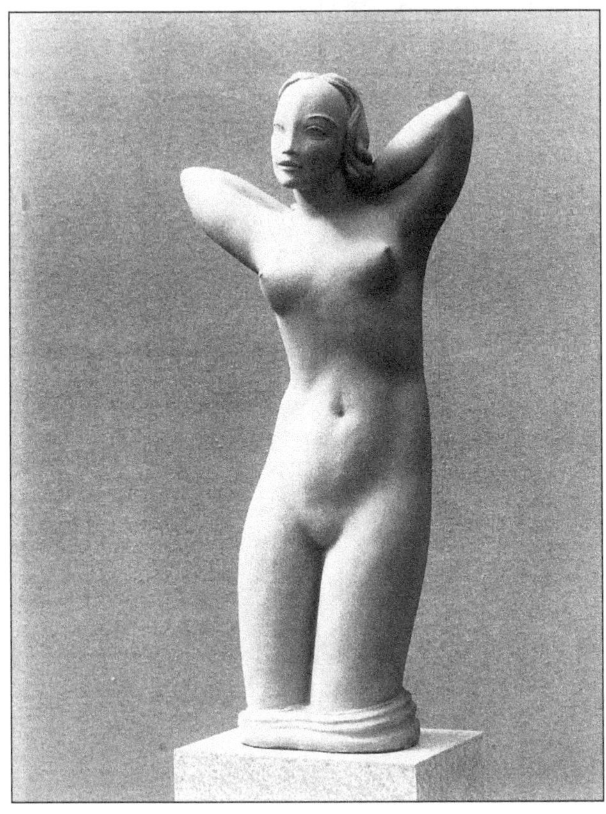

The Bather, c. 1940s, was a Gregory work. The artist's Mountain Top Studio was surrounded by gardens in which he displayed his larger works. He moved here, according to his wife, because he needed space for kilns "big enough to house a couple of horses comfortably. . . ."

BALLOT No. 394

TO BE TORN OFF BY JUDGE OF ELECTION — Fold to this line

SCHOOL ELECTION BALLOT

TOWNSHIP OF WARREN, N. J.
TUESDAY, FEBRUARY 13, 1934

Polling District No. 1
(Entire Township, including the Districts Nos. 1, 2, 3, and 4)
New Warren Township School
Mt. Bethel Road

William B. J. Reitze
District Clerk

For Membership to Board of Education, Full Term (Vote for 3)

To vote for any person whose name appears on this Ballot mark a cross (X) or plus (+) mark with black ink or black lead pencil in the place or square at the left of the name of such person.

- ☐ CHARLES A. ERICSON
- ☐ JACKSON M. METLAR
- ☐ (Mrs.) MARION MORTON
- ☐ VICTOR POSSIEN
- ☐ WILLIAM B. J. REITZE
- ☐
- ☐
- ☐

To vote in favor of the proposal place a cross (X) or a plus (+) mark in the space opposite the word "YES."
To vote against the proposal place a cross (X) or a plus (+) mark opposite the word "NO."

	YES	CURRENT EXPENSES $15,508.50
	NO	

Only Coontown was without its own schoolhouse. There was but one school election district for the whole township in 1934, the year the entire township budget was $15,508.50. Paper ballots were used in Warren elections until the 1940s.

Mount Horeb Road boasted paving and a row of gawky utility poles but little else in this 1953 photograph. John Suckoe, who lived on Broadway Road near the Wurmser family, joined the Mount Bethel Volunteer Fire Company in 1939 and rose to become its chief. He was also an active member of the special police.

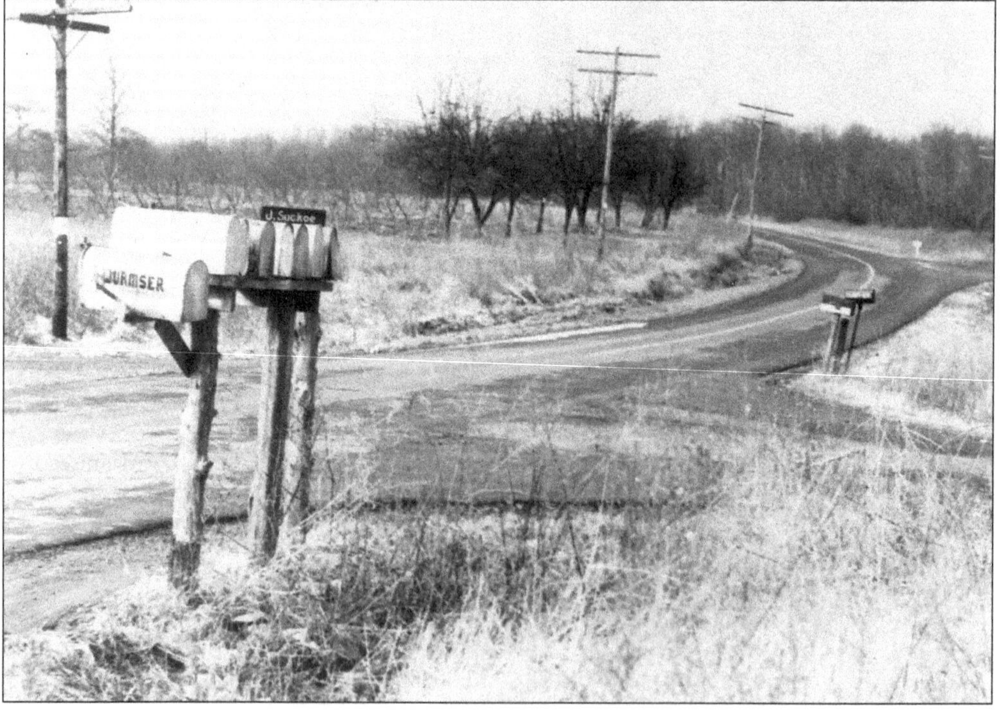

Five

Mount Horeb and Dead River

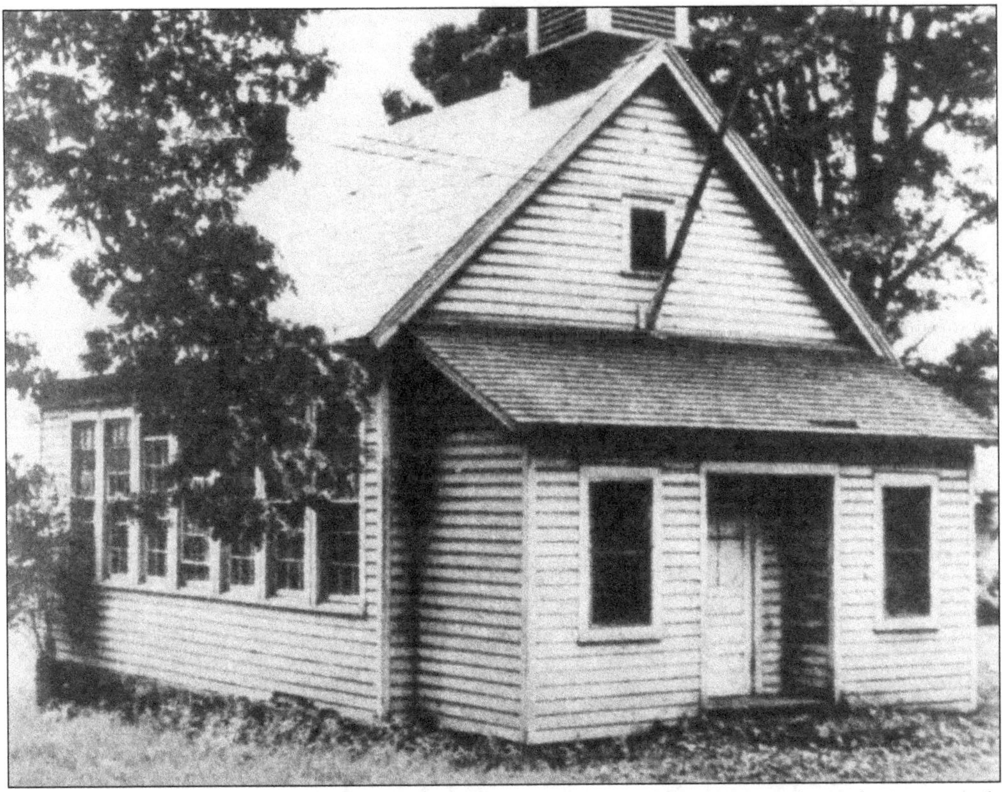

The westernmost part of Warren has been known as Mount Horeb since the early nineteenth century when Methodists built their church at the corner of Mount Horeb and Liberty Corner Roads. The original Round Top School near the corner of Mount Horeb and Dock Watch Hollow Roads was built c. 1857 on land donated by Jacob and Lydia Giddes. The present building was erected after a fire destroyed the second schoolhouse at the site.

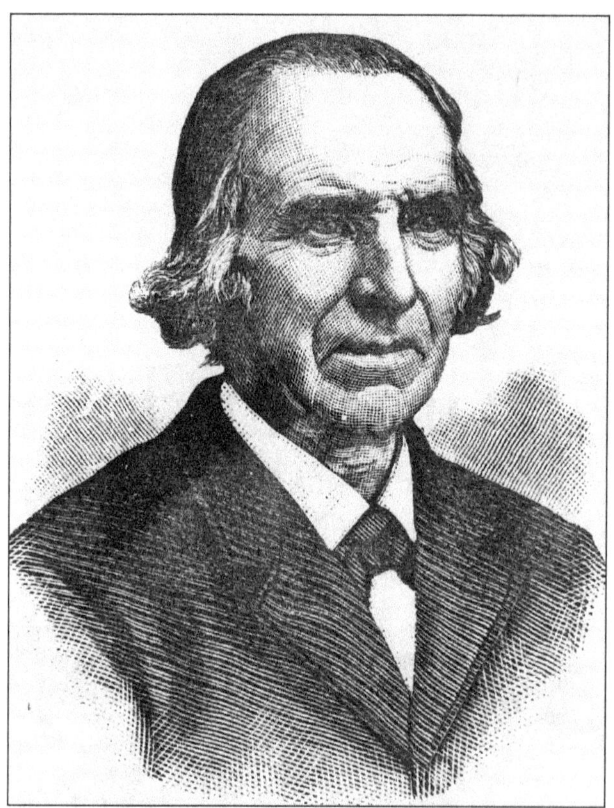

Samuel Giddes (1816-1891), a farmer at Mount Horeb, was "universally esteemed for his integrity. . . ." His great-grandfather, John, was the first of the family to settle here.

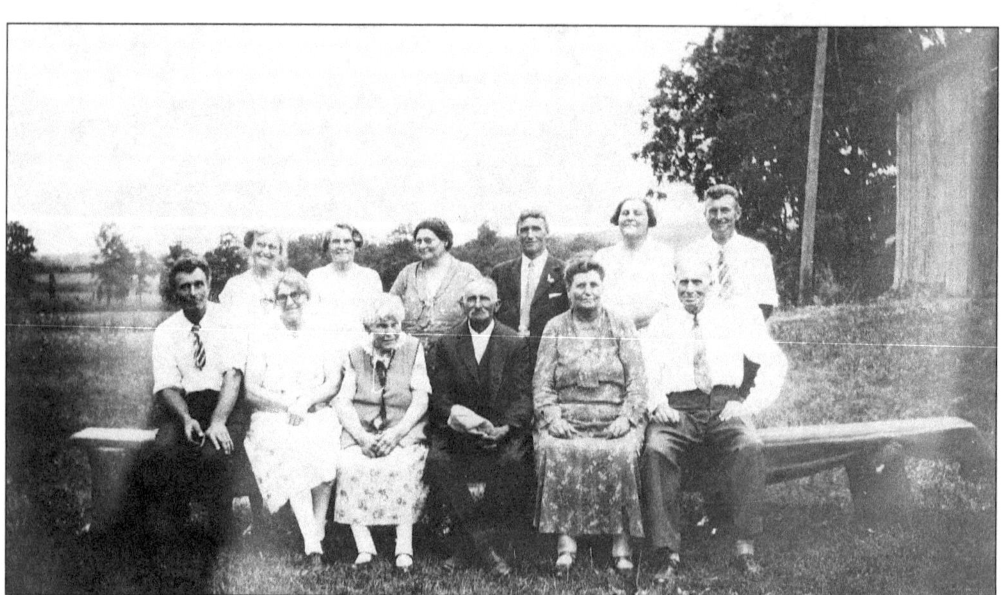

Members of the Giddes family still call Mount Horeb their home. A Giddes family reunion in 1927 included Emma, Lillian, Jenny, Eugene, Edith, LeRoy, Rufus, Phebe, Estelle, and Jacob, the children of Cornelius and Fanny Moore Giddes.

Ethel Giddes Osmon (1910-1988) and her cousin, Jenny Thoresen, are shown here c. 1925. Ethel was born and died in the same house at 59 Mount Horeb Road.

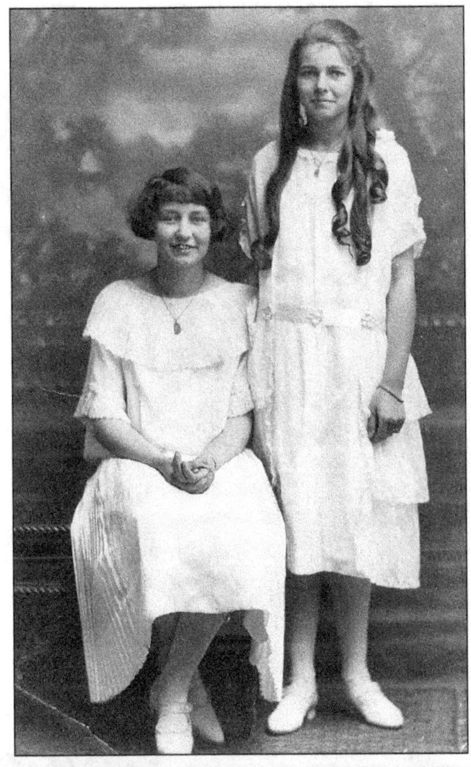

The Mountain Jewish Community Center (now Temple Hor Shalom) came to Mount Horeb Road in 1981. Gerald Flanzbaum, Murray Howard, Bernard Berkowitz, and Ida Friedman (all shown here) led the center's first meeting at the Rescue Squad building in August 1970.

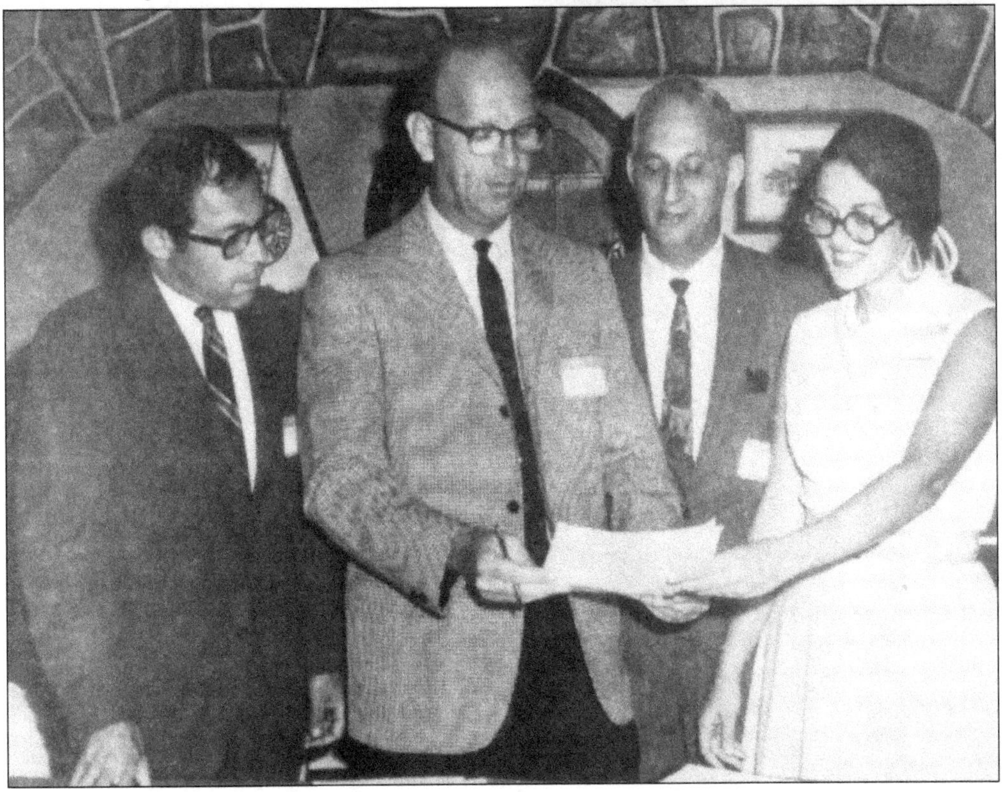

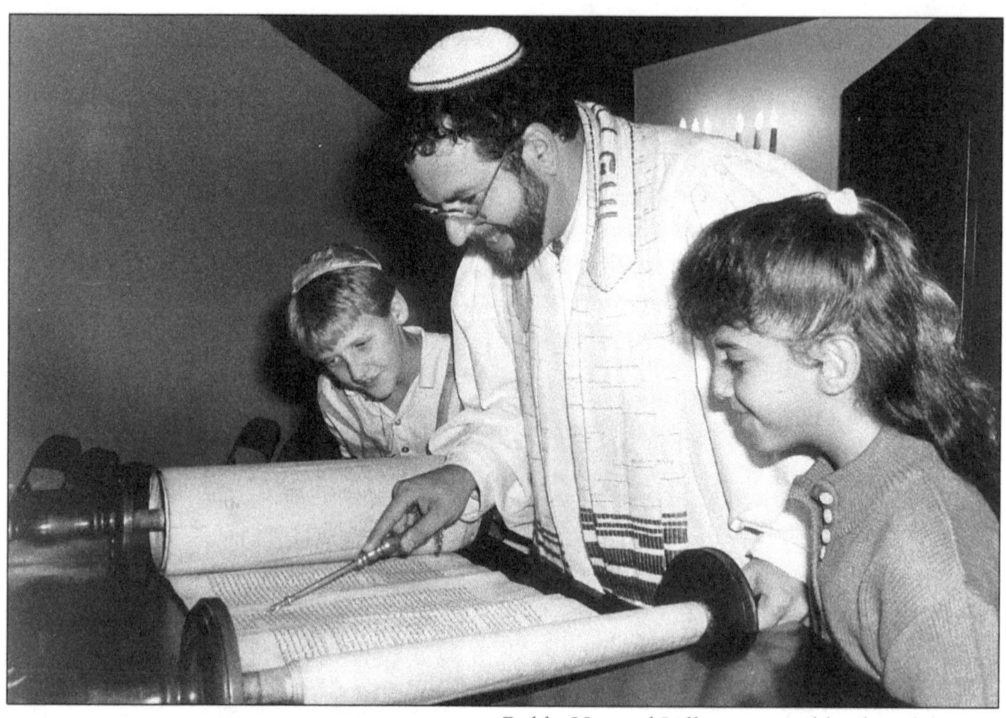

Rabbi Howard Jaffee, spiritual leader of the temple since 1988, reads from the Torah to Douglas Silversten and Sandra Menasha. The temple traces its history to July 1970, when five couples gathered at the home of Marilyn and Gerald Flanzbaum.

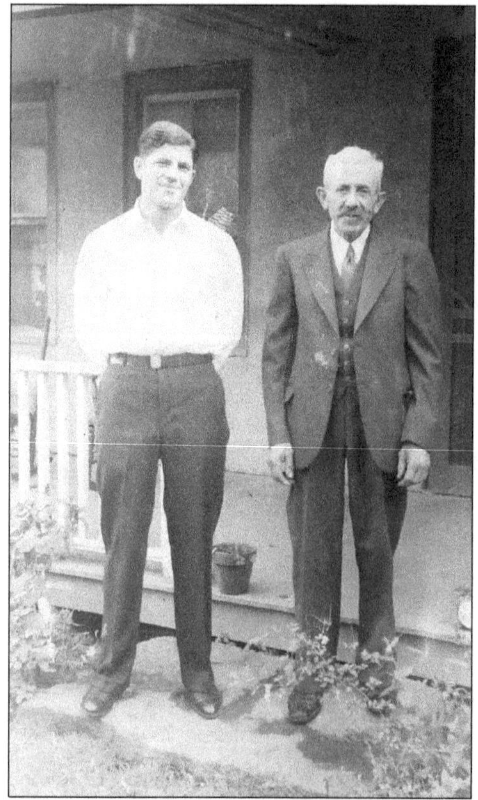

Frank Salvato Sr., shown here with his son, Frank, came to Warren soon after the turn of the century, buying the old Blazier place on Mount Horeb Road A dairy farmer, he made provolone, Romano, and mozzarella cheeses.

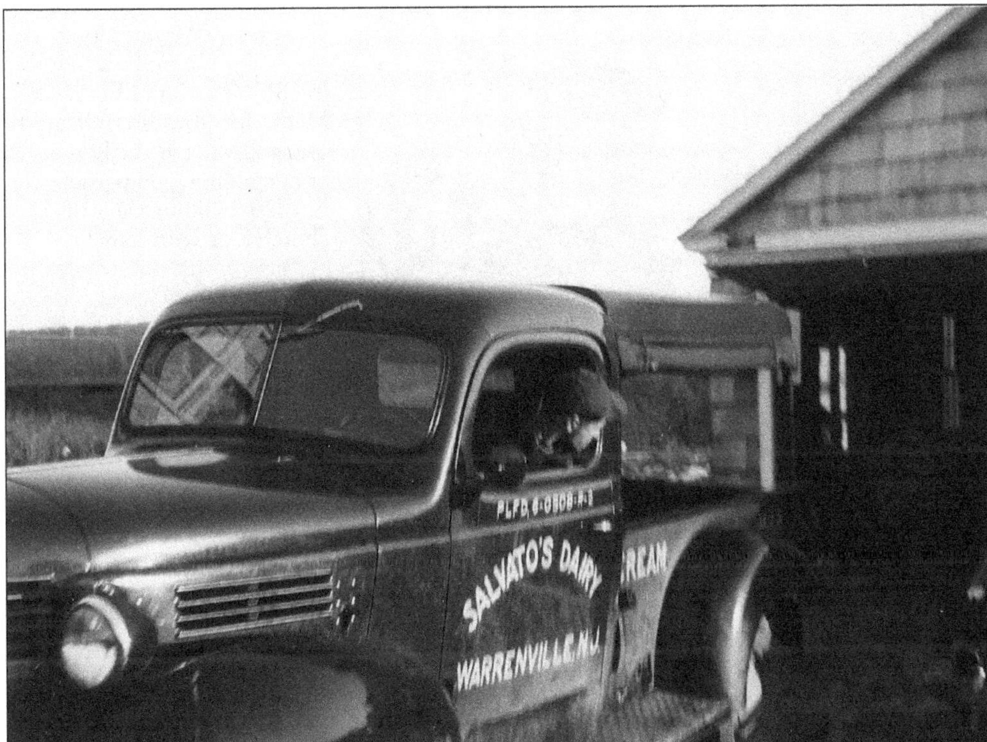

Frank Jr., shown here in 1941, was a dairyman and farmer like his father. He entered politics in 1939 when he was elected to the township committee. He returned to the township committee in 1985 after twenty-seven years on the regional high school board of education.

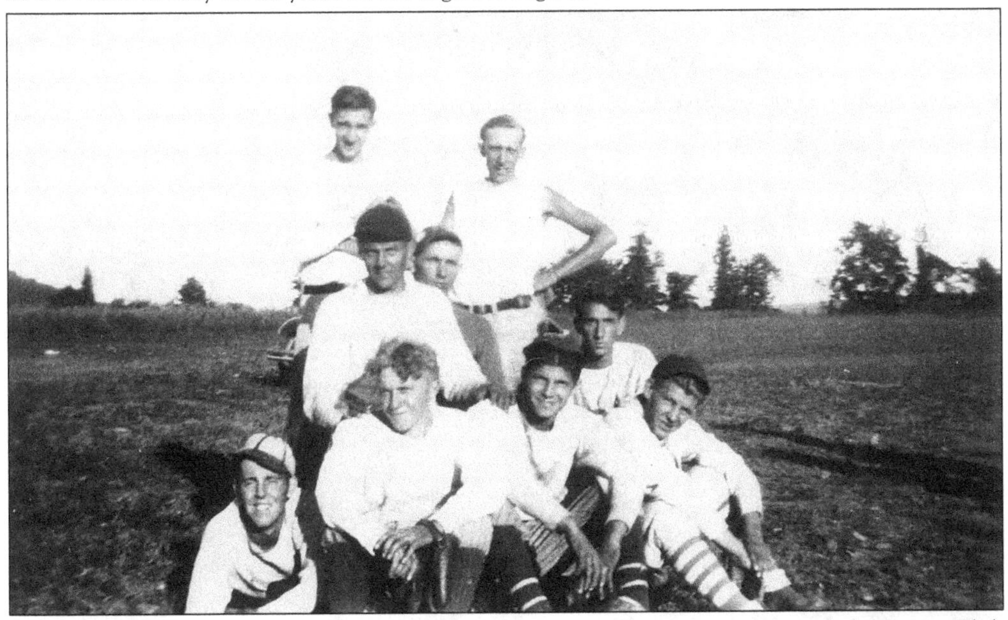

Salvato played with the Blue Jays baseball team in his youth, then managed the Lions Club Little League team in the early 1950s. Blue Jays Frank Mangee, Philip Berberich, William Newland, and Frank and Dan Salvato pose in this 1932 snapshot.

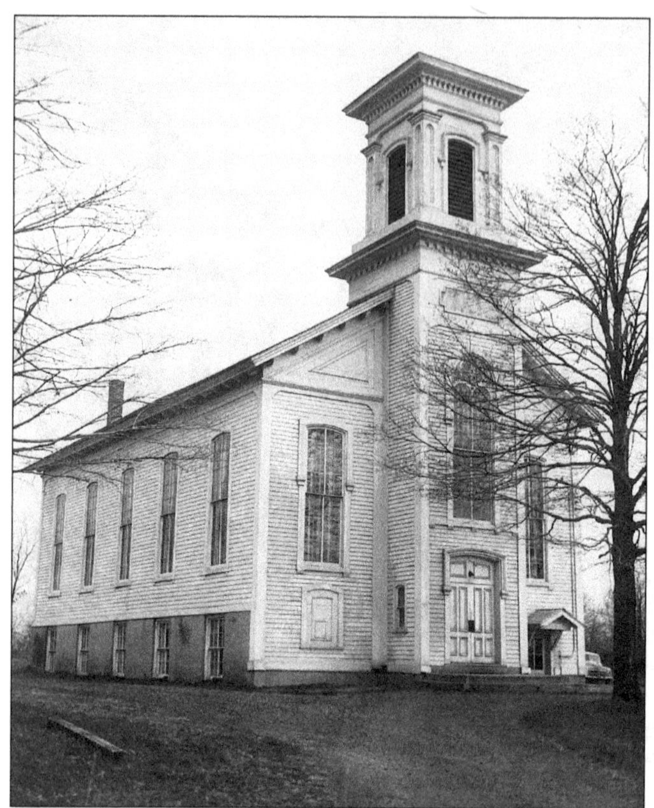

The present Mount Horeb Methodist Church was built in 1867 at a cost of $11,000. Methodists in western Warren originally met at the home of Benjamin Coddington in 1820, building their first church four years later.

The original Mount Horeb Methodist Church parsonage was erected in 1846 and burned in 1963. The seven-room house did double duty as a stagecoach stop before the Civil War.

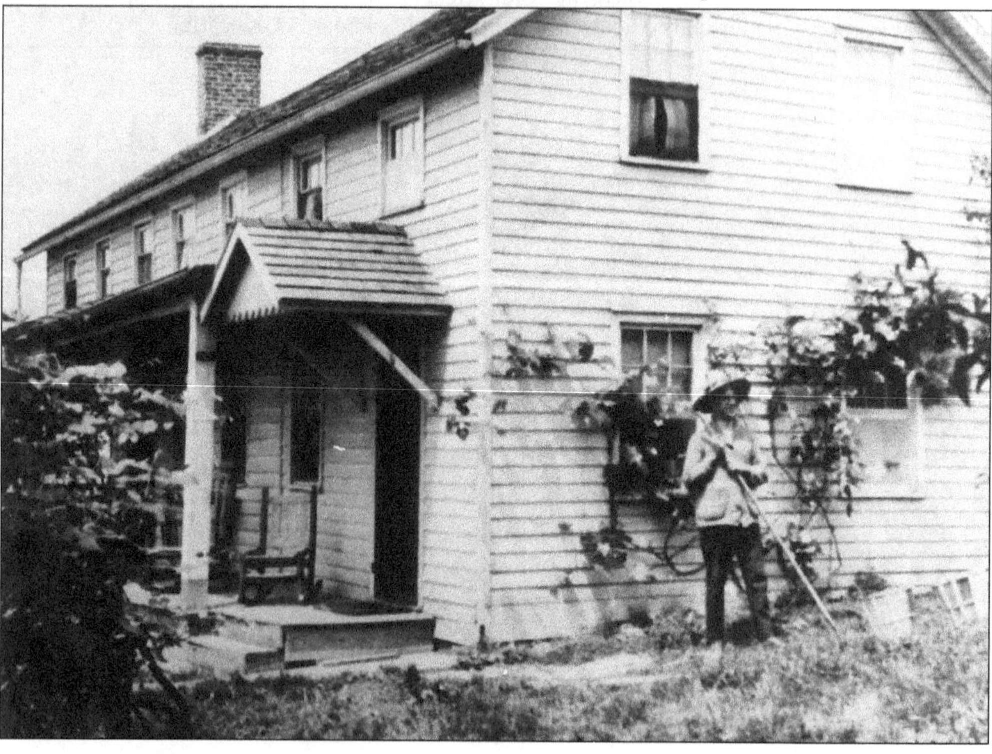

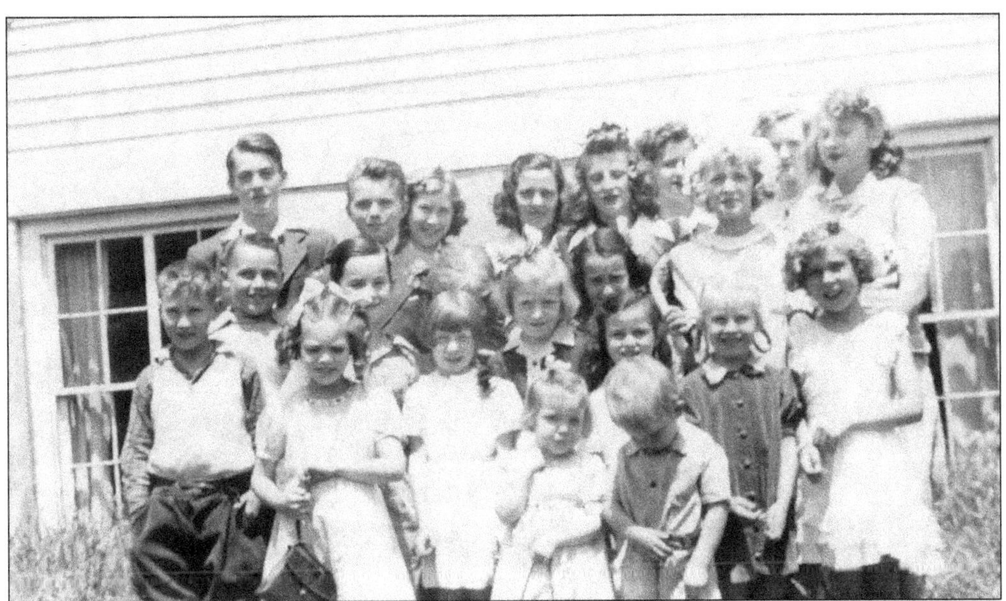

Children's Day was celebrated in 1944 at the Mount Horeb Church. Pictured are Carol Ann, Jean, Sally, and Lawrence Richards; Henry Lounsbury; Dolores Wojnar; Dolores Gaffney; Katherine Mervine; Marie, Tony, Peter, James, and Florence Plummer; Charles Mangee; Helen and Joe Salvato; June Gibbs; Virginia Hompech; Janet Osmon; and Joan and Sally Spencer.

PUBLIC SALE.

WILL be sold at Pulic Sale, on the premises, on TUESDAY the 13th day of March next—that handsome

PLANTATION,

late the property of Archibald Corrington, deceased, containing about two hundred and fifty acres, situated in Warren township, and county of Somerset. This Farm is supplied with abundance of timber, and well watered. On the premises is a handsome DWELLING-HOUSE—Cider & Distilling Establishment, Blacksmith's Shop, with a variety of other Buildings, all in good order—a fine Apple Orchard and other Fruit trees.

The property is to be sold under a decree of the Orphan's Court of the county of Somerset, and will be sold in lots as will best suit purchasers

☞ Vendue will open at 10 o'clock of said day, and attendance, with terms, will be given by

Charles Toms,
William C. Annin, } *Com'rs.*
Andrew Howell,

Somerville Dec 25. 1823. ts

The Coddingtons once owned the largest amount of land in Mount Horeb. Archibald Coddington (1756-1822) was a soldier in the Revolution.

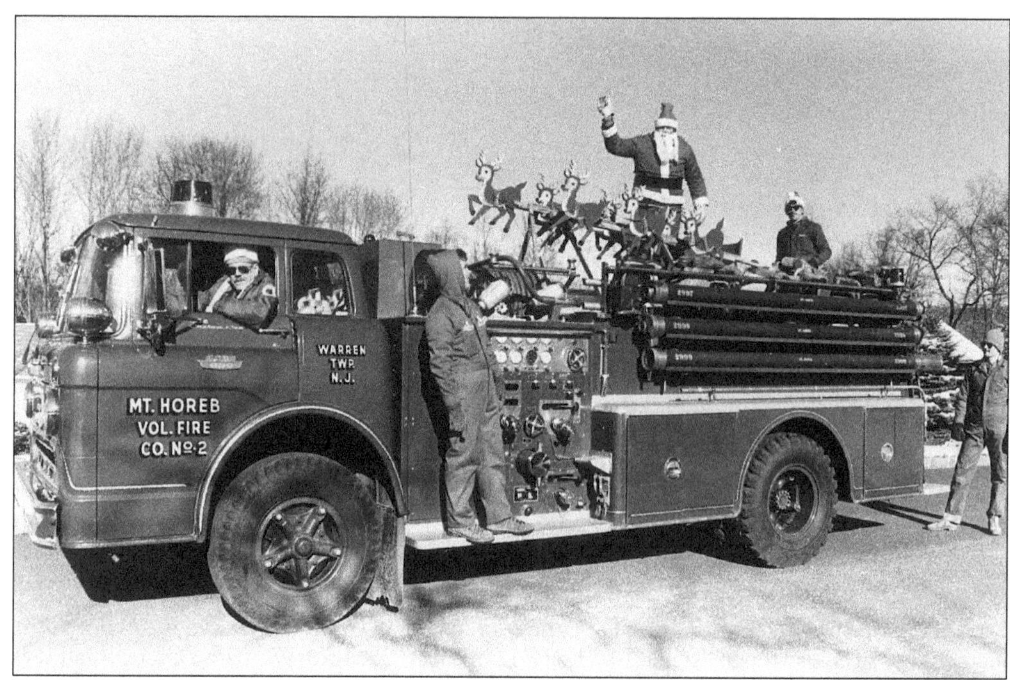

Mount Horeb volunteer firemen take Santa on a ride through Warren streets in this 1986 view. The Mount Horeb Volunteer Fire Company dates to 1948, when members of the Mount Bethel company, working with residents of Mount Horeb Park, formed the Mount Horeb Park station.

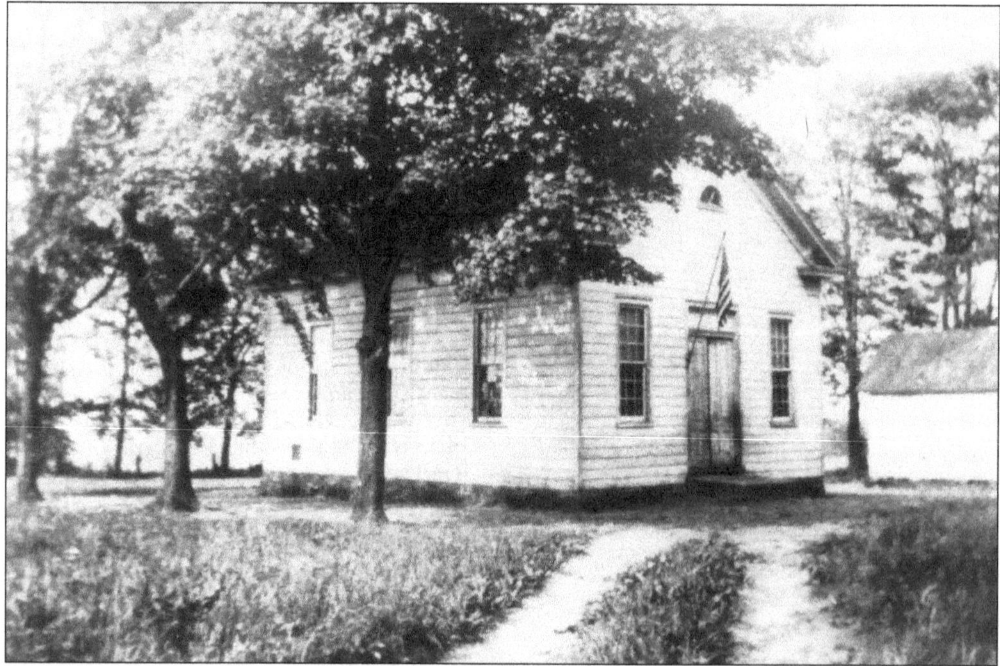

The Dead River School, now part of a private residence on Mountainview Road west of Round Top Road, was built on land acquired in 1874 from Jacob Giddes and Jonathan Moore. It replaced an old stone schoolhouse known as the Back River School, which was built about 1840 but is no longer in existence.

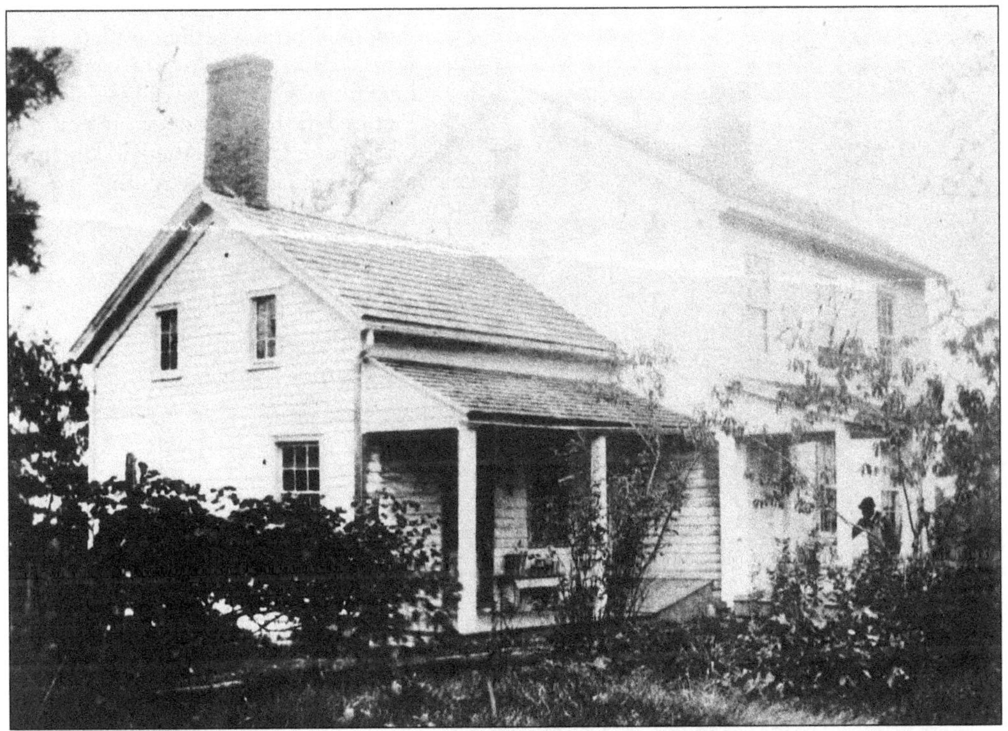

The Wallace house at 88 Round Top Road stands on property acquired by Joseph Manning in 1777 and the oldest part of the house may date from that time. Later, when the Coddingtons owned the place, it was known as Oakwood Farm.

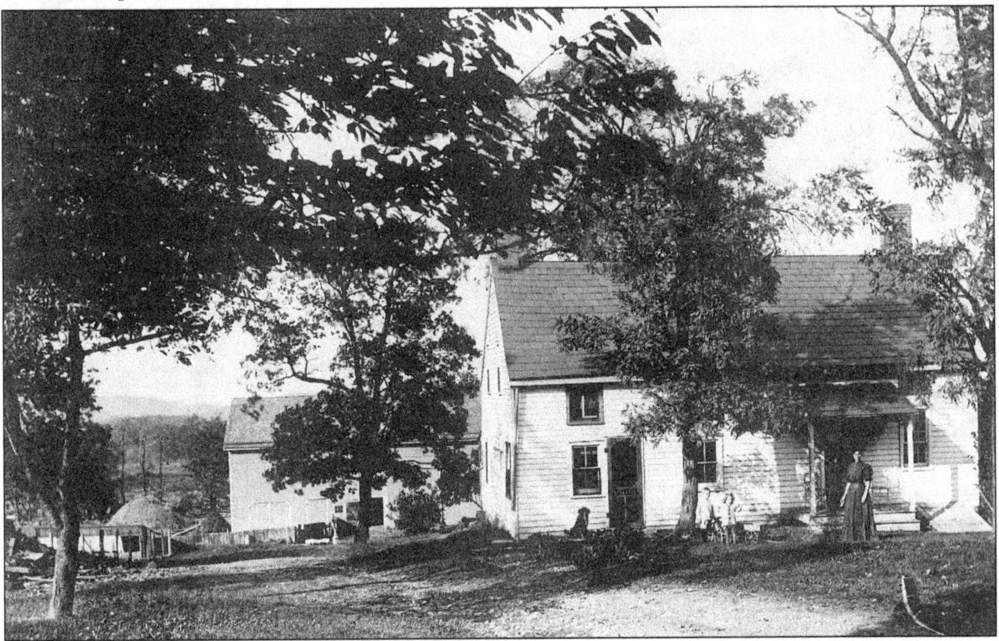

This house at 5 Mountainview Lane was built prior to 1850. Dairy farmer John Betzold bought the farm after the Civil War, raised milk cows, and delivered milk door to door under the name Star Dairy Farm. Pictured is Mrs. Adam Betzold with two of her children.

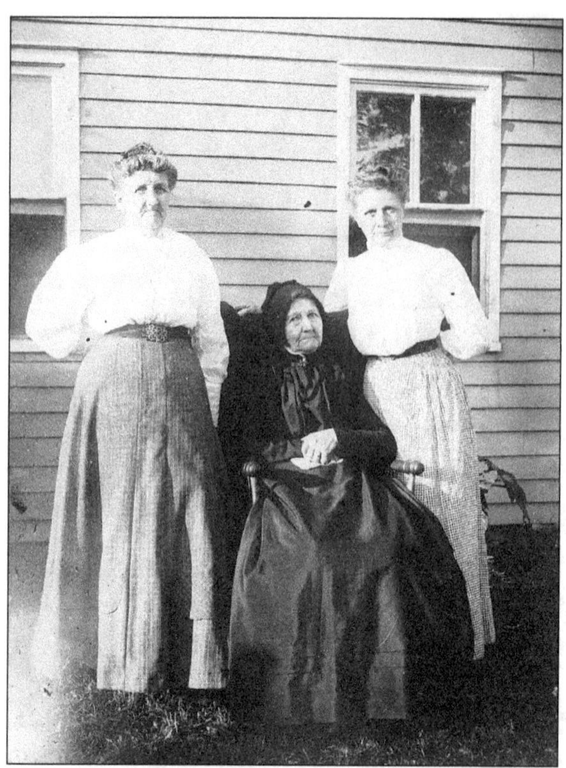

Among Warren's earliest settlers were the Coddingtons, who came here from Woodbridge *c.* 1740/45. Pictured in this 1890s view are Aunt Christiana, Grandmother Coddington, and Mary Coddington Smith.

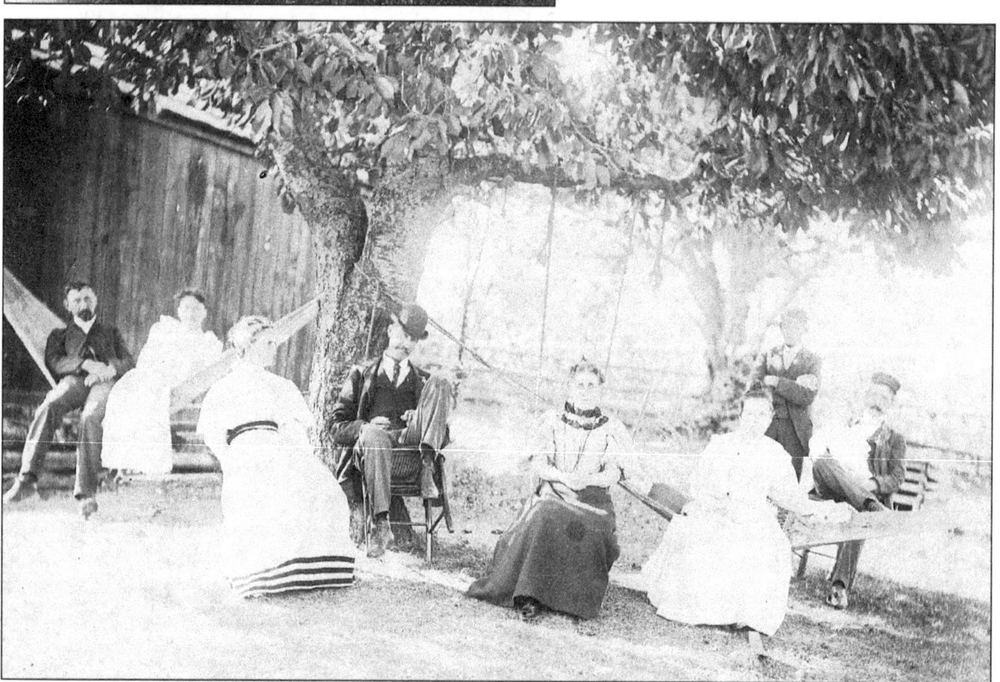

Tradition has it that during the Revolution, George Washington and his troops passed the Coddington home on Mount Horeb Road. Members of the family, including Ruben (1860-1929) in the chair and Charles (1862-1957) on the hammock, are shown here relaxing at the family farm near Round Top Road in the 1890s.

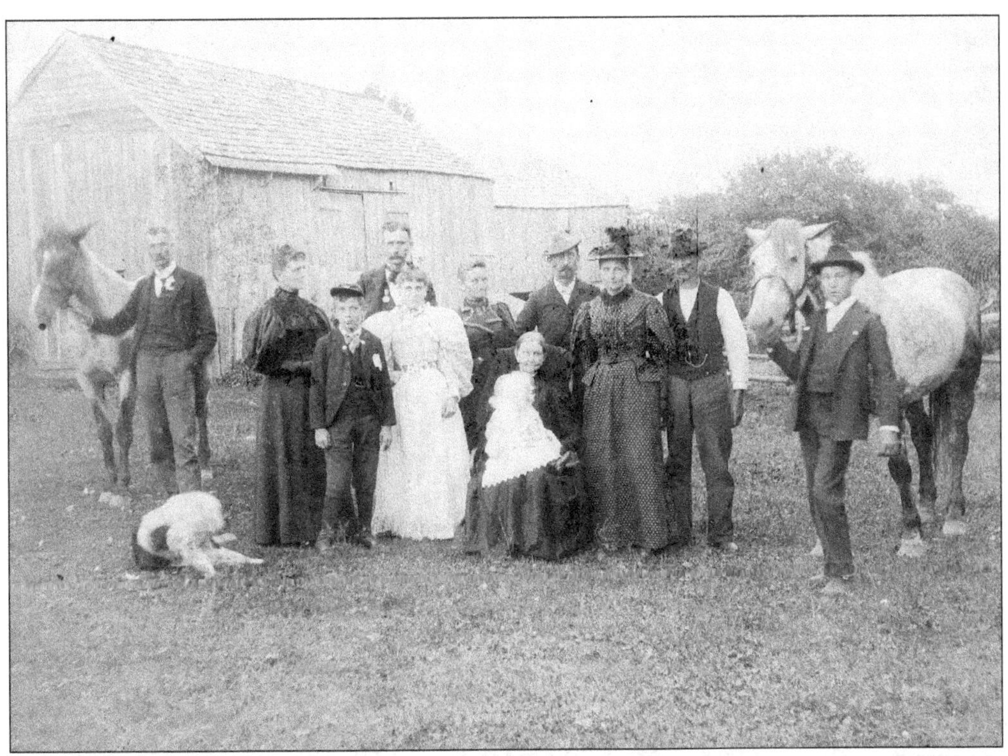

In 1896 the family gathered at Hill Top Farm near Round Top Road. A 1907 township tax list showed twenty-two Coddingtons owning 1,161 acres. Members of the Coddington family still live in the township.

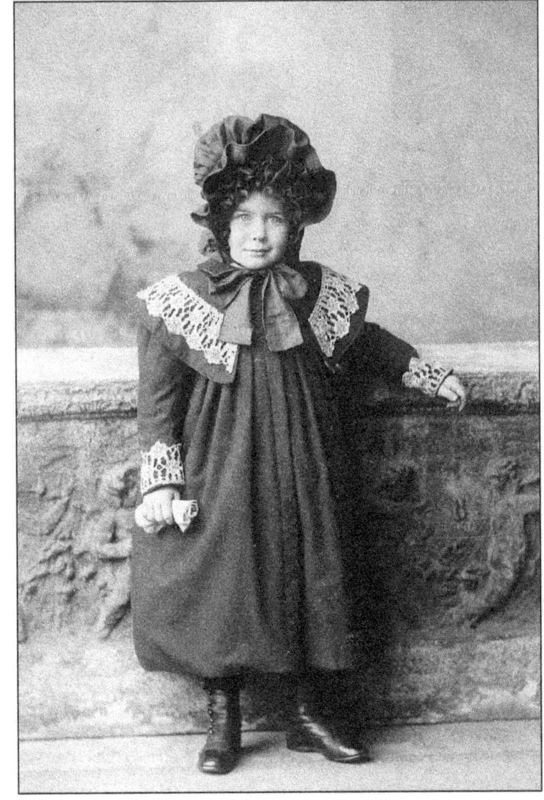

Ariadne, daughter of Bartholomew Coddington, married John Bricknell at Mount Horeb Church in 1894. Their daughter, Geraldine, was four when this portrait was made in 1904.

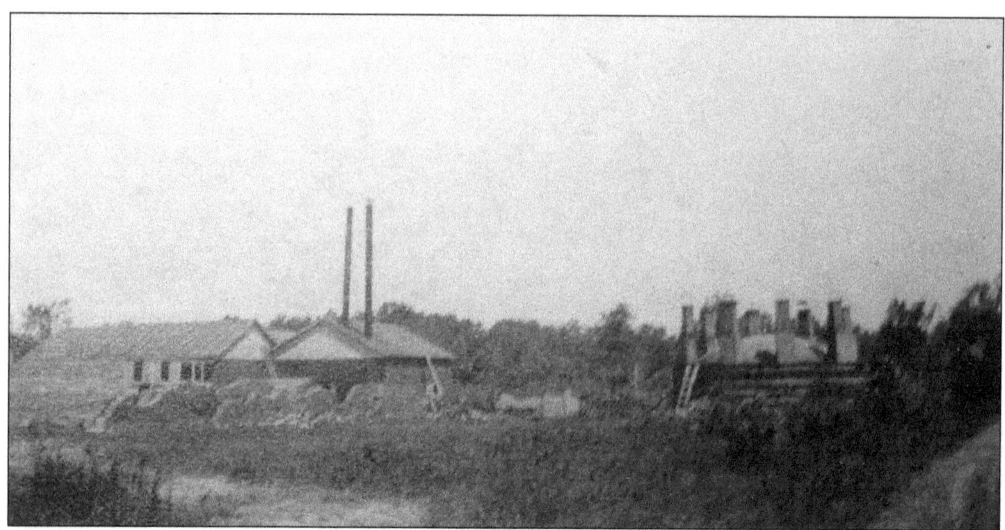

The Dead River, so named because of its sluggish flow, borders the northwestern part of the township. In 1908, Charles L. Crabb founded the Crabb Clay Products Company to manufacture building tiles from the vast clay deposits laid down during the last Ice Age. Ruins of his abandoned buildings at the foot of Dead River Road were still visible forty years ago.

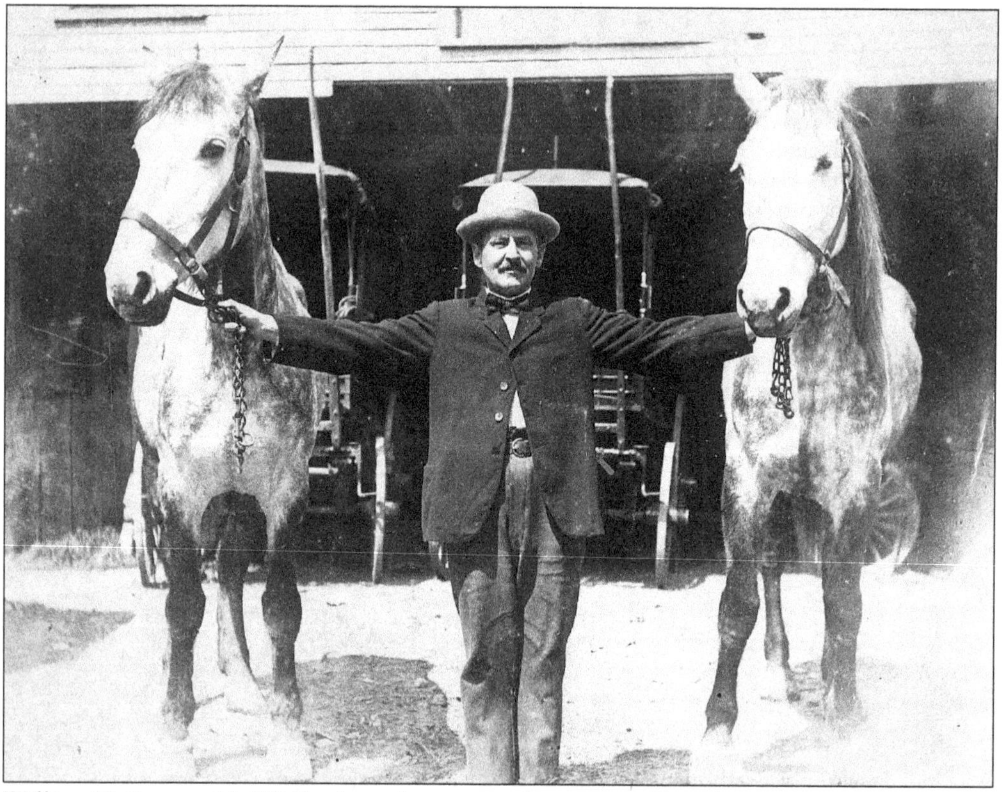

William T. Gregory (d. 1936), whose farm was at the corner of Broadway and Mountain Roads, moved to Warren at the turn of the century. By 1910 his place had become a summer vacation spot for travelers. His daughter, Hazel, transported boarders from the Millington train station in a horse-drawn buggy.

Gregory dammed the stream flowing through his property, calling the resulting pond "Crystal Bowl." Ruth Williams and Hazel Gregory Walter make light work of plowing in this 1930s snapshot.

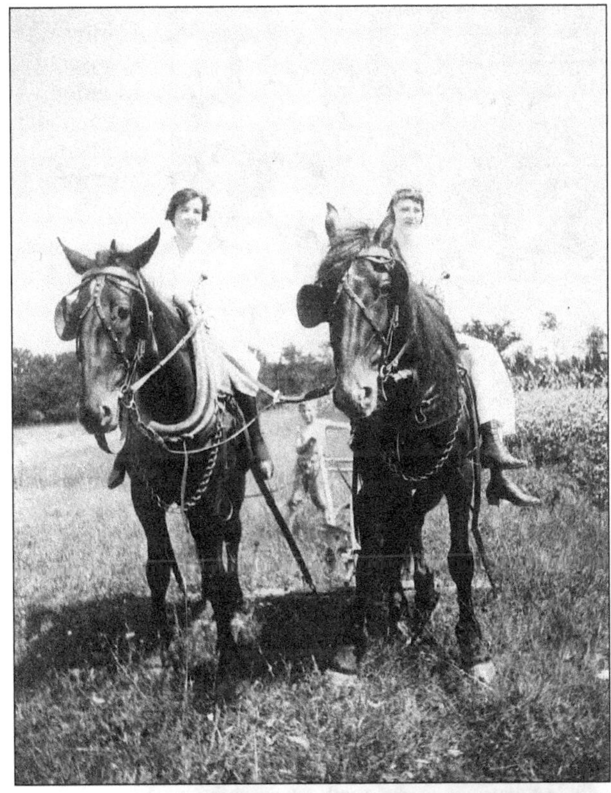

On a lazy Sunday afternoon in the summer of 1935, the men of the Gregory family tune up their bicycles. William Gregory's barn looms behind them.

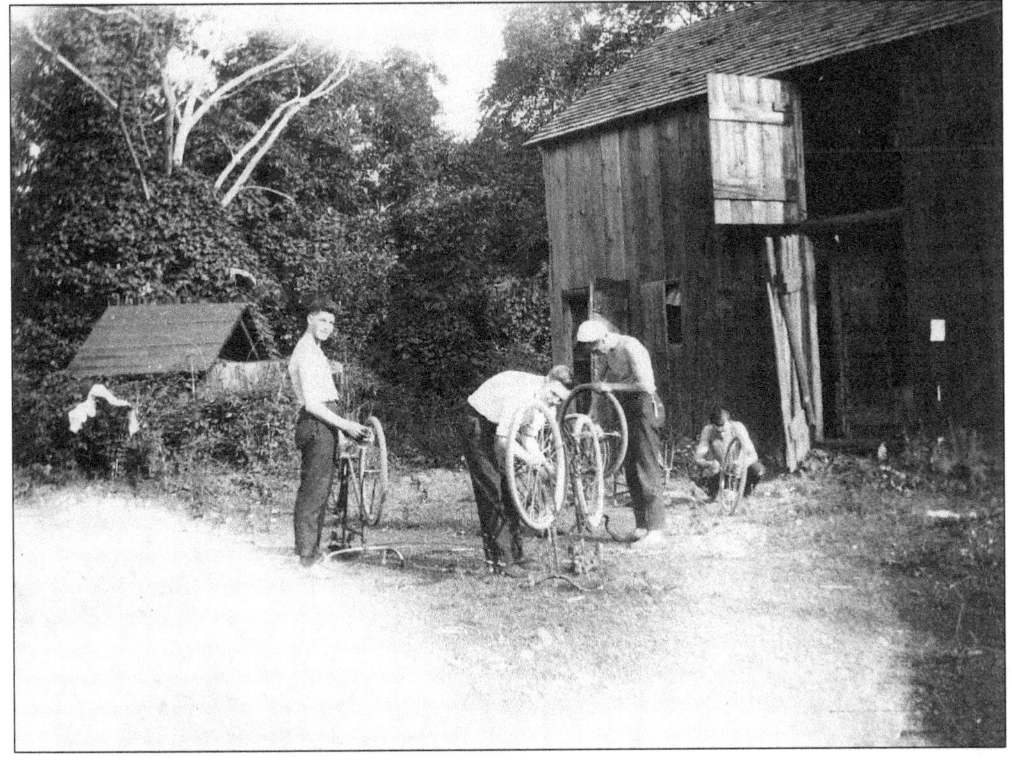

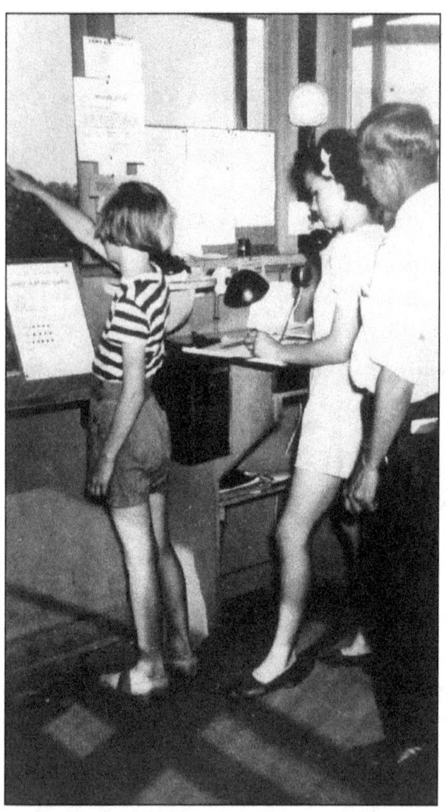

During World War II the American Legion sponsored an aircraft spotting tower on Mountainview Road. Here Jack Metler, post commander and chief observer, watches as Elaine Yannuzzi (left) and June Sachs take turns looking for enemy planes.

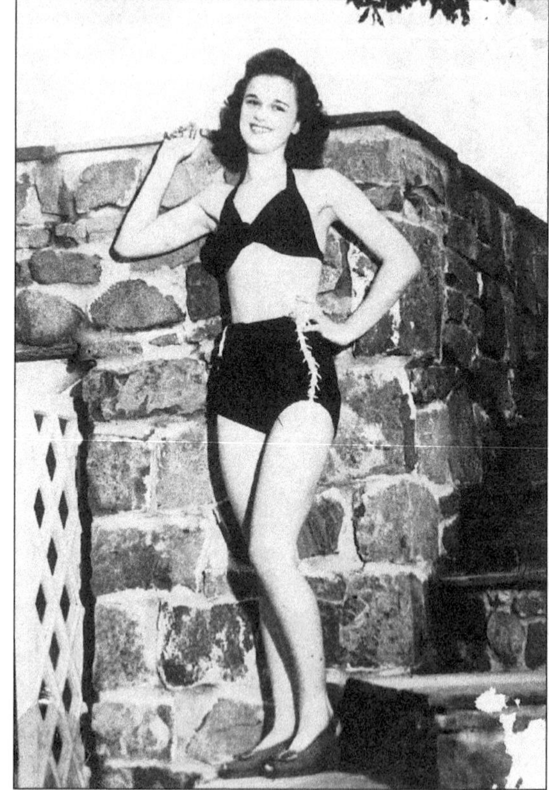

The Sachs family lived on Mountainview Road since the nineteenth century. June Alice Sachs was chosen Miss Warren Township in 1945.

Six

Springdale and Dock Watch Hollow

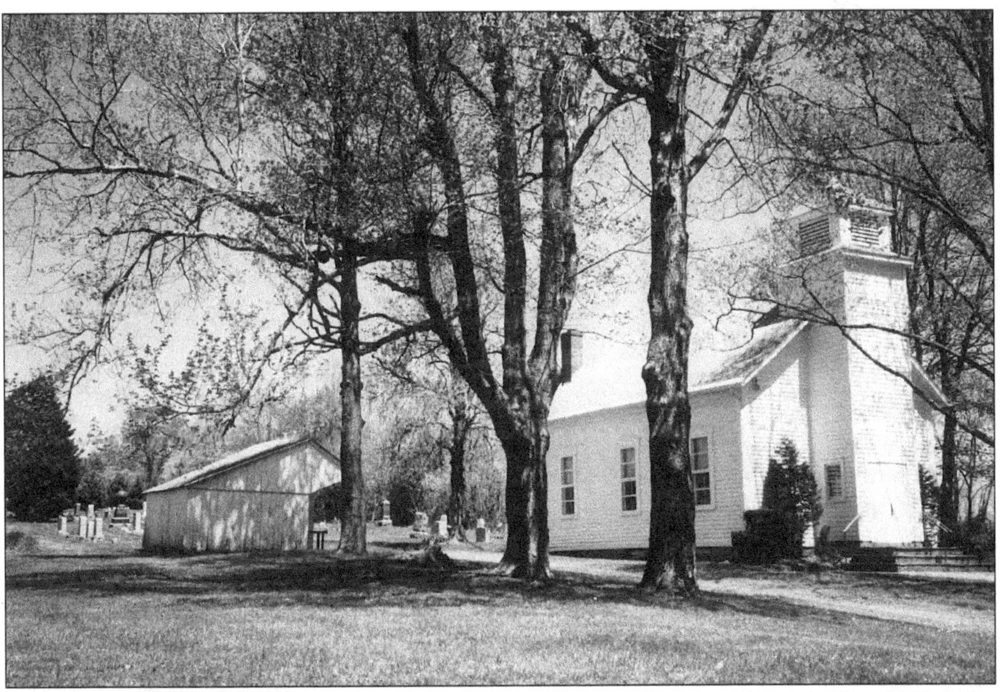

Stretching along Washington Valley Road from Warrenville toward Dock Watch Hollow, Springdale takes its name from a fresh-water spring on the Sage property near the corner of Quail Run and the valley road. The Springdale United Methodist Church was built about 1840, two years after the congregation first began meeting at the schoolhouse nearby. A horse shed still stands to the left. Bornmann, Winans, Flammer, Gaddis, Jennings, Lawler, Mundy, and Toms are some of the names on the tombstones that dot the still-active cemetery to the rear of the church.

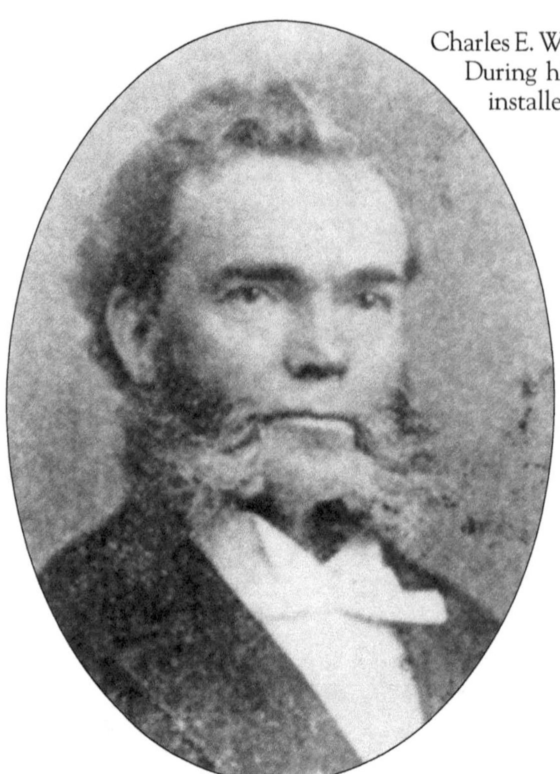

Charles E. Walton was Springdale's pastor from 1902-04. During his tenure, the church erected a belfry and installed a 365-pound bell costing $105.

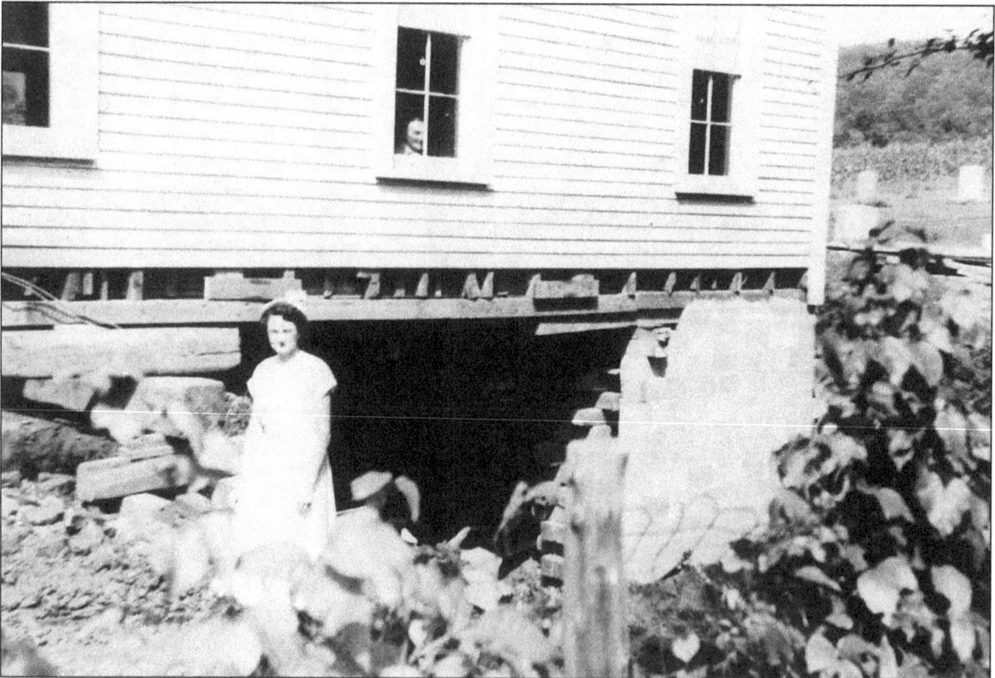

Closed after a 1951 hurricane destroyed its belfry, the church reopened in 1953. The men of the congregation, led by Frank Mundy and Wilbur Mobus, excavated a basement by hand in 1956-58. An admiring Ruth Wilson stands by the gaping hole.

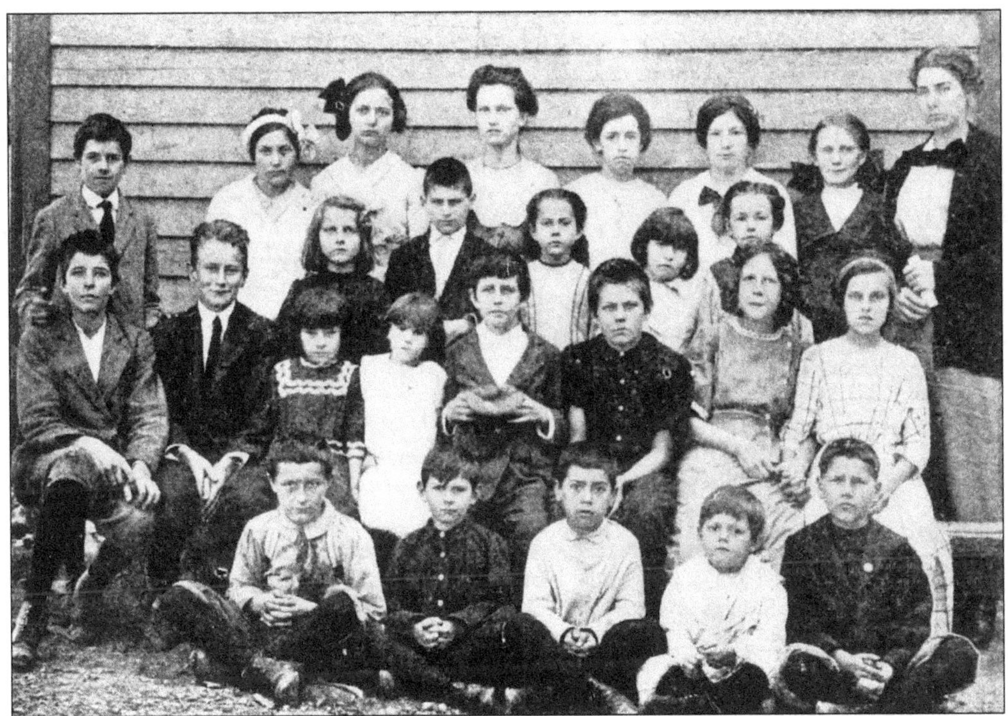

These children attended Springdale School in 1913. "It was a one-room schoolhouse with a potbellied stove in one corner," remembered Claire Mundy Steeber, who studied there in the late 1920s. "When you were bad the teacher made you stand behind it. The older boys put snow in the furnace to put the fire out. Without heat, the teacher had to send us home."

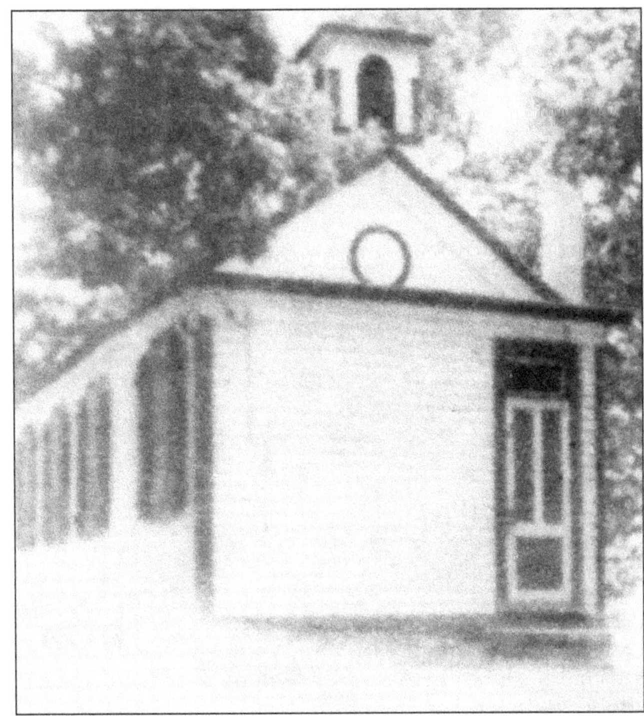

The school stood on land acquired in 1872. Pupils sat two to a desk—desks that Harold Mundy recalled were so riddled with carved initials that students could barely write on them. The school is now a private home.

THE PRESENCE OF YOURSELF AND COMPANY IS RESPECTFULLY SOLICITED AT

An + Evening + Sociable

TO BE HELD AT THE RESIDENCE OF MR. JOHN KOECHLEIN,
WASHINGTON VALLEY, N. J.,
ON WEDNESDAY EVENING, DECEMBER 4, 1889.

LADIES REFRESHMENTS. GENTLEMEN ASSESSED.

COMMITTEE:
P. W. MUNDY, FRANK ALOTTE.

MUSIC BY PROF. O'REILLY.

John Koechlein (1839-1895) and his wife Margaret lived on Washington Valley Road near the church. An evening of music and refreshments—such as this one in 1889—was the high point of the holiday season.

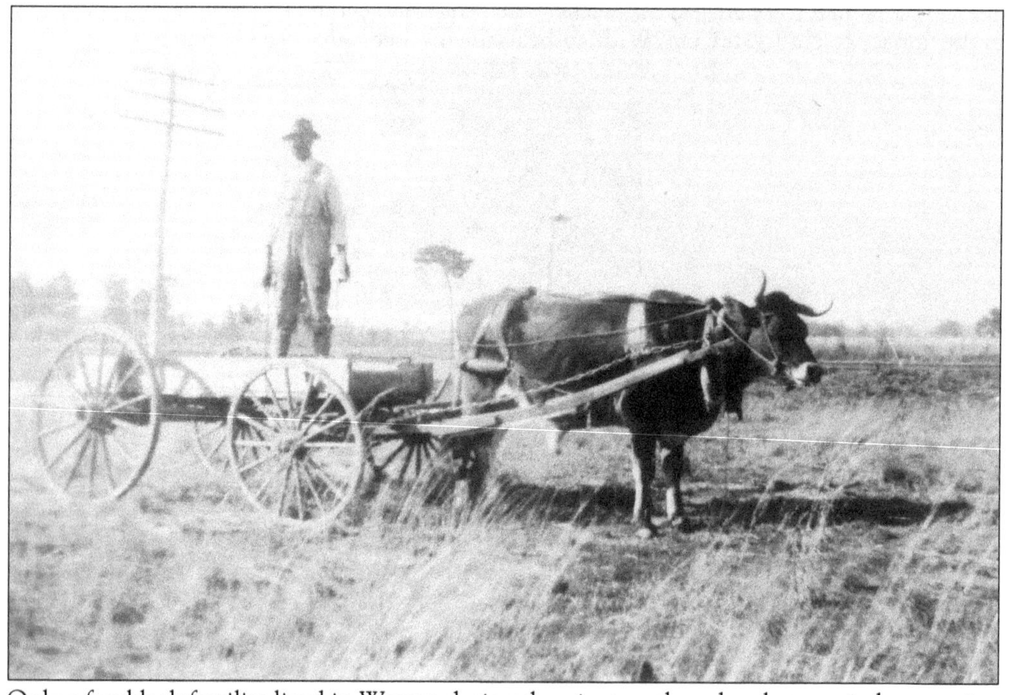

Only a few black families lived in Warren during the nineteenth and early twentieth centuries. Bill Smith, shown here *c*. 1920 farming near the corner of Washington Valley and Morning Glory Roads, lived on Broadway Road

Organized in 1939 by Charles Flint, Charles O'Brian, Alfred Wicht, and Edwin, Harold, and Robert Mundy, the Washington Valley Volunteer Fire Company has raised funds with its pancake breakfast for nearly forty years. In 1967 Mayor John Lloyd bought the first ticket from Chief Gus Mobus.

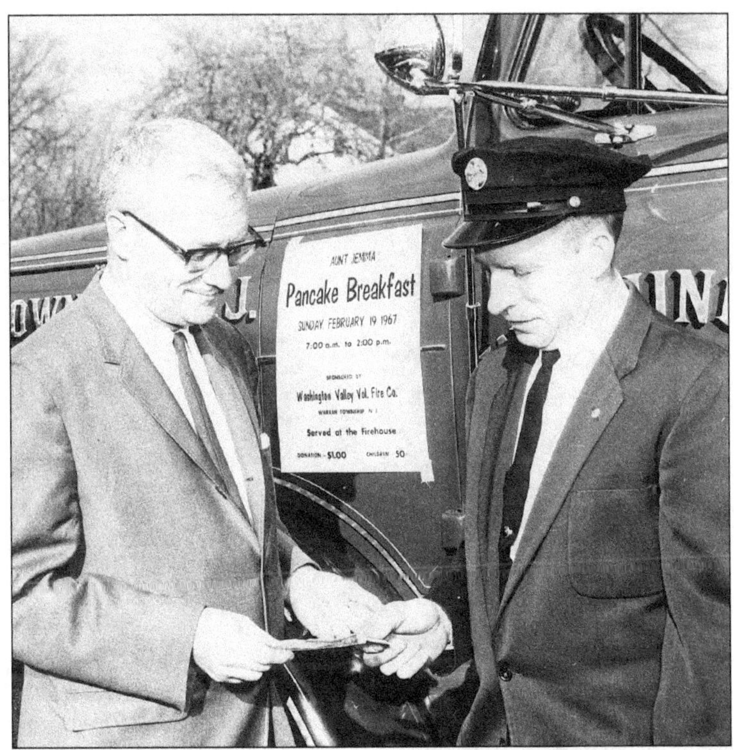

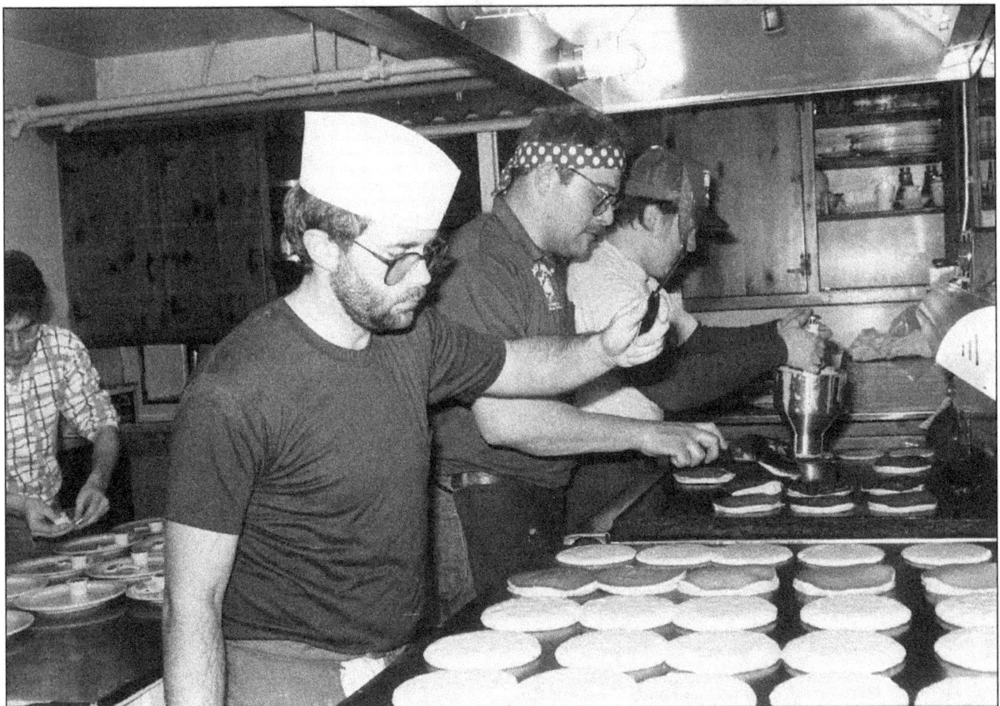

From left to right, Walt Tucker, Tom Norris, and John Dumont slave over the hot griddle in 1989, the year a Soviet ballet troop decided to pay a call at the last minute. The Soviets were incredulous when told that township firefighters worked without pay.

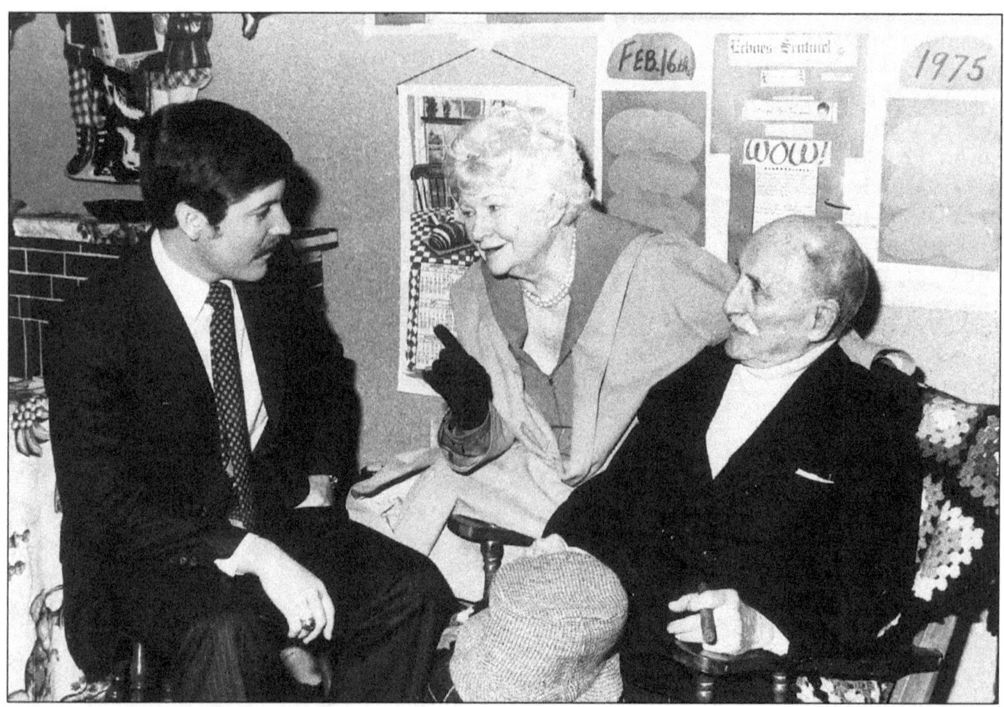

In February 1975, Pegeen and Ed Fitzgerald of WOR radio fame paid a visit. Ed Fitzgerald was honorary chief of the fire company. Chatting with them is Mayor John E. Coley Jr.

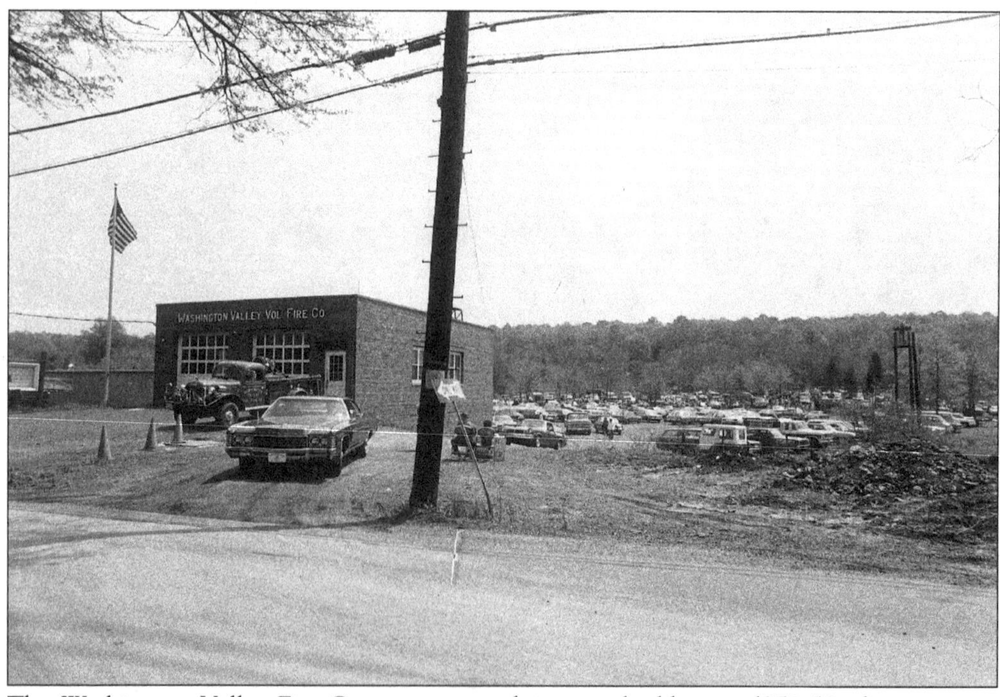

The Washington Valley Fire Company erected its own building in 1950-52 after nineteen members personally guaranteed the mortgage. The flea market opened in 1975 with proceeds used since then to purchase much-needed fire equipment.

Janet Flint, first president of the Washington Valley Fire Company's Ladies Auxiliary, compiled a township history in 1956 and wrote and produced musicals performed locally. Her husband, Charles, served as school board president in the late 1940s.

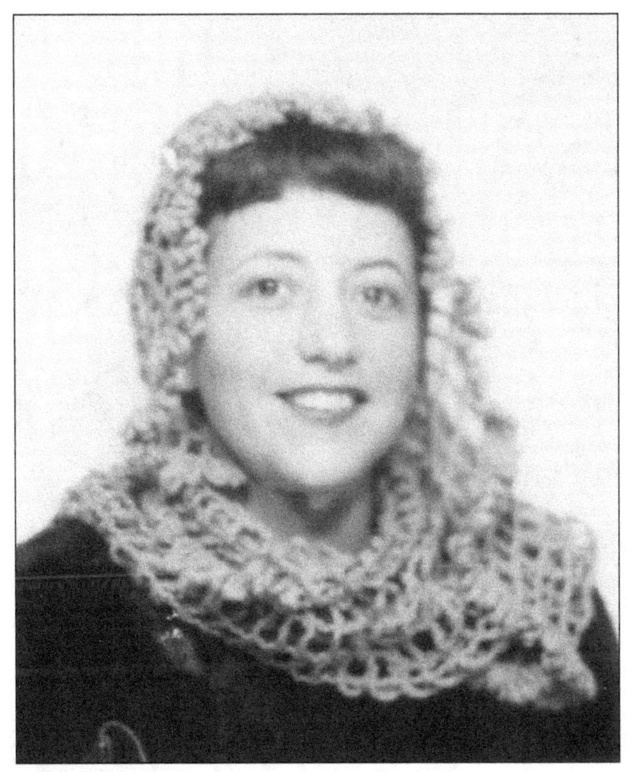

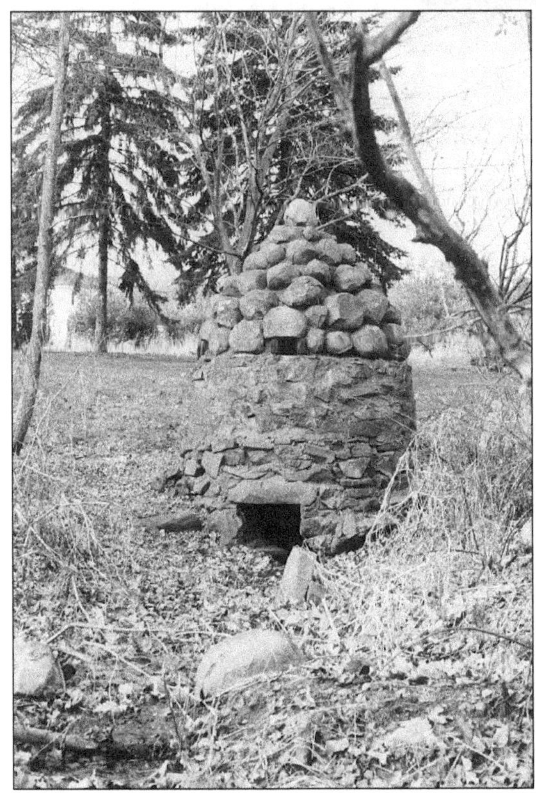

Springdale was first settled in the 1720s. Its spring is mentioned in pre-Revolutionary War road descriptions. The spring house, built by Philip Mundy, can still be seen from the valley road.

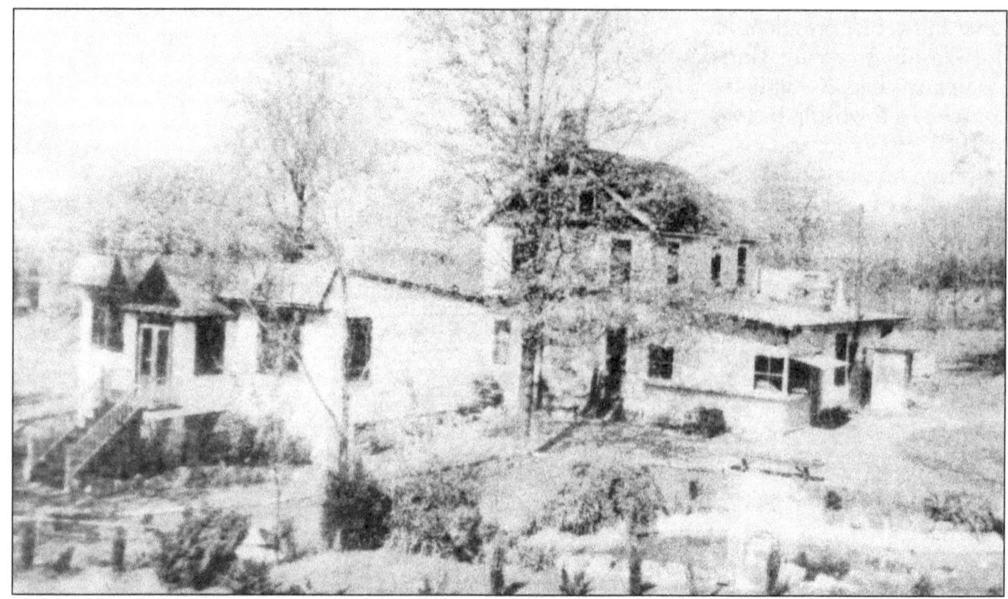

The Schwaebische Alb restaurant has been a local fixture since the repeal of Prohibition, when Herman Mauser, William Schwartz, and Herman Fry—all failures at chicken farming—decided to open a restaurant (the structure on the left) on Mauser's farm.

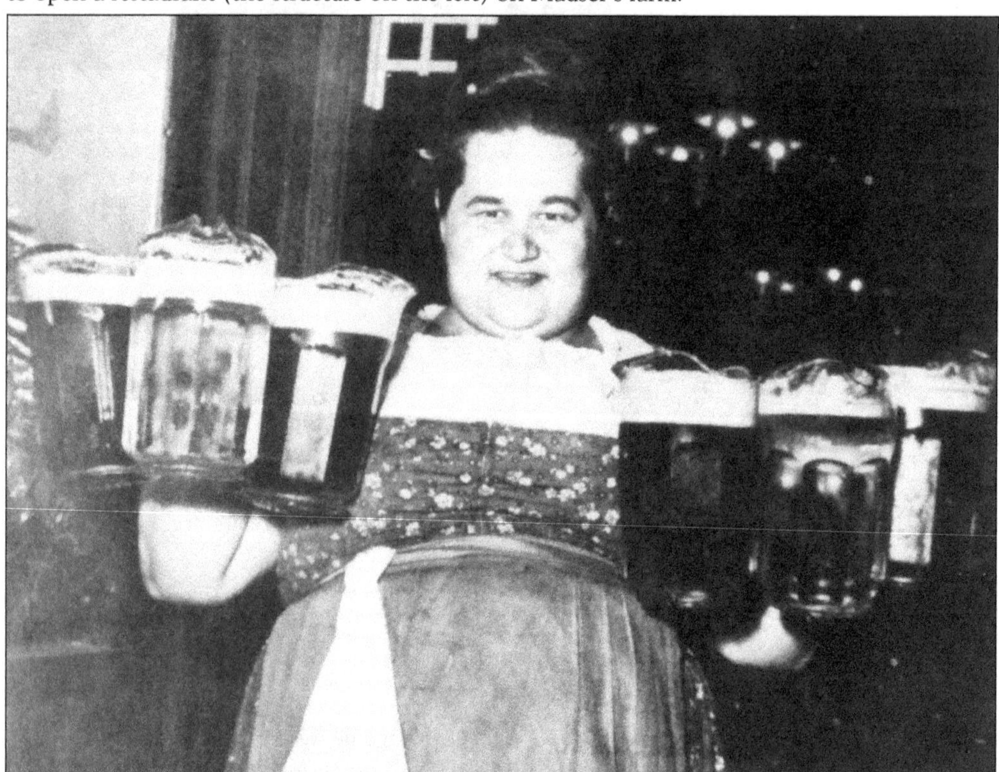

Rosemary Mueller easily handled eight pitchers of German beer in the 1960s after Richard and Elizabeth Bachert became owners. The famous Trapp family singers used to hold their annual reunions at the Schwaebische Alb.

Washington Valley was dotted with farms that have now given way to housing developments. In the late 1940s Bill and Russ Horster, whose father's farm was at the corner of Washington Valley and Morning Glory Roads, help George Dealaman, who sits on the combine, thresh wheat.

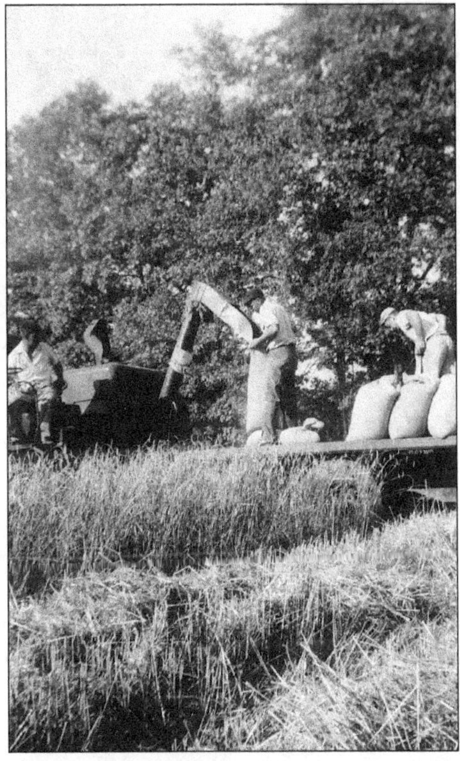

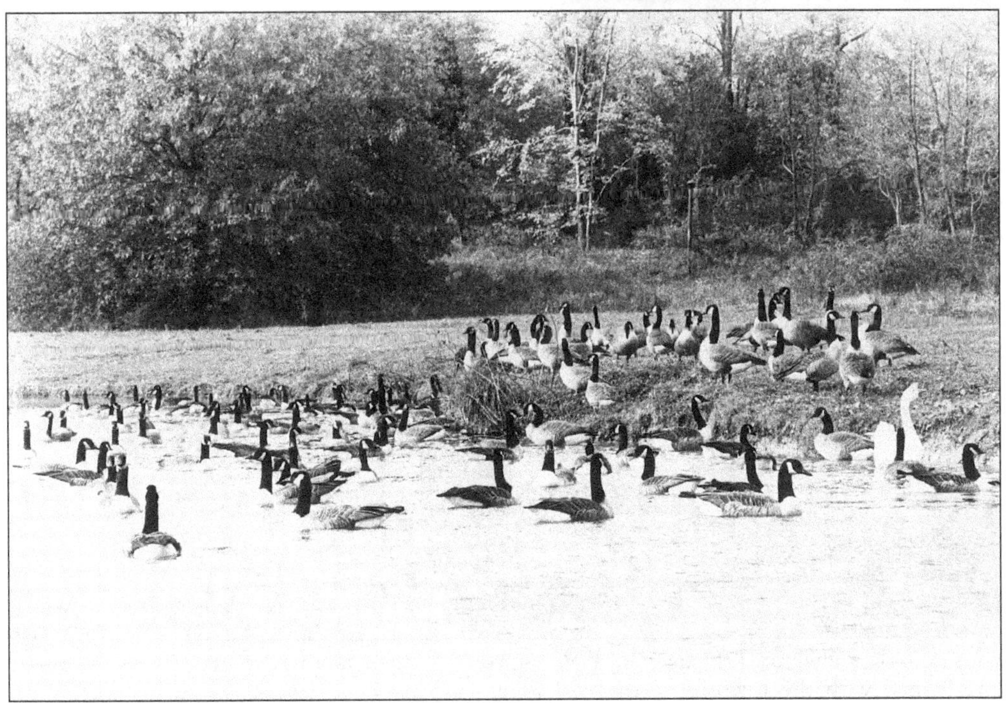

In October 1988, Canadian geese claim the pond at the rear of Malanga's produce stand on Washington Valley Road. Hundreds of deer, otter, raccoons, skunks, and an occasional bear make their homes in Warren as well.

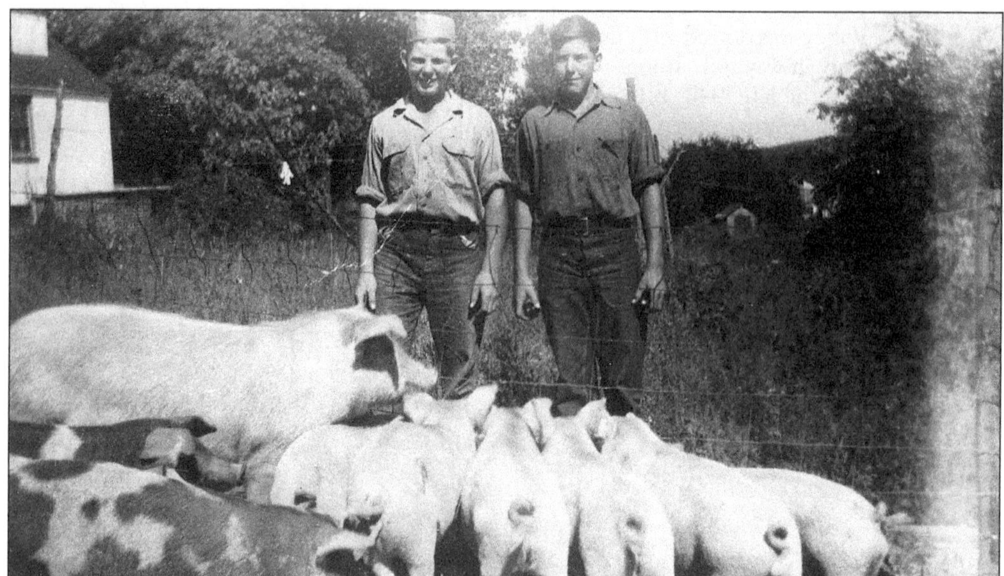

Carl A. Horster (1905-1976), a bricklayer and farmer, served as Warren's mayor for nine years during the 1950s, and as tax assessor for eighteen years. His sons, Bill and Russ, are pictured here in October 1944 slopping pigs on the family farm.

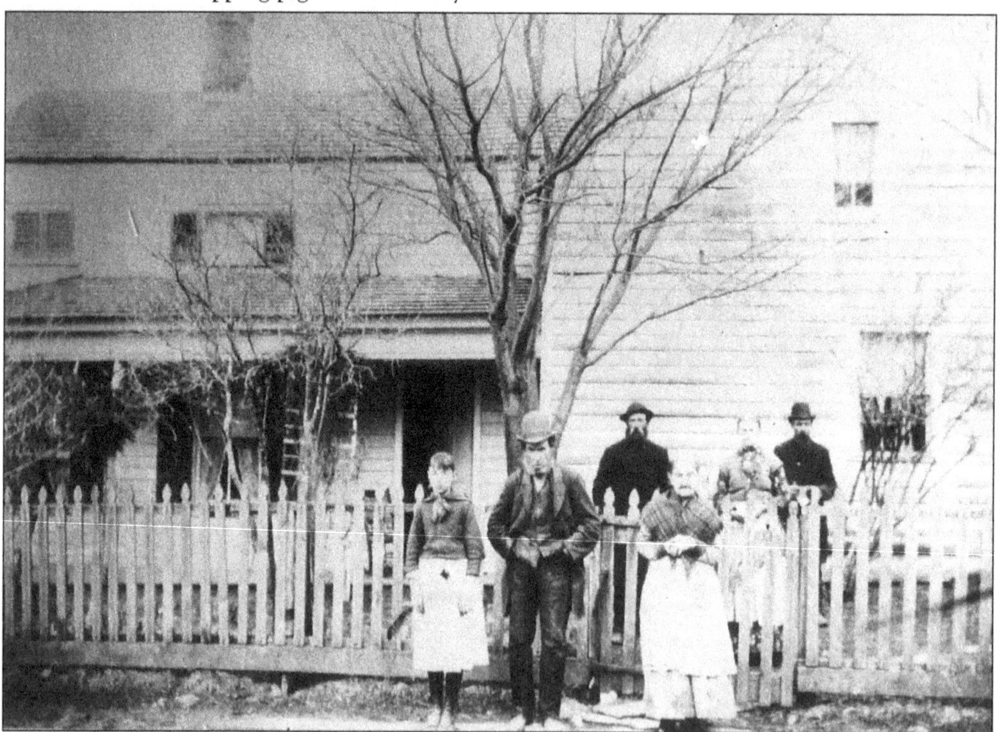

Enos Mundy came to Springdale in 1792, starting a small family dynasty whose history is intertwined with the township's. In 1890 Peter D. Mundy (1819-1903) and his wife Mary Ann Moore (1828-1905) pose in front of their home on Morning Glory Road. Descendants of their children, Marabel, Harriet, David, William, Ellah, Philip, Sarah, and Elmer, still live in the township.

Peter's son, Philip D. Mundy (1860-1928), conducted a coal and feed business in partnership with his brother, Elmer.

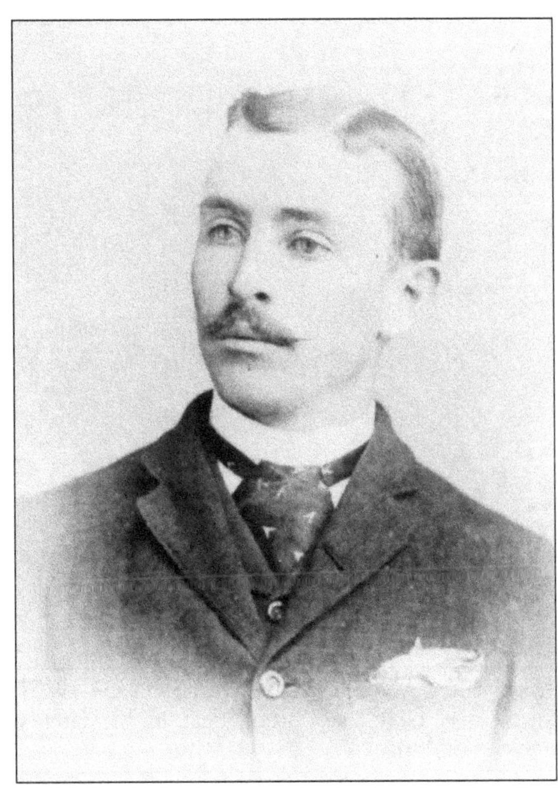

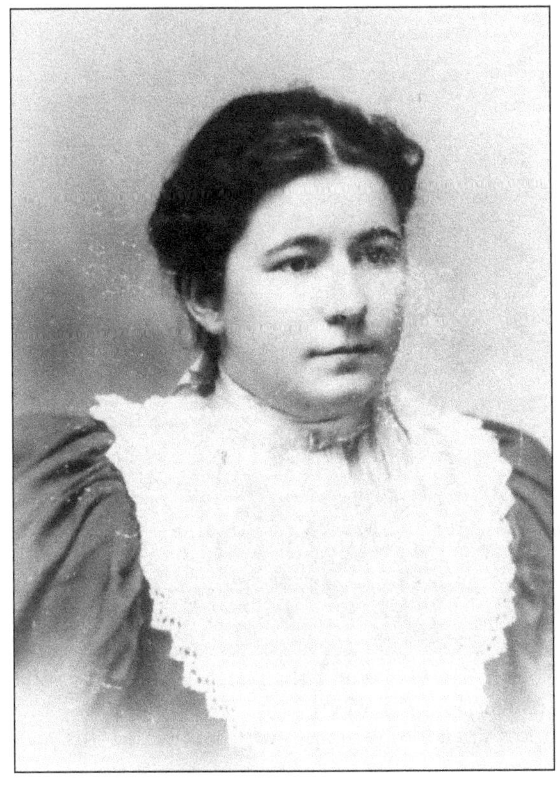

Philip and his wife, Carrie Eager Mundy (1877-1942), lived in a fine home on the corner of Washington Valley Road and Quail Run. The Sage family is there now, next to their produce stand.

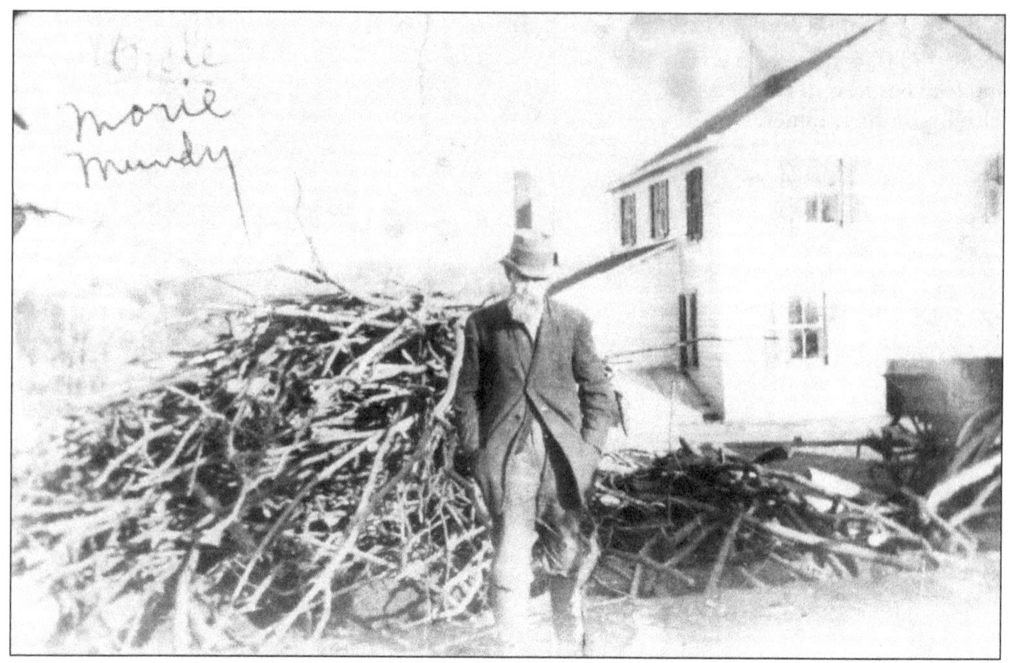

A carpenter, William Moore Mundy (1854-1935) lived his entire life in Springdale. Uncle Morie may have been stone deaf in his later years, but he could gather an impressive stack of kindling.

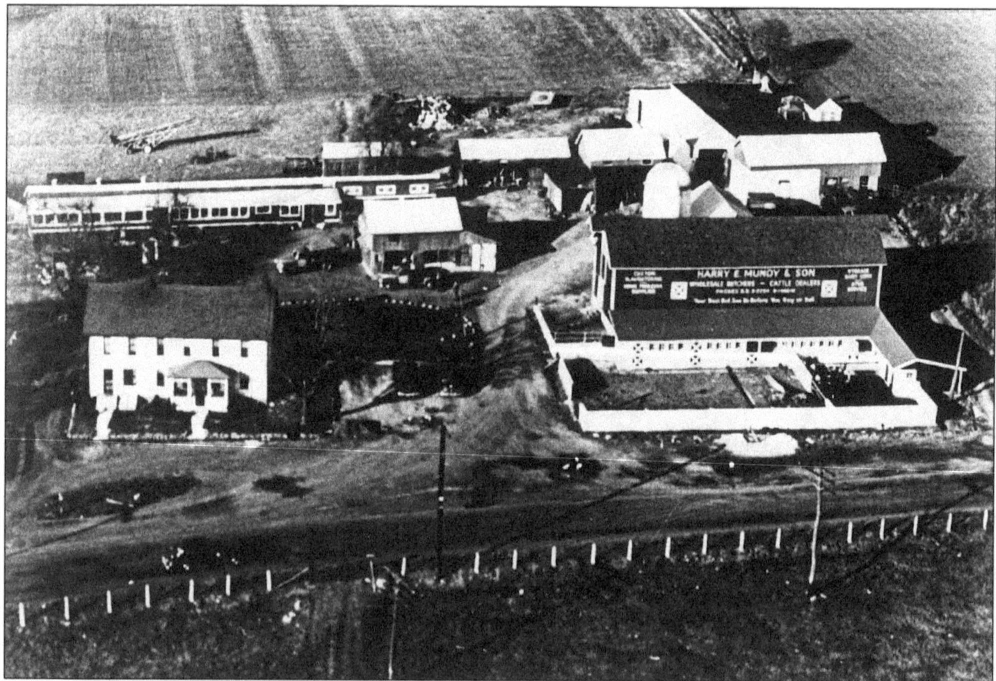

Cattle dealer and dairyman, Harry E. Mundy (1901-1964) operated the Harry E. Mundy & Sons Slaughter House on Washington Valley Road until 1963 when a fire destroyed barns and equipment. The Mundys had owned the business since 1881. A mini-mall that opened this year now occupies the site.

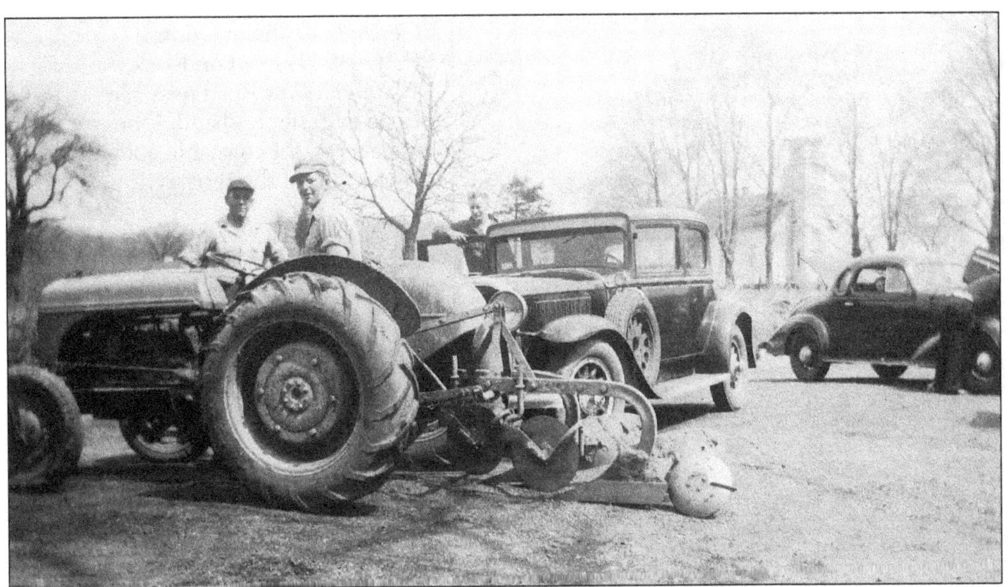

A Saturday afternoon in 1947 found Russ and Bill Horster tinkering with the family's new Ford tractor. Richard Cramer stands proudly next to his '31 Buick while Herb Thrum repairs his '35 Chevy. Springdale Church can be seen faintly in the background.

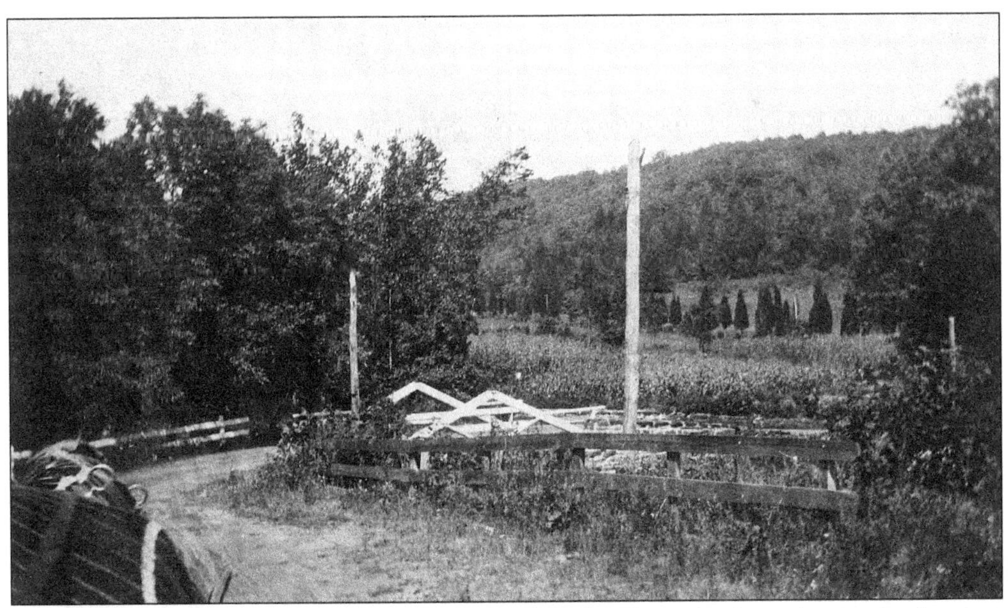

Dock Watch Hollow is less a village than a neighborhood strung along the stream that cuts through Second Mountain to empty into Middle Brook. During the eighteenth and early nineteenth century, saw and grain mills dotted the brook; ruins of mill dams can still be seen. The A-frame bridge over the brook is pictured here in 1912.

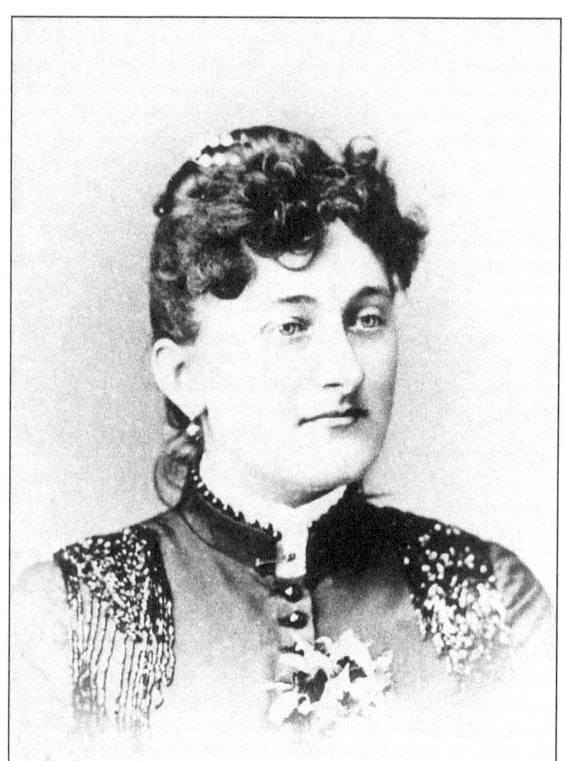

Gertrude Wilhelm Gunton (1866-1939) lived on Dock Watch Hollow Road near Blazier Road with her husband, John, a member of the township committee at the turn of the century.

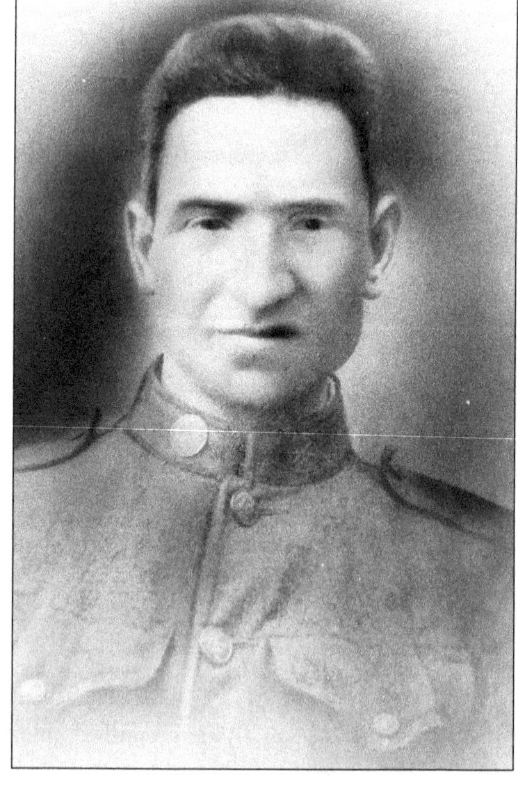

Andrew Mantz dug for copper along Dock Watch Hollow Brook. His son, Judson (b. 1894), joined the army and died in 1918. The Mantz-Cavaliere Post 293, American Legion, is named in honor of Mantz and Carmen Cavaliere, both of whom died in World War I.

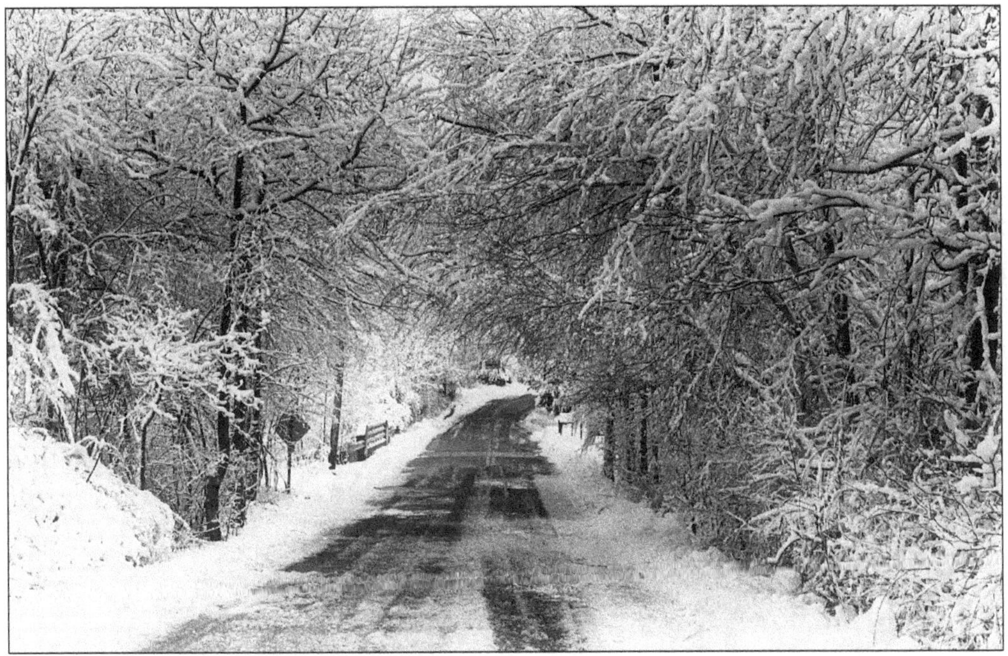

Ilse Landau's photograph of Ferguson Road after a snowstorm in 1985 captures the romance of Dock Watch Hollow, a place of great natural beauty in every season. In the Lenape Indian language, "dogwatcha" meant "I am cold," a sentiment easily associated with a place known for its cool air currents on even the hottest days.

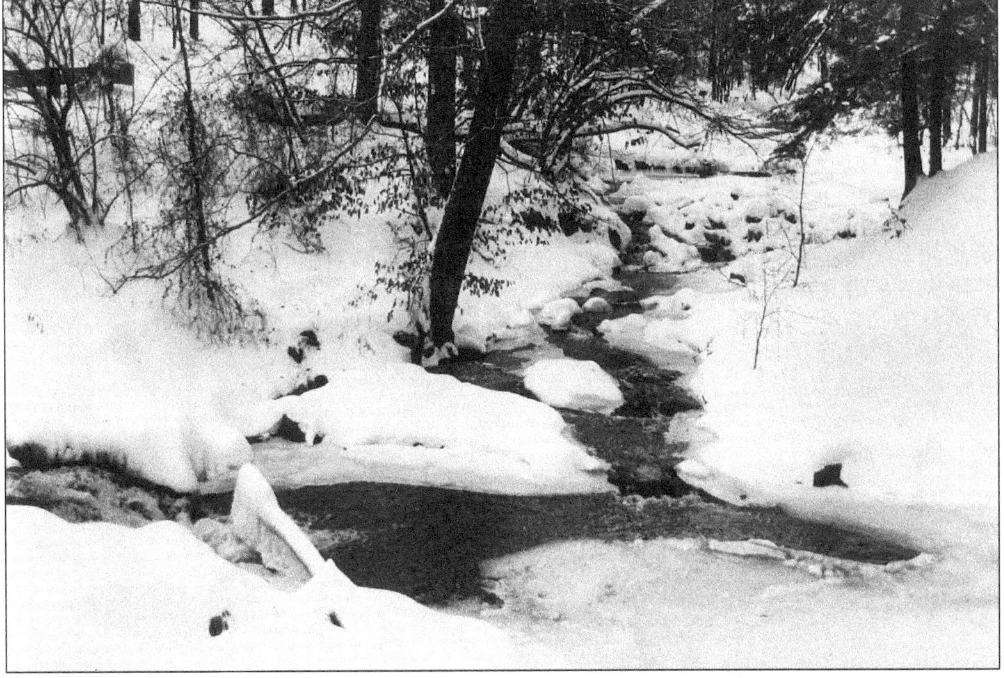

Dock Watch Hollow is mentioned in historical records as early as 1708. Although the name originates from an Indian word, tall tales of a Chief Dock Watch—with a pot of gold buried at his feet—or a Hollander named Dockwatch—resting eternally under giant oaks—still abound.

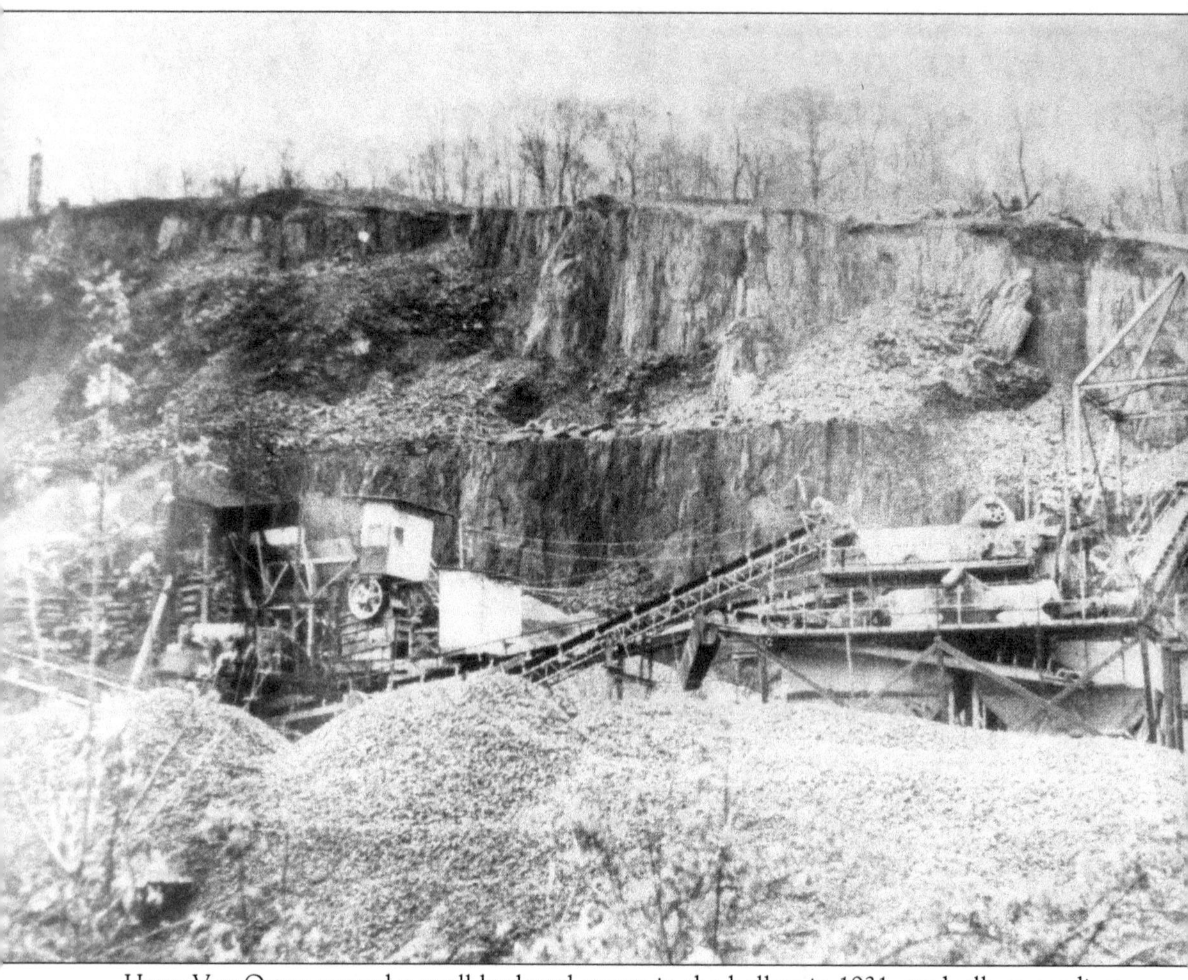

Harry Von Osten opened a small backyard quarry in the hollow in 1931, gradually expanding his operation until much of the hillside had been removed. After the quarry closed in the mid-1980s, eager developers proposed ten-story apartments, a ski slope, an amphitheater, and sixty-five town houses for the site.

Seven

Warrenville

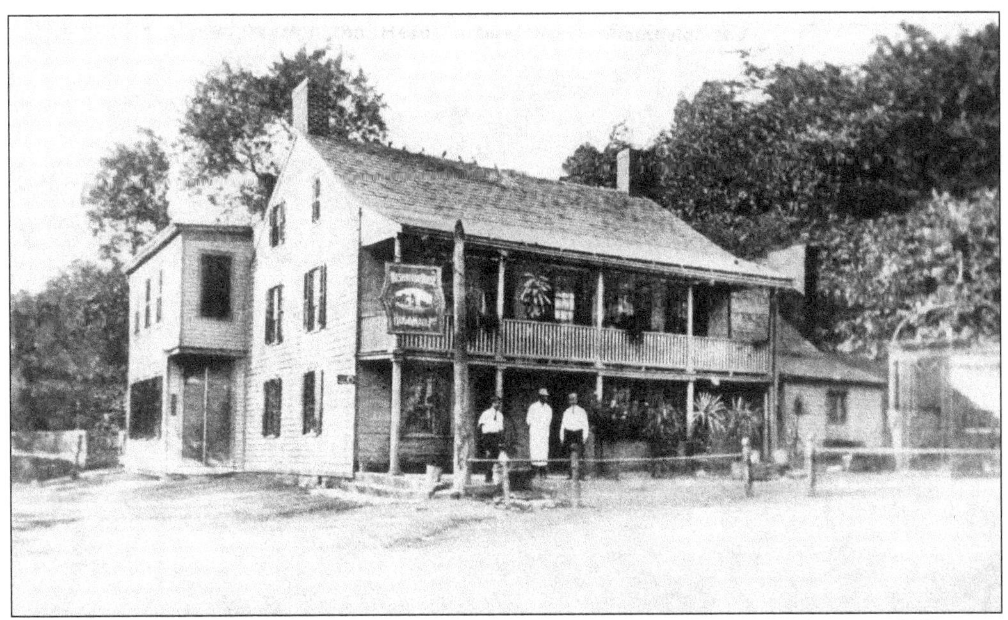

David Stewart's tavern on Somerset Street in what is now Watchung was the site of Warren's first township committee meeting on April 14, 1806. Inhabitants of the easterly portions of Bernards and Bridgewater asked to be set off as a separate township as early as 1799, but it was not until March 1806 that the state legislature agreed. After electing Jacob Smalley as moderator, voters approved a $900 budget.

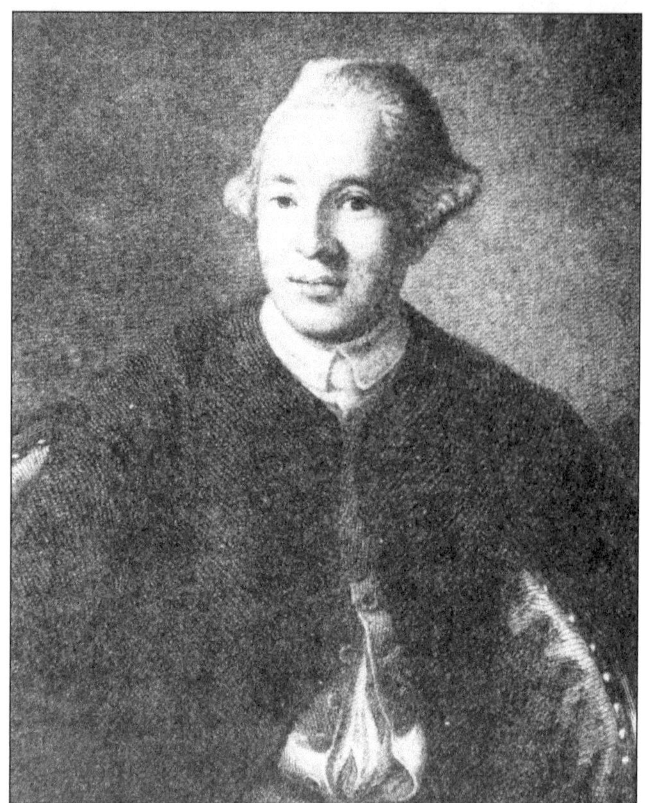

Warren is named in honor of Dr. Joseph Warren (1741-1775), a fiery patriot and martyr to the cause of liberty who lost his life at the Battle of Bunker Hill. Warrenville, the area around the intersection of Mountain Boulevard and Mount Bethel-Warrenville Road, has been the town center only since the 1960s.

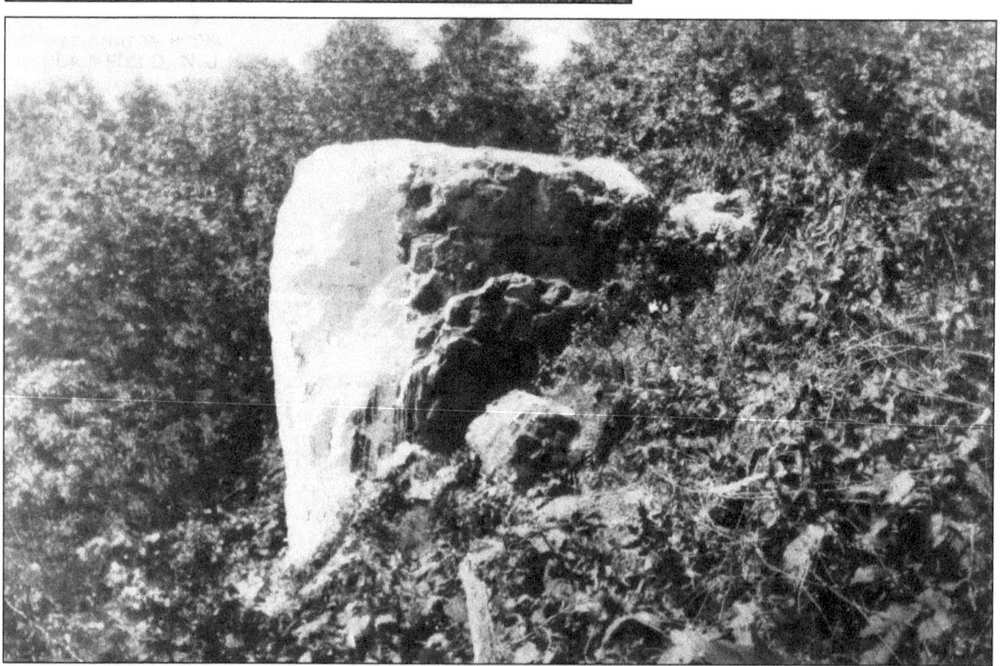

Washington Rock, now in Green Brook, was within Warren's bounds until 1872 when the lower portion of the township became North Plainfield. It was in 1777 that General Washington stood atop this rock to view the movements of British troops on the plains below.

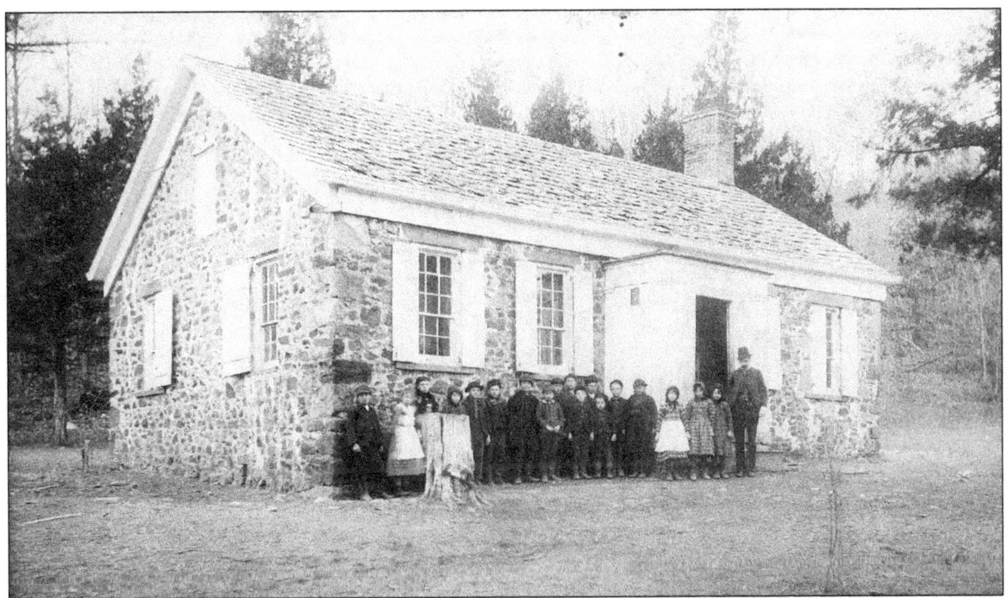

The Warrenville schoolhouse at 67 Mount Bethel Road was built in 1847 to replace an earlier school erected prior to the Revolution. Now a private home, the building still retains the carved remnants of students' names and initials on its window frames.

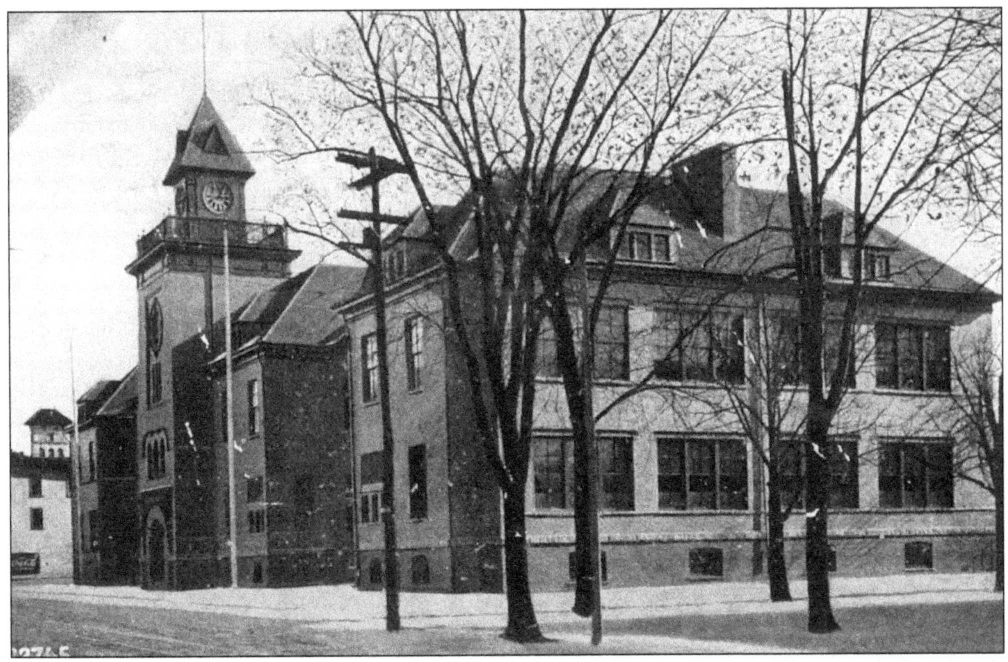

During the early part of this century, most of Warren's high school students attended North Plainfield High School on Somerset Street. Until World War I, they journeyed by horse-drawn coach driven by Reverend George Bowers or his daughter, Maude. The first stop was Mount Bethel at 7am.

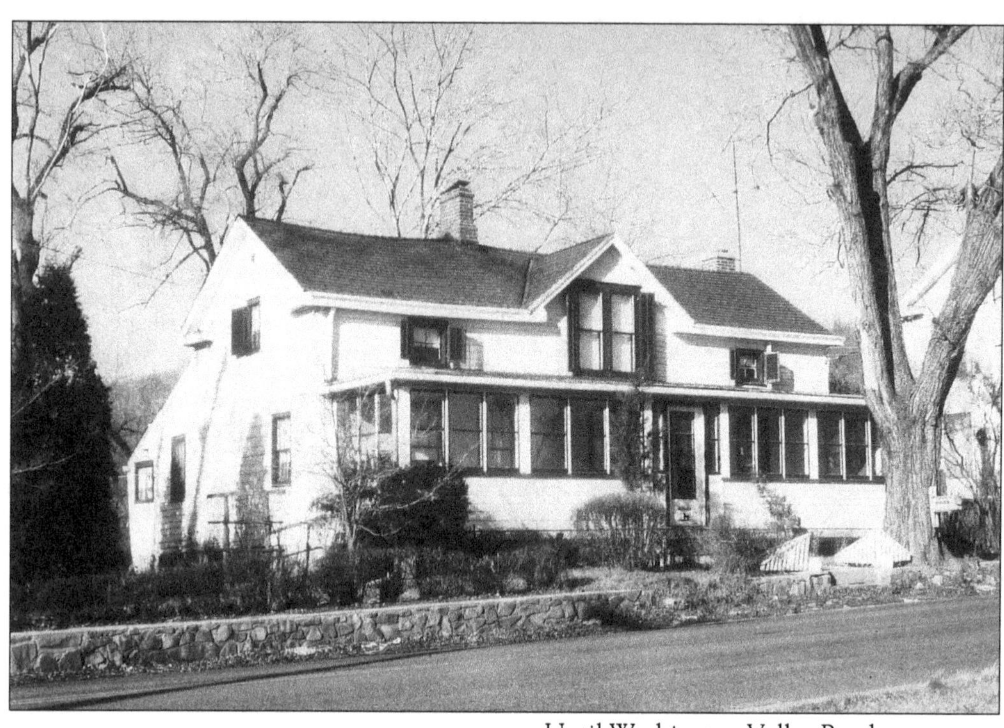

Until Washington Valley Road was extended to Mountain Boulevard in 1973, the Herlich house stood on Mount Bethel Road opposite the end of Mountain Boulevard. Built before the Revolution, the house passed through the Jobs, Tingley, Stewart, Cole, Drake, and Wilson families before Adam Herlich acquired it in 1853.

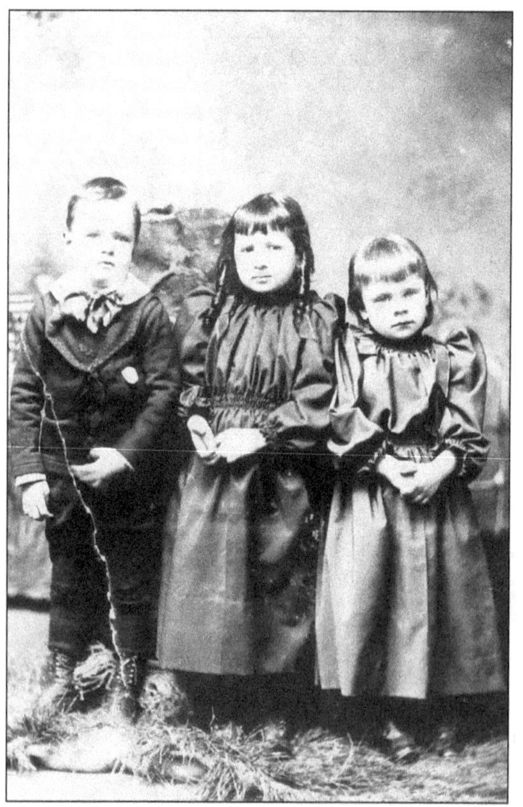

The Herlichs lived in the house for one hundred and twenty years. Robert Herlich and his two sisters, grandchildren of the original owner, pose for this *c.* 1895 portrait.

The Bornmann family owned the general store and post office in Warrenville from 1866 to 1916. John D. Bornmann and Catharine Newmiller (pictured here) were married April 2, 1893.

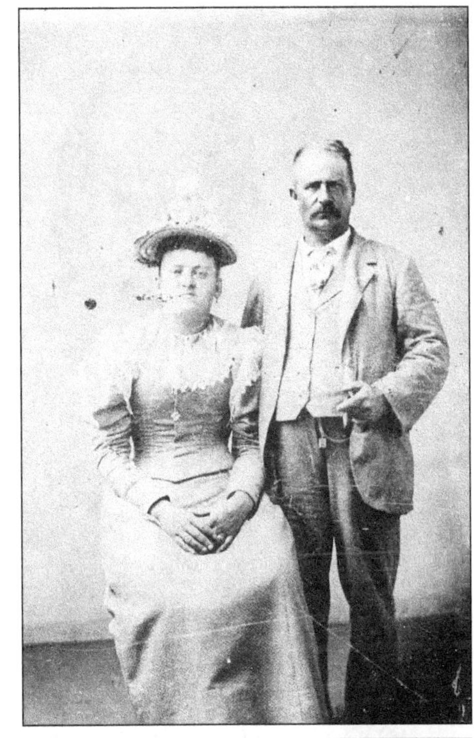

Daniel Cory was Warrenville's first postmaster in 1851. Daniel Bornmann was appointed in 1866 and his daughter, Lizzie, held the post from 1882 until 1916. Their general store, built prior to 1847, occupied the site where the Warrenville Tavern later stood.

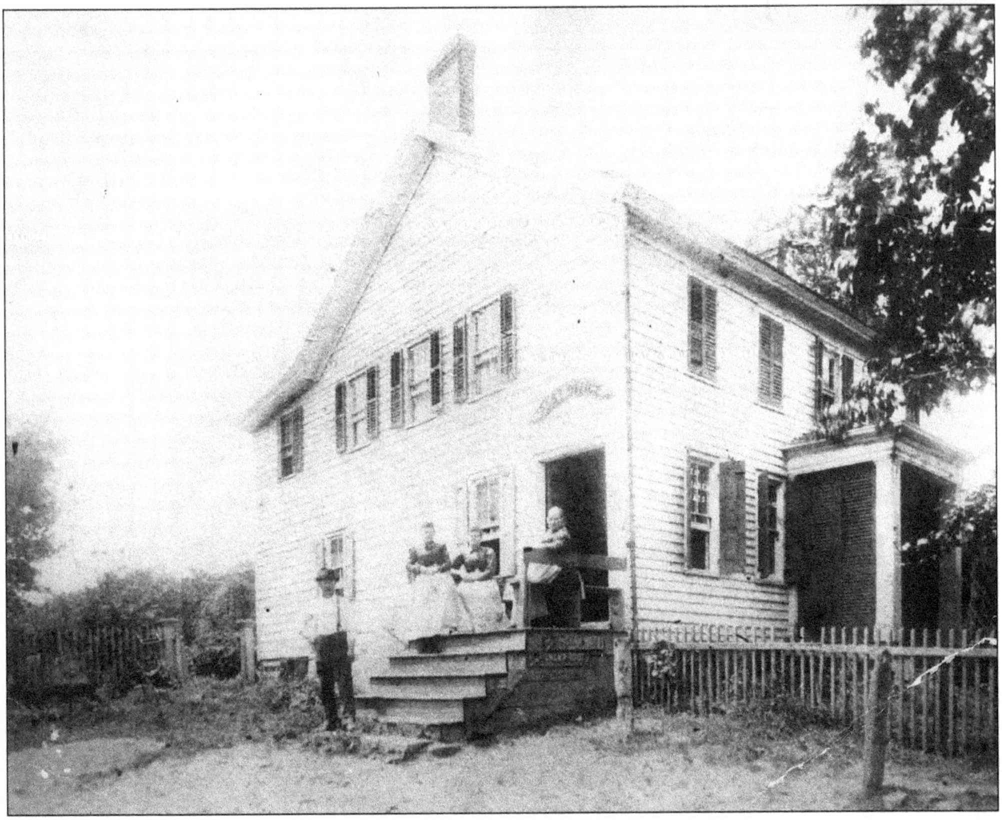

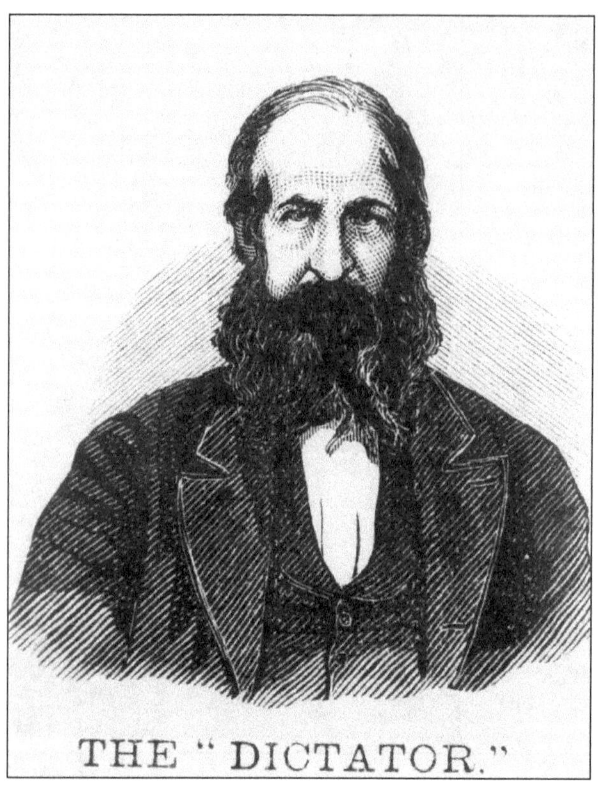

Daniel Cory (1808-1895), who lived in a fine home near the intersection of Mount Bethel and Mount Horeb Roads, was a county freeholder and assemblyman. He was charged with corruption and convicted in 1881.

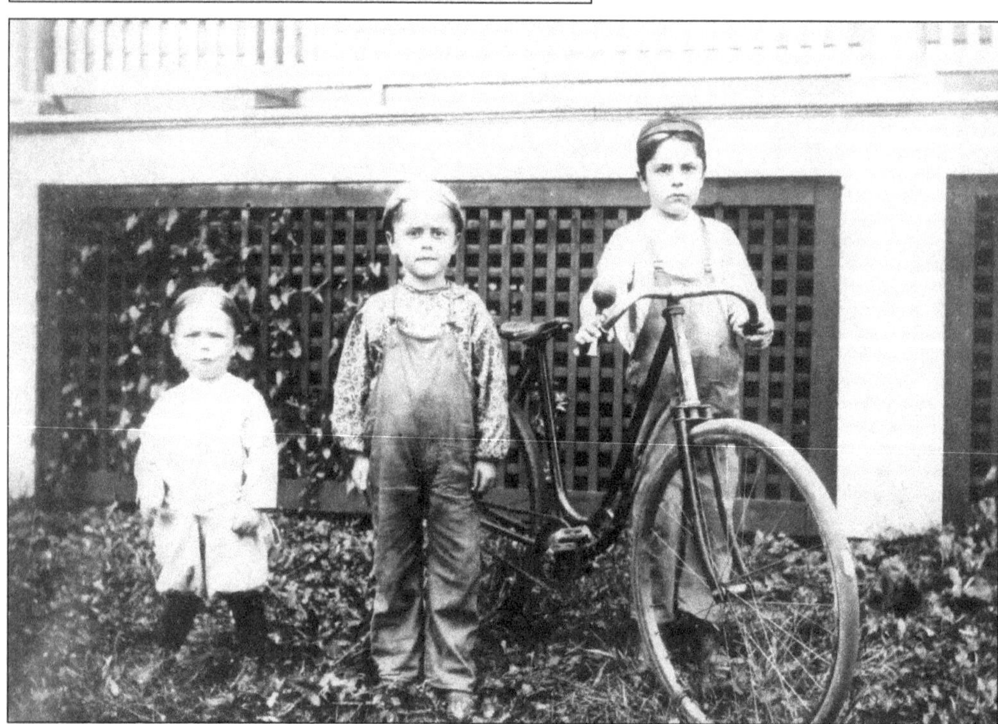

Near what is now the town hall stood the home of the Bowers family. Ranceford, Ellsworth, and Gerald, seen here in 1900, were the sons of John and Laura Bowers.

Millionaire investor and businessman Nathan Hofheimer (1836-1921) retired to Warren, bought 350 acres in the downtown area, and built a $50,000 home (now the town hall) with twenty-one rooms and five baths.

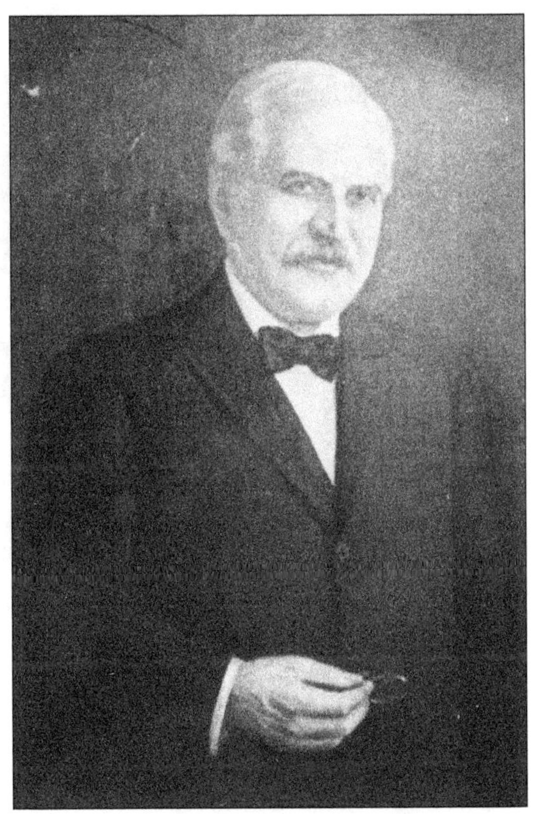

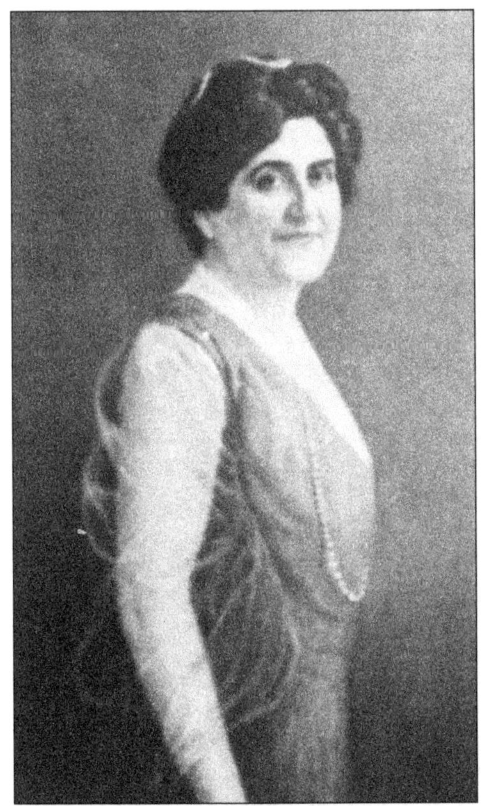

His wife, Lena Hofheimer (d. 1922), is shown here. The family compound contained tennis courts, stables, a pool, two ponds, a six-hole golf course, and several houses.

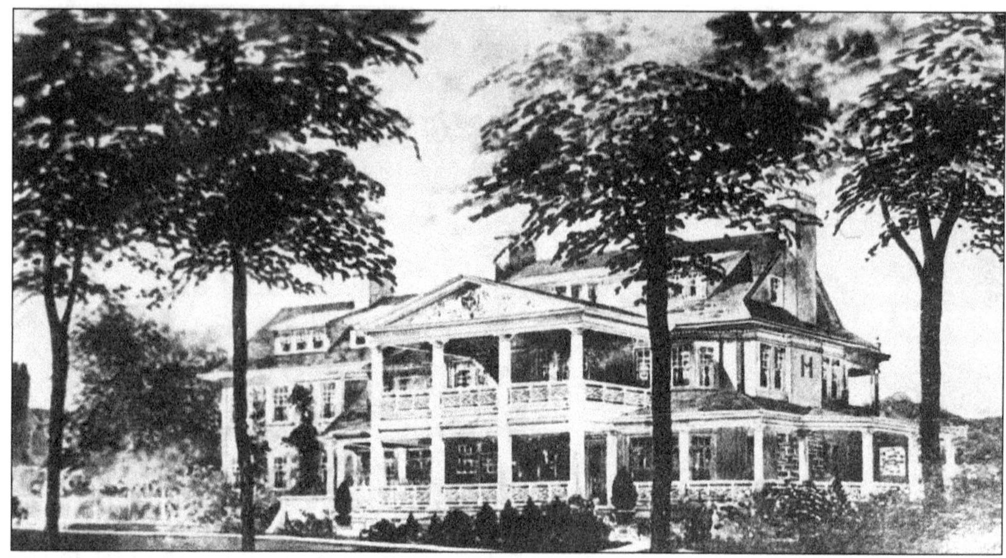

The Hofheimer estate included the present-day Pheasant Run Plaza. Nathan's son, Arthur, built "The Eaves" on the northwest corner of Washington Valley and Warrenville Roads. It burned to the ground shortly after Arthur died in 1927.

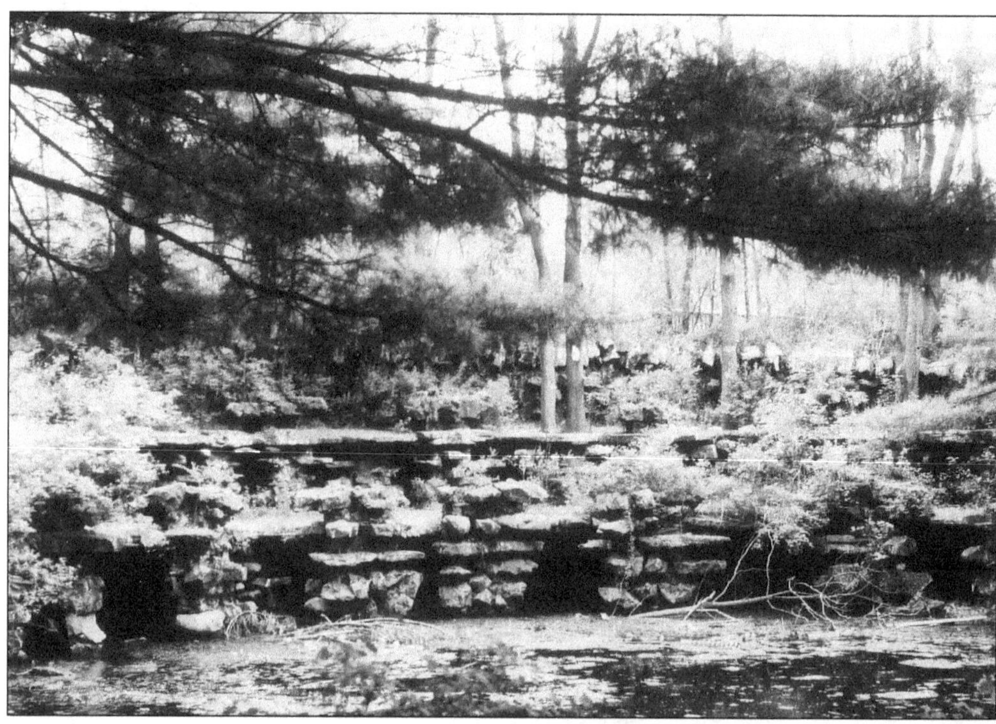

The Elks Club was also part of the Hofheimer compound. To the rear is this natural stone grotto built over an old copper mine shaft by Nathan Hofheimer to resemble a place he remembered in Germany. Hofheimer also dammed Middle Brook, stocking the resulting ponds with trout.

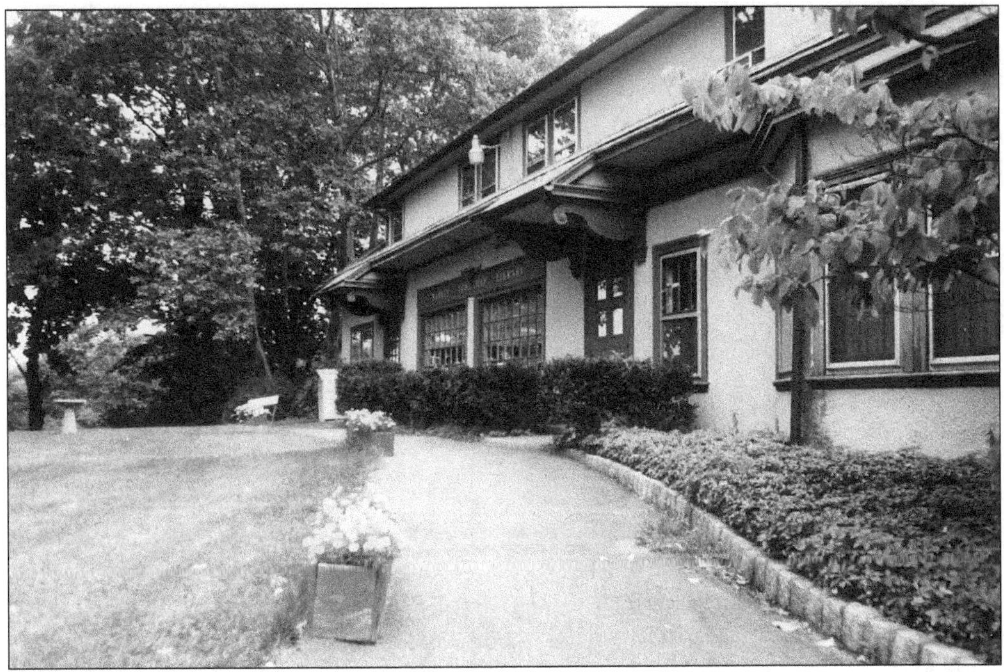

The former township library was Hofheimer's coach house and servant quarters. The public library, which began in 1946 with a collection of books in a Central School hallway, occupied this building from 1964 to 1995.

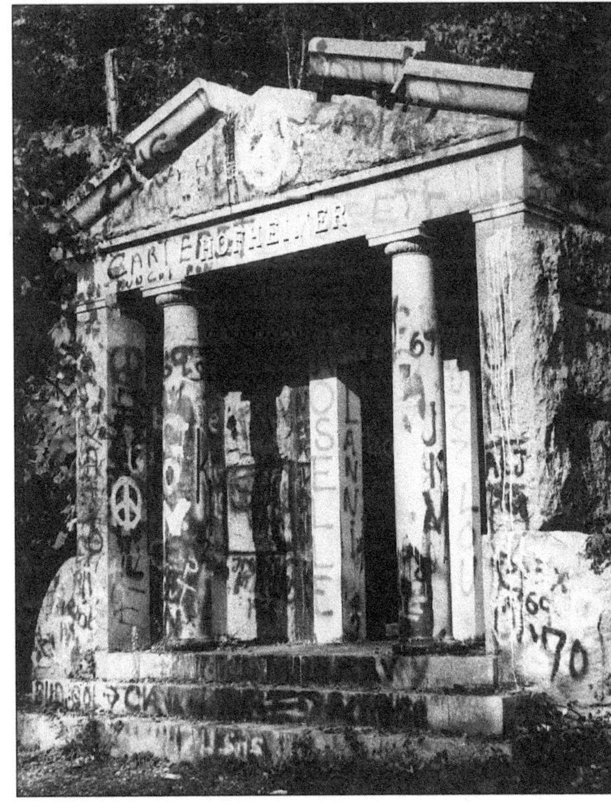

The Hofheimer mausoleum to the rear of town hall contained sixteen crypts. The bodies of Nathan, Lena, and Arthur rested here until the family sold the estate to the township in 1956. Now heavily vandalized, the mausoleum cries out for restoration.

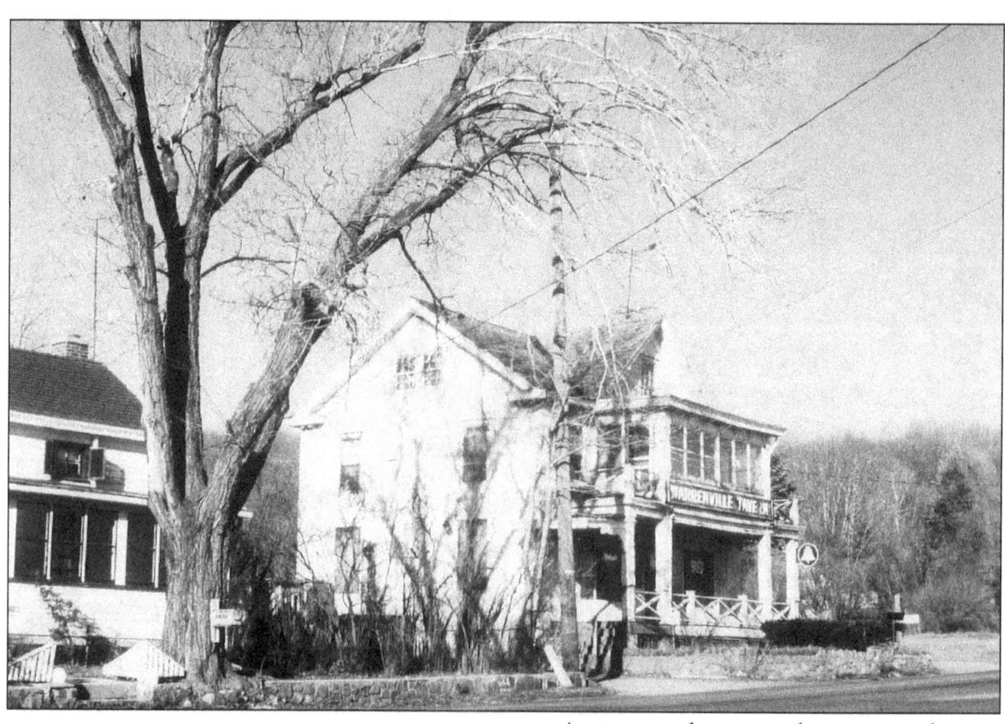

A nineteenth-century house moved across Mount Bethel Road when Hofheimer developed his estate. The Warrenville Tavern was the town's best-known watering hole and unofficial political headquarters until it was demolished in 1973. The tavern was torn down when Washington Valley Road was extended easterly to join Mountain Boulevard.

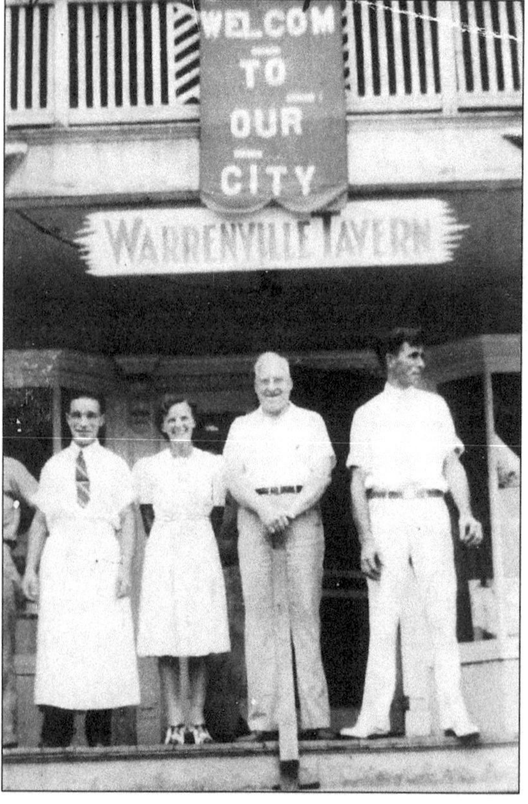

Charles B. Wicht is seen here with Margaret and Walter Mundy and Freddie, Wicht's bartender, reviewing a parade held in 1939 to mark the founding of the Washington Valley Fire Company. Wicht was an early supporter of the fire company. His wife, Catherine, was the daughter of one of the owners of the Mount Bethel Inn. Spelling was apparently not one of Wicht's strong points.

Russian and German Jews came to Warren from New York City in the early twenties to find a healthier life. Samuel and Sophie Ratner, with son, Louis, arrived in 1926.

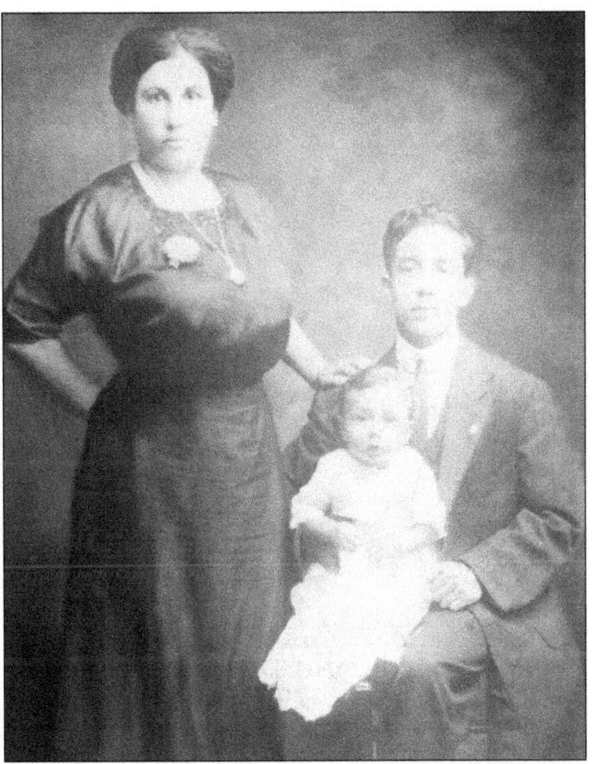

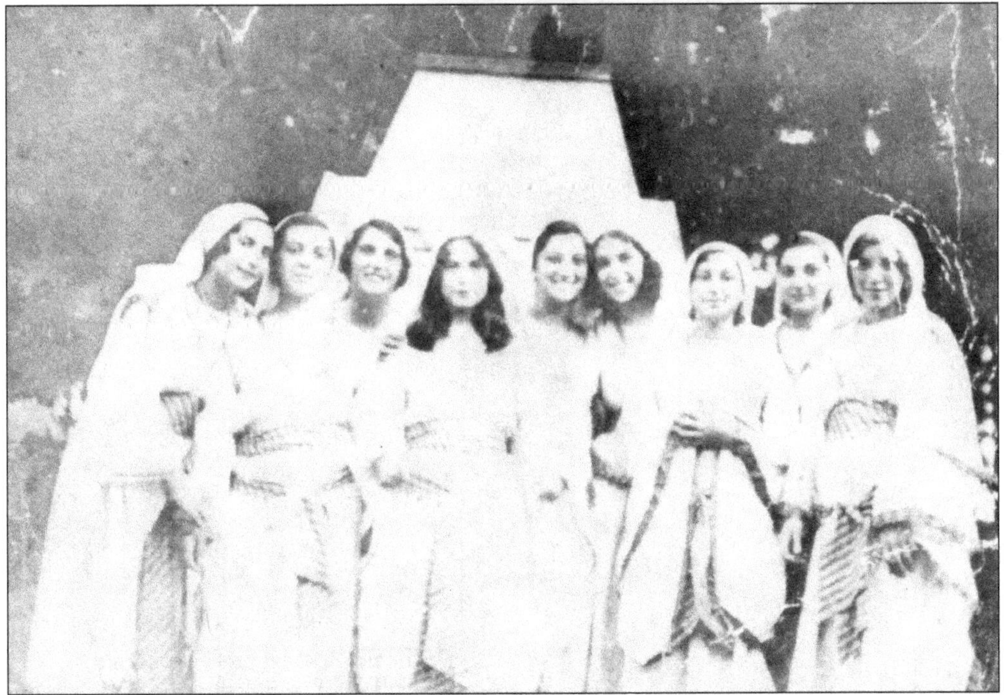

Israel Steinbaum founded Camp Harmony at the corner of Harmony and Mount Horeb Roads in 1926. Dressed in period costume, a group of young ladies staying at the camp in the summer of 1930 put on a Biblical play.

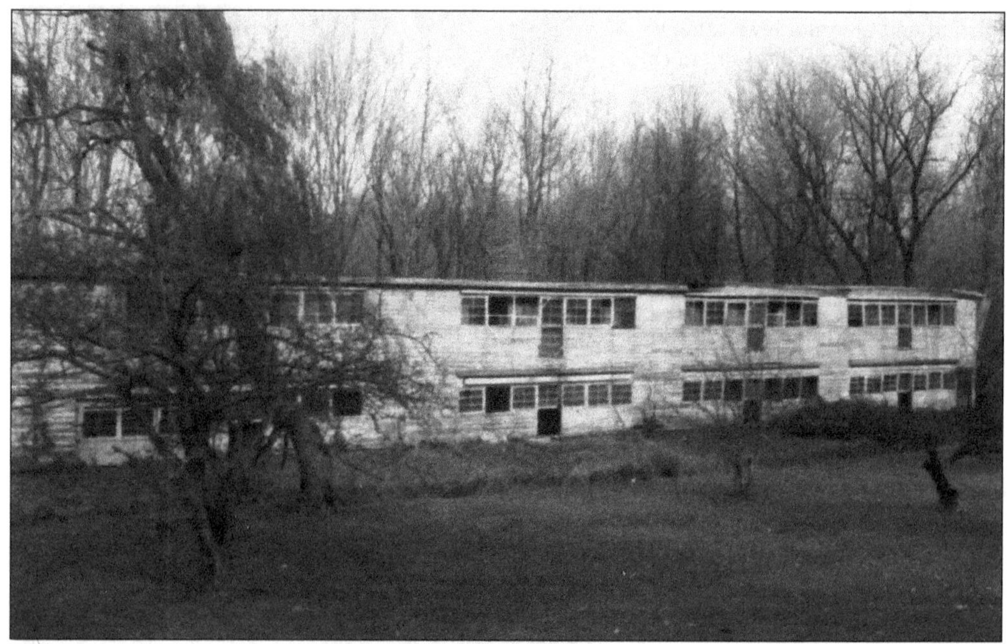

These dilapidated chicken coops on Mount Horeb Road opposite Camp Harmony were torn down in the late 1980s. The Epstein, Ratner, Margolis, Regenberg, Magid, and Steinbaum families were among those who built small homes on Harmony Road and nearby.

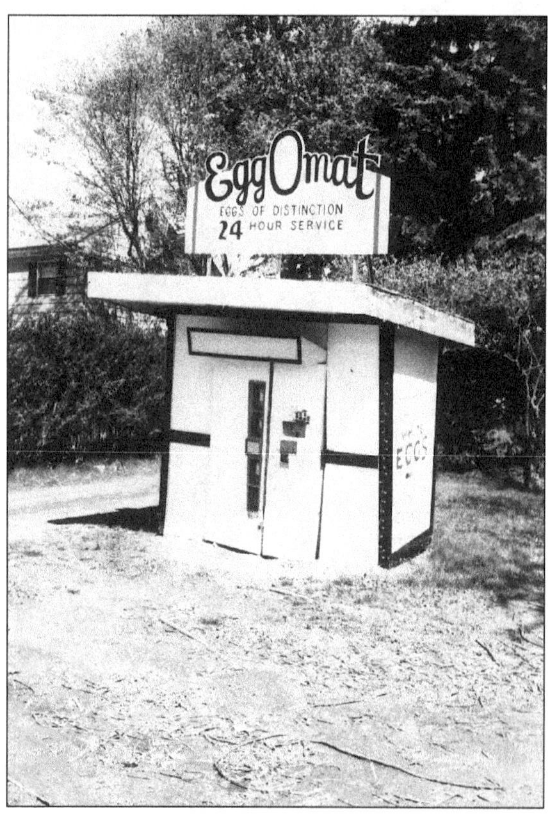

The Egg-O-Mat at 41 Mountain Boulevard, installed in the early 1950s by Camillo Epstein, was a coin-operated, refrigerated egg vending machine.

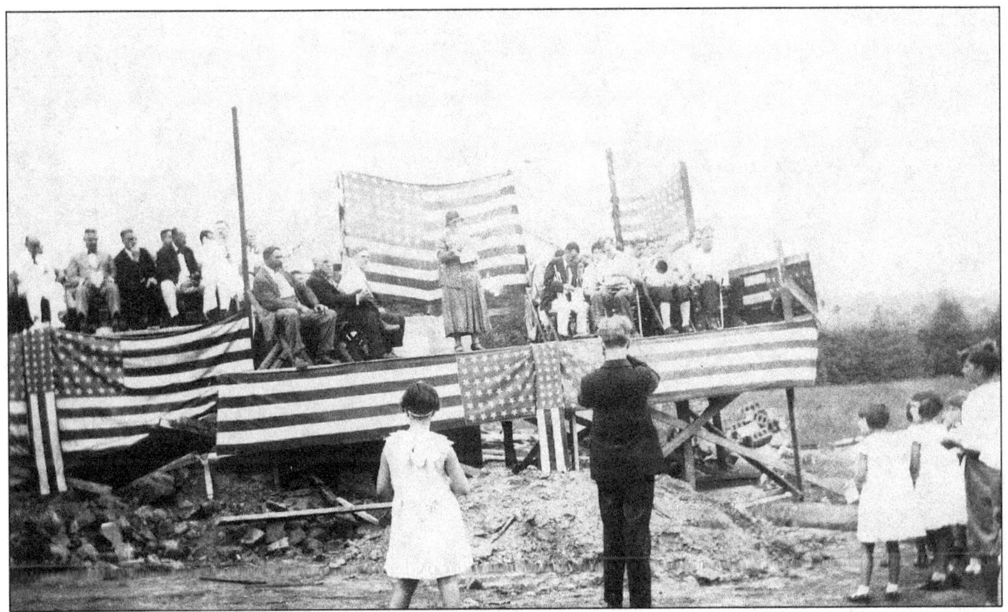

Both county and state school officials were highly critical of Warren's six one-room schoolhouses, citing as problems their poor sanitary facilities, polluted wells, and overcrowded conditions. Bernadine Nuse, who taught at South Stirling School, reported in 1929 that she had forty-eight students but only twenty-nine seats. After five failed attempts, Warren voters approved a plan to abandon their one-room schoolhouses in favor of a central elementary school in December 1931. Groundbreaking ceremonies pictured here were held on July 23, 1932. School board vice president Laurabelle Goodwin is speaking.

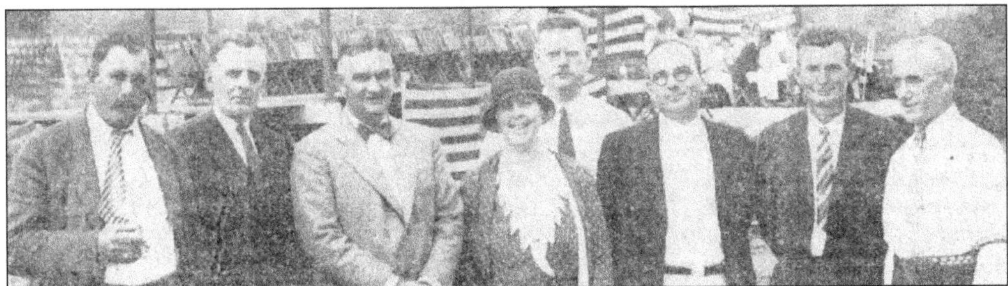

From left to right at the groundbreaking ceremony are: John F. Mundy (board president), Robert Sanford (county superintendent), John Spargo (assistant commissioner of education), Lauabelle Goodwin, W.J. Brown (school custodian), William B. J. Reitze (district clerk), and Roy Giddes and Oscar Fingerhut (members of the board). It was an act of considerable faith for Warren voters to approve the building of a new school in the midst of the Depression. In 1932, teachers agreed to "voluntarily contribute" 10% of their salaries back to the school district to help reduce taxes.

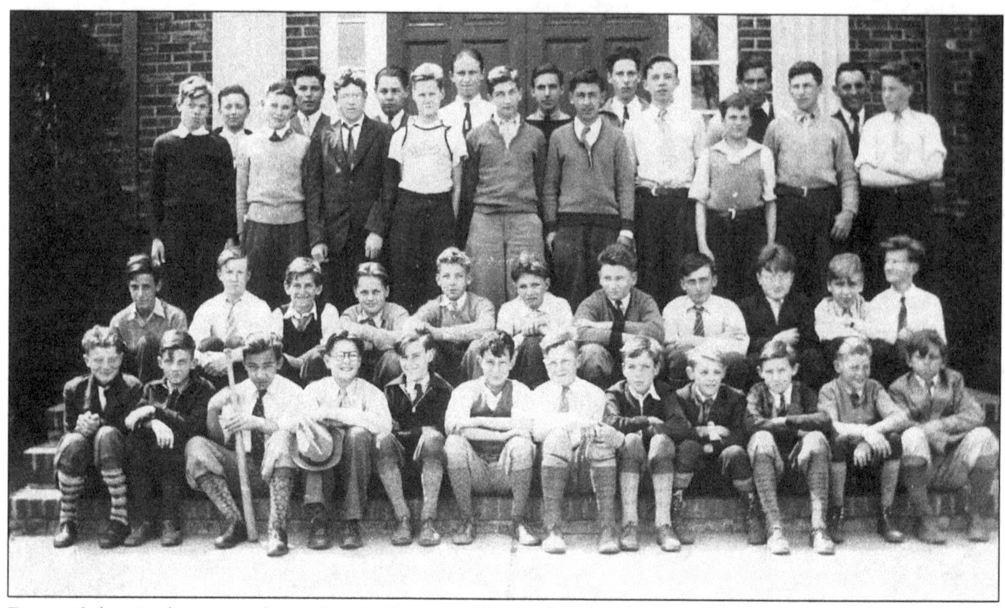

Boys of the sixth, seventh, and eighth grade Central School classes pose in 1936. The students include: Frank and Philip Freehauf, Jack Engstrom, Charlie Ross, Fred Weigand, Charlie Smith, John Magnani, Alfred Saddington, Angus MacLaren, Fred Reinmann, Louis Rosenberg, Henry Jennings, Emil Bielko, Art Gray, Howard Perry, Ted Koss, Bill Reitze, Adam Adami, and Billy Betzold.

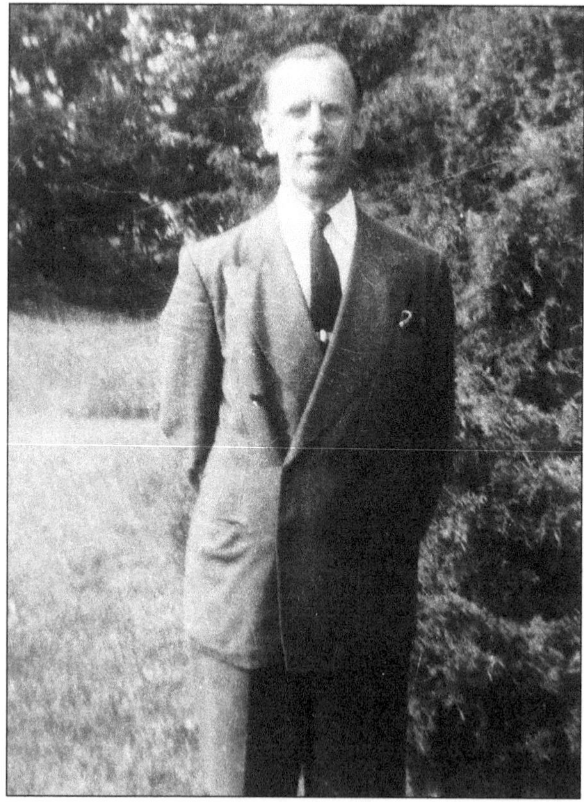

Ralph Juppe was Central School's second principal, succeeding Helen Smalley. The school was built at a cost of $80,000.

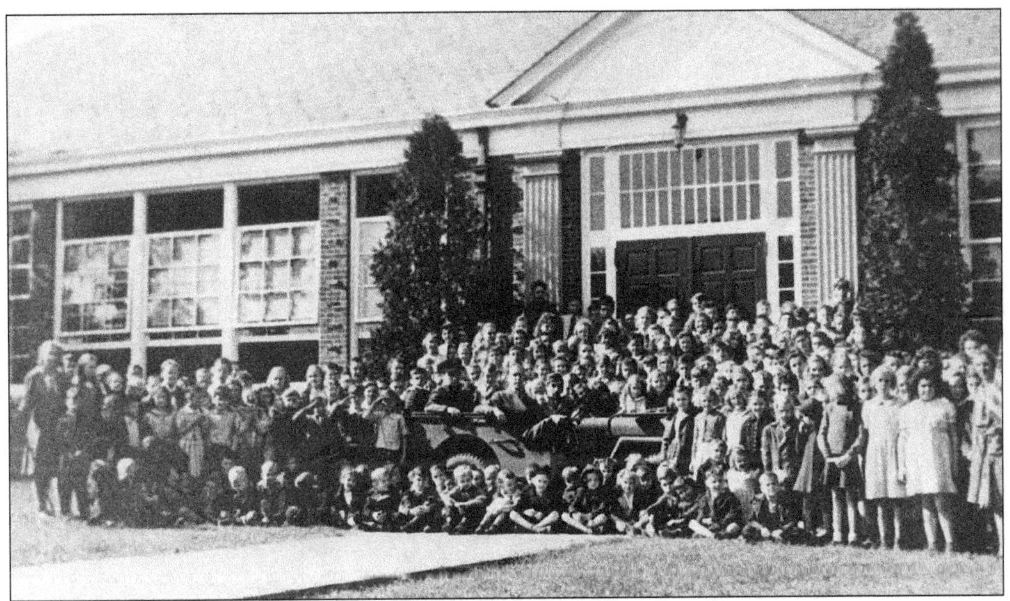

Principal Juppe sits proudly in a jeep purchased with money raised by Central School students in one of the many war stamp and bond drives held in Warren during World War II.

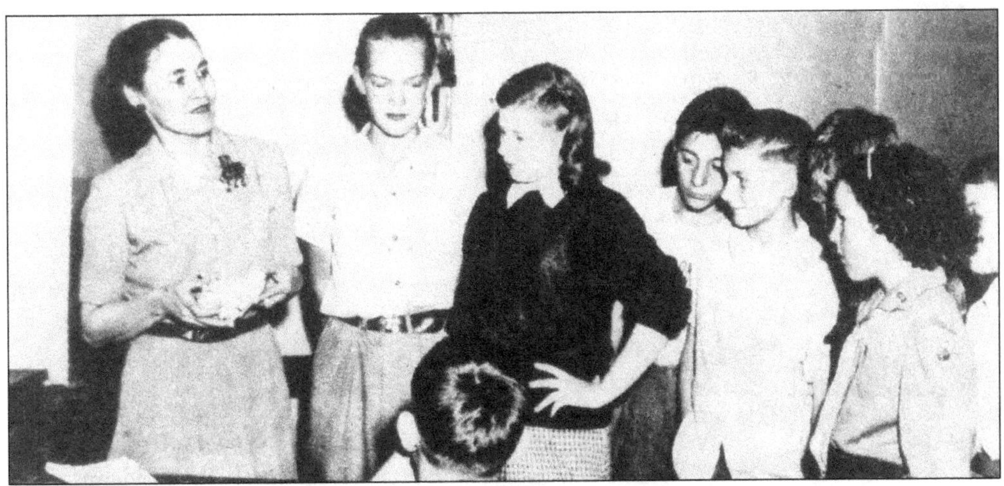

Mrs. Edith Binker, who taught English and science and supervised Central School's glee club, was named "Best Teacher of 1945" in a nationwide contest. Her yearly salary was $1,950.

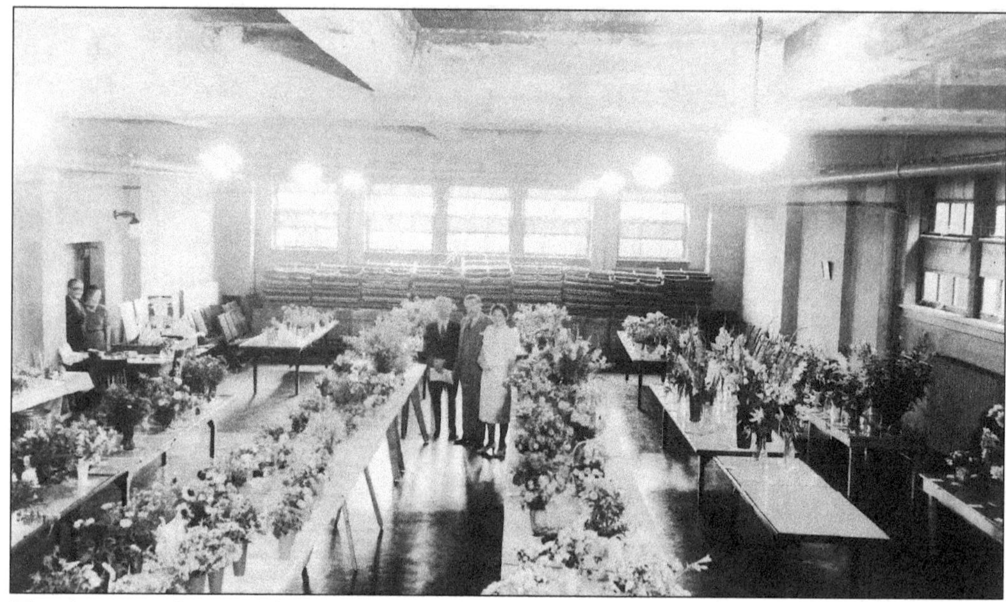

The Autumn Flower and Vegetable Show in August 1940 was one of many events held at Central School. The show was sponsored by the Warren Township Garden Club, Ethel A. Reitze, president, and admission was 25¢. Congressman Charles A. Eaton from Watchung presented the grand prize of $5.

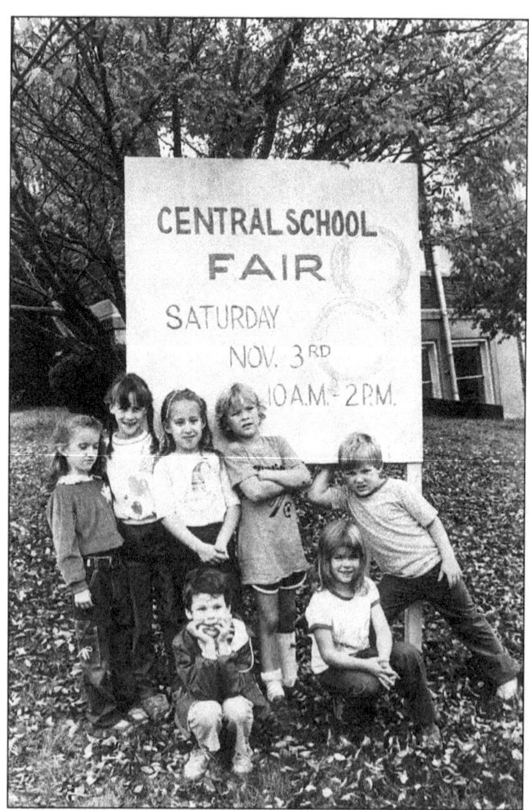

From left to right at the annual Central School Fair in November 1984 are: (front row) David Malpas and Rachel Porzig; (back row) Jenna Keimmel, Robin Truxel, Denise Smith, Armin Porzig, and Jay Aldrich.

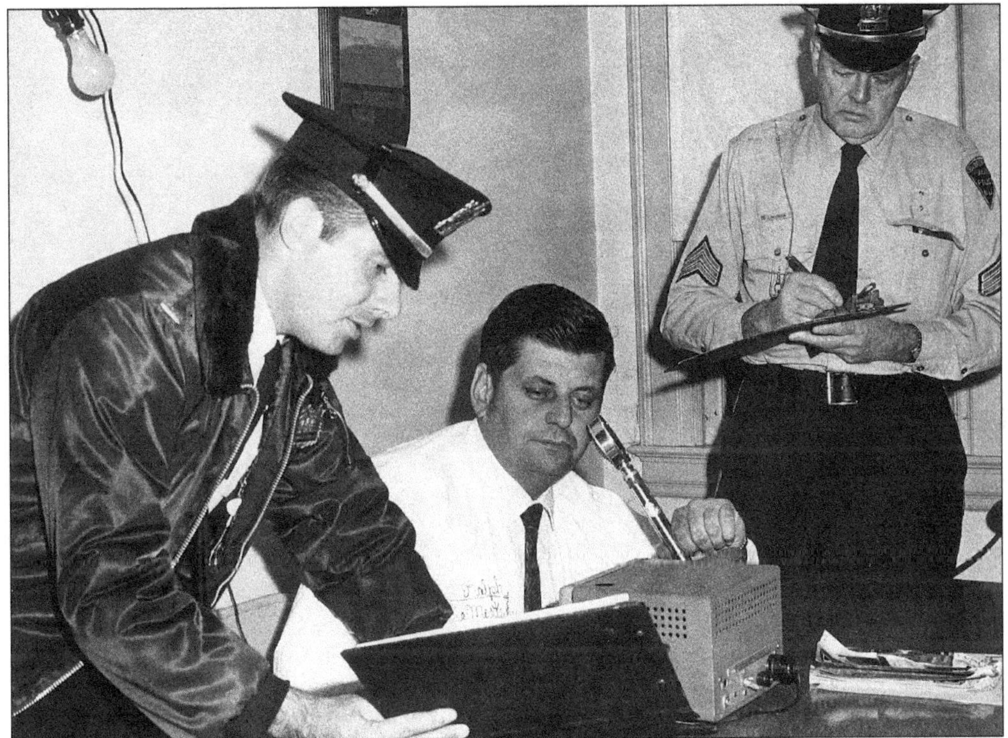

After the township disbanded its first police department as a Depression-era economy measure, state troopers from the Scotch Plains barracks provided coverage. Auxiliary police also patrolled the township in their private cars. In 1970, Dick Weinschenk and John Hickerson participate in a training exercise.

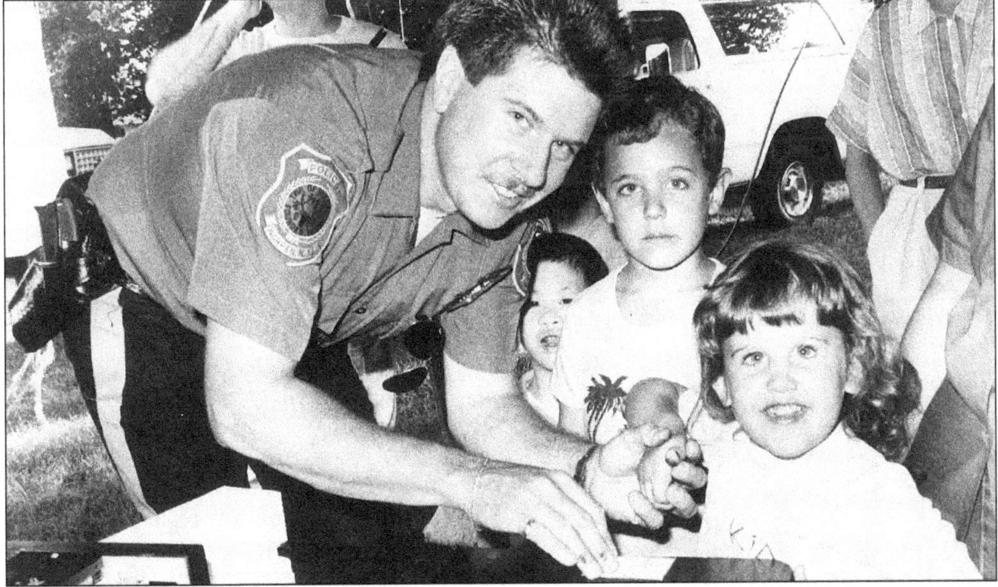

The police department was founded in 1972. Leonard Visotski, the first chief, had fourteen men under his command. In 1985, Patrolman Russell Leffert fingerprints schoolchildren as part of the department's crime prevention program.

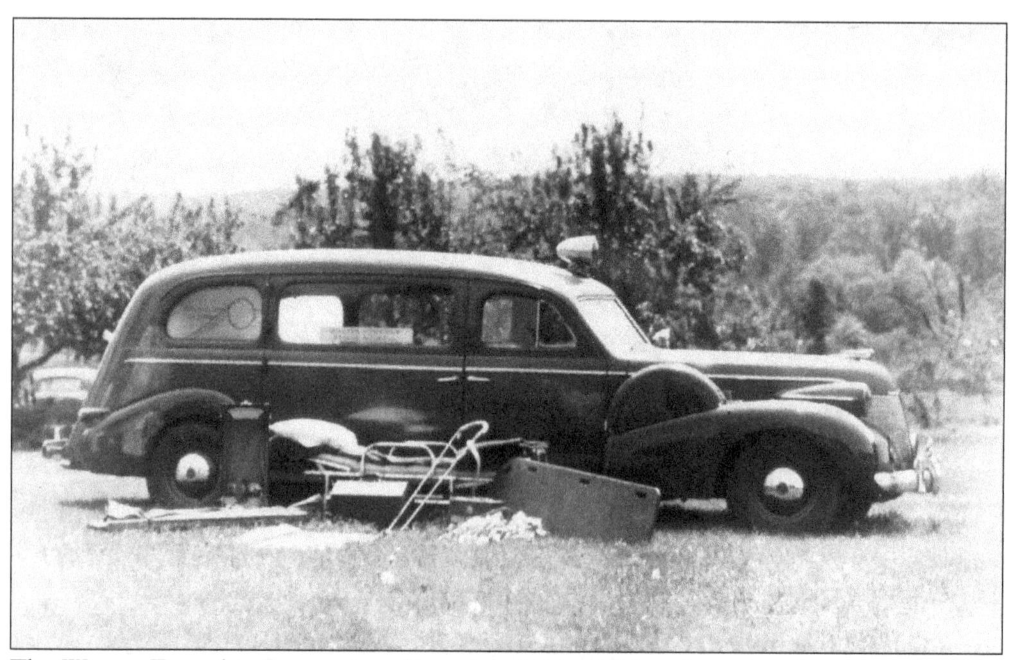

The Warren Township Rescue Squad was founded in 1940 with twelve charter members. Its first ambulance was a second-hand Meteor, a converted hearse complete with flower vases that cost $200. The squad moved into its new building behind the town hall in 1971.

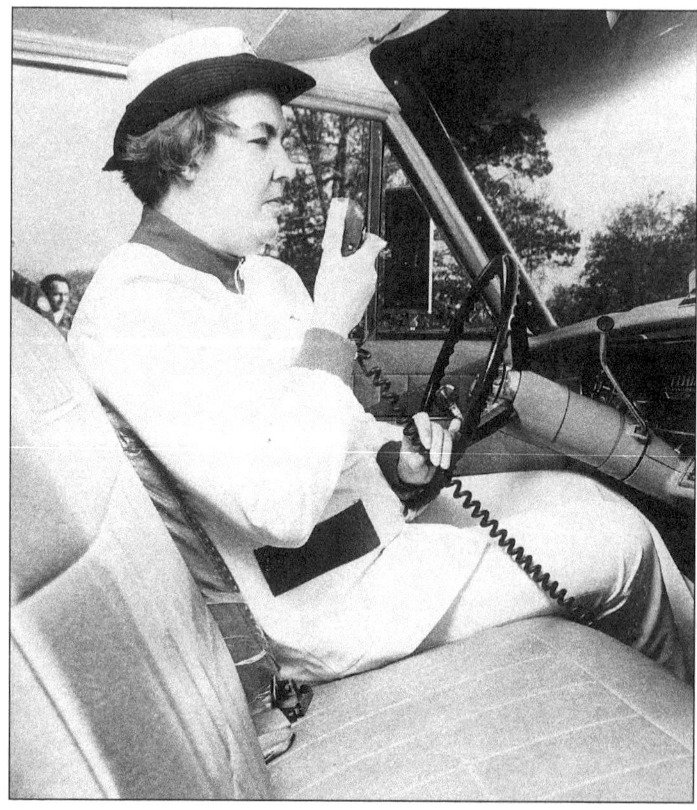

Elizabeth Aulicky tries out the rescue squad's new short wave radio system in 1970. Esther Kingman, elected squad captain in 1972, was the first woman so honored.

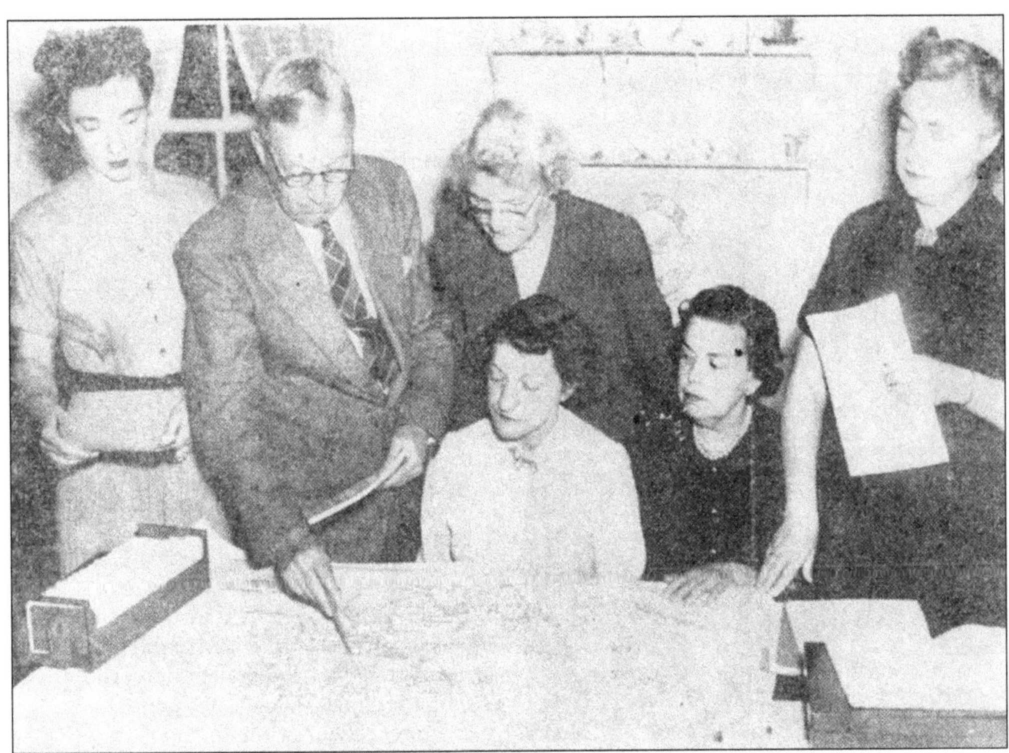

The Warren Township Civic Association, formed in the late twenties, issued a new town directory in 1952. Pictured here working on the project are, from left to right: (front row) Mrs. Reuben Cain and Mrs. Joseph Paine; (back row) Mrs. Robert Wallace, Sidney Curren (association president), Mrs. Charlotte Heilman, and Mrs. Alma Sharrett.

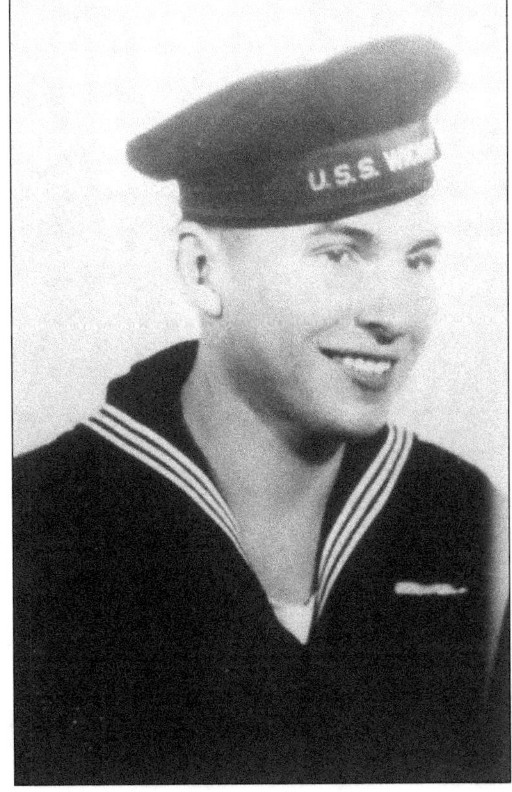

Navy man Emil Bielko died when the USS *Tasker Bliss* went down off the coast of Morocco early in World War II.

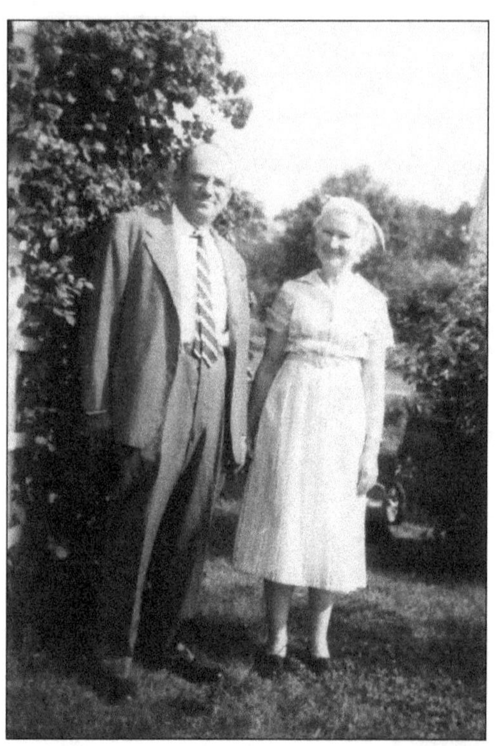

William B.J. Reitze and his wife Ethel are shown here in 1956. Reitze served as a member of the board of education for over twenty years, including several terms as president.

Alfred Allen was installed as Exalted Ruler of Watchung Hills Lodge 2252 B.P.O.E. in 1980. Founded in 1966, the lodge acquired its present home in 1964. Once part of the Hofheimer estate, the grounds include a grotto, two ponds, a picnic area, and a swimming pool.

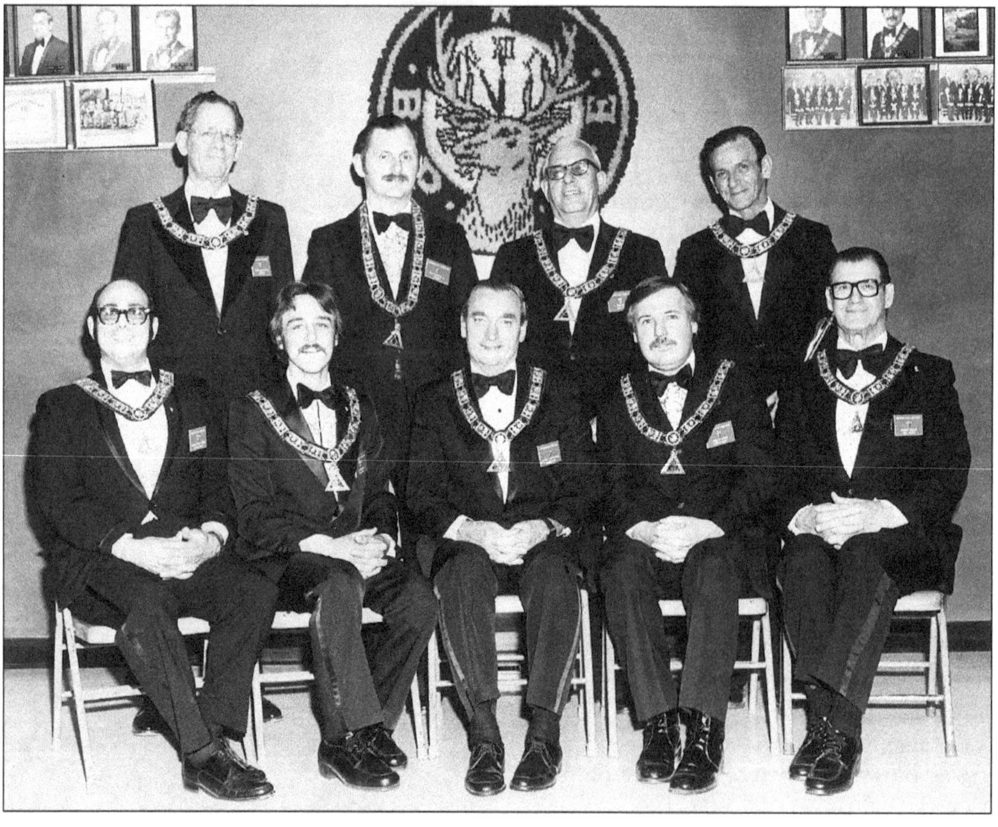

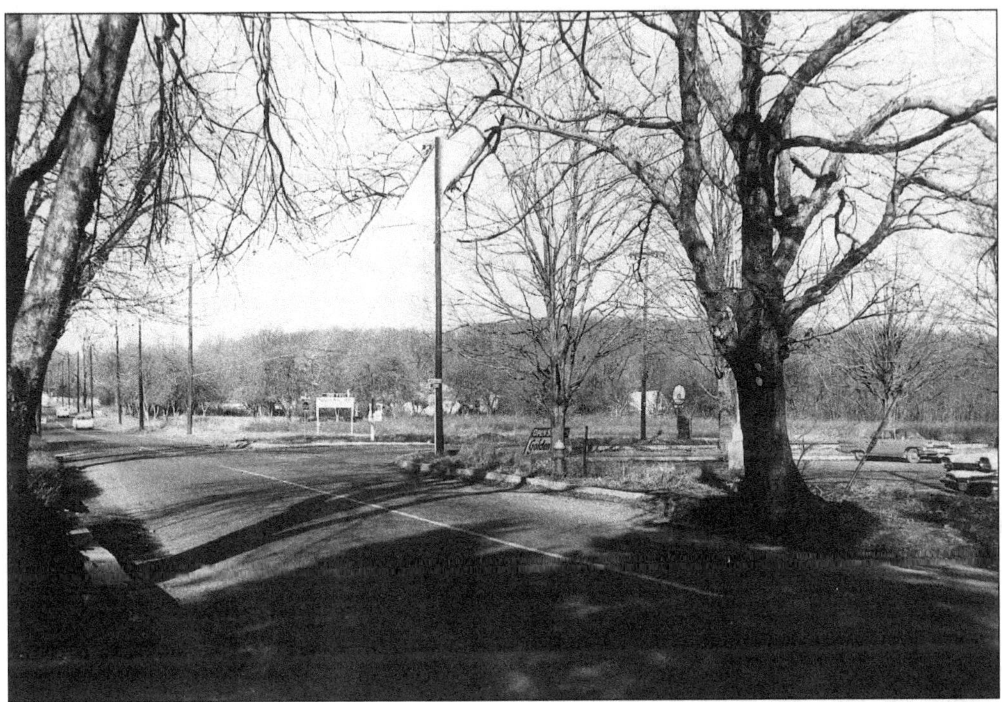

This is downtown Warrenville in 1964. To the right is the Bardy Farms Shopping Center. In the center will be Weichert Realtors and Warrenville Hardware. A Stewart's Root Beer stand was a thousand feet east of the intersection. To the left but out of view is the Herlich house and Warrenville Tavern.

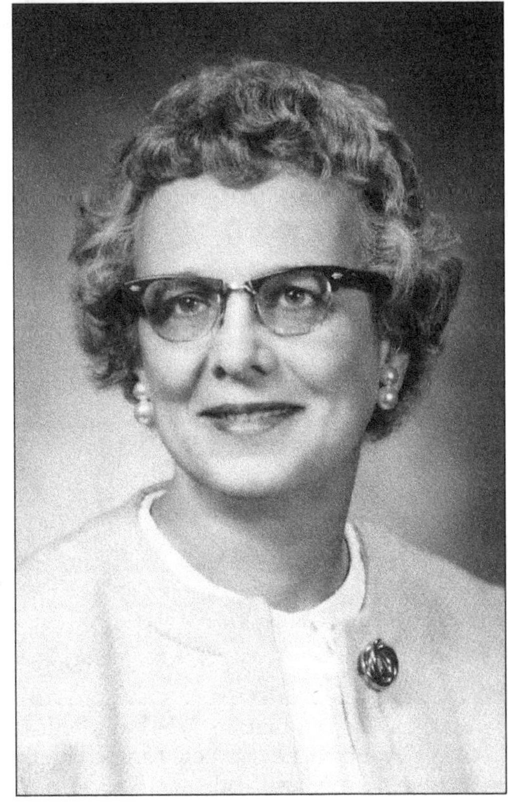

Elected tax collector in 1945, Myrtle Conover (1905-1978) was the first woman to hold municipal office in Warren.

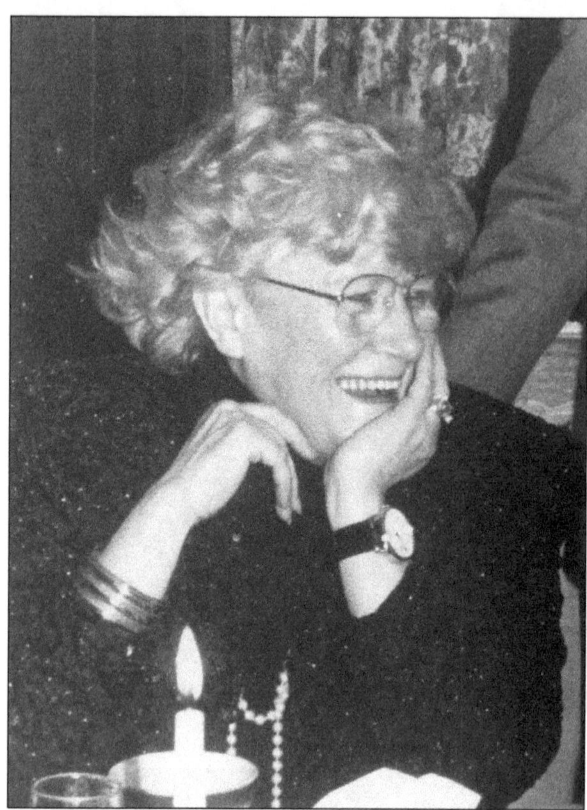

Florence Higgins was a reporter and editor of the *Echoes-Sentinel* newspaper until she retired in 1987. Flo's column, "On the Scene," was the first part of the paper her loyal readers turned to each week.

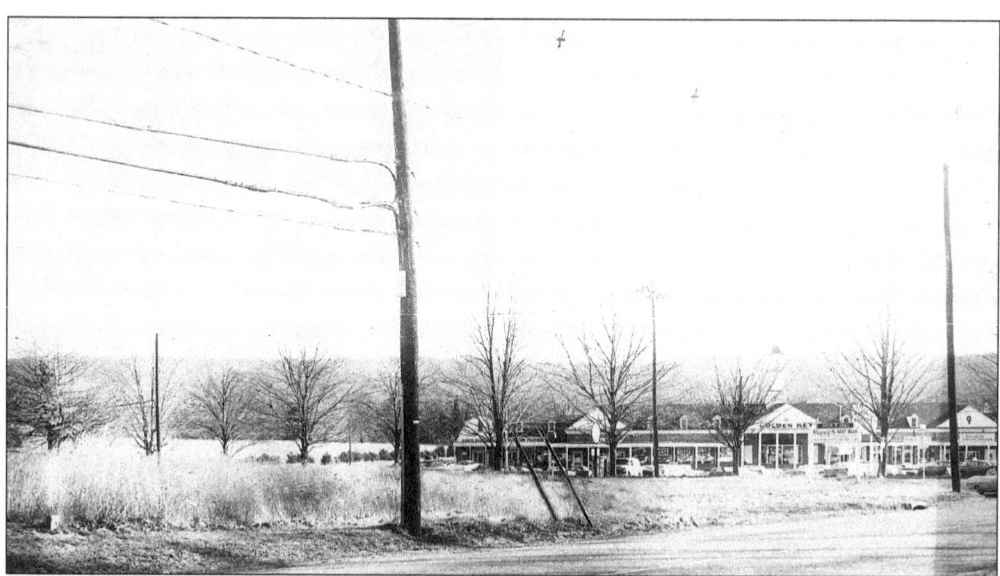

Bardy Farms, shown here in 1964, was built by Jack, Edward, and Philip Bardy in 1961. The Golden Key supermarket is now Kings. The Bardy family still operates a large produce market on Washington Valley Road.

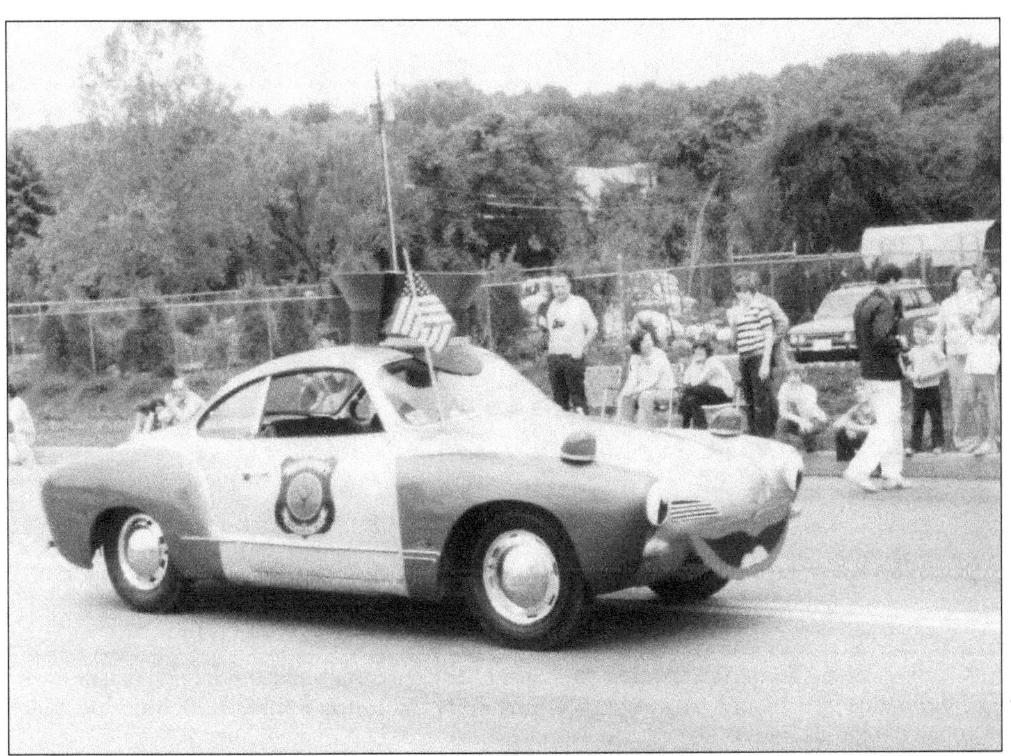

Otto the Auto, seen here rolling down Mountain Boulevard in a 1970s Memorial Day Parade, helped township police teach safety to school children. The talking auto, a Volkswagen of indeterminate age, featured headlamp eyes, a broad smile on his grill, and a police cap on the roof.

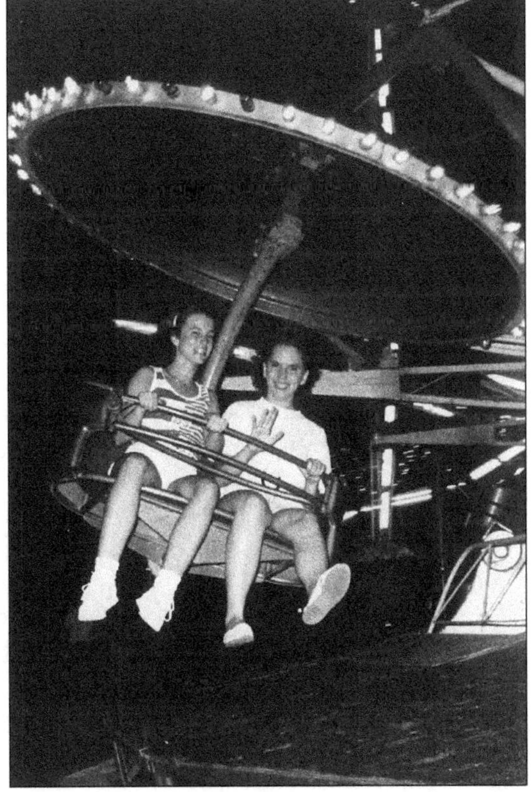

Staci McLaughlin and Tammy Weisser enjoy a ride at the Warren Expo in 1990. The Lions Club's first expo was held on the municipal grounds in 1967.

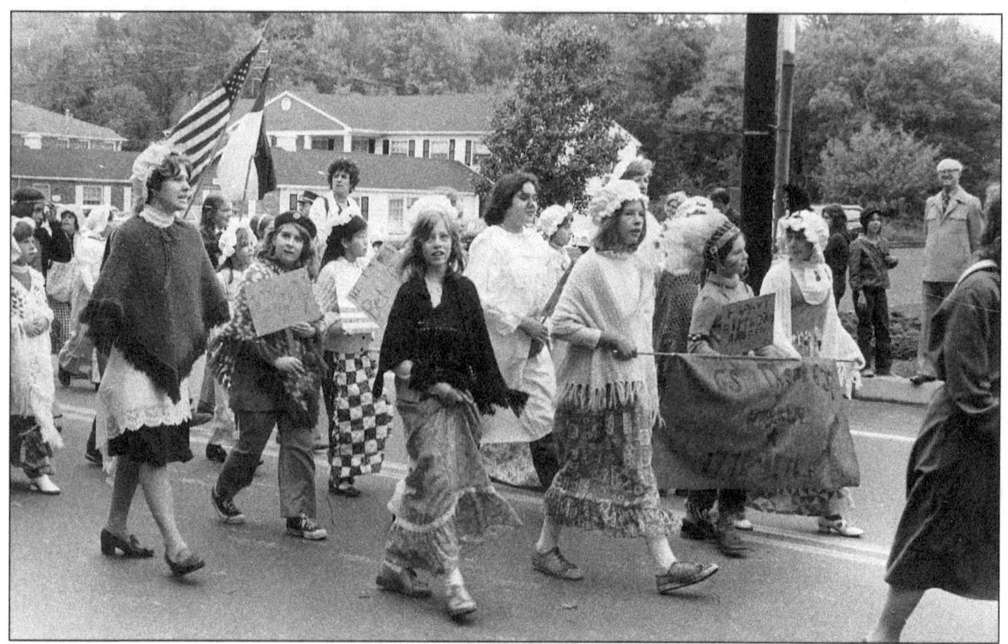

In October 1976, Warren celebrated the nation's bicentennial with its largest parade ever. The girl scouts were among a score of marching units competing for prizes. Mount Horeb Fire Company's reproduction of the Round Top School won as best overall entry.

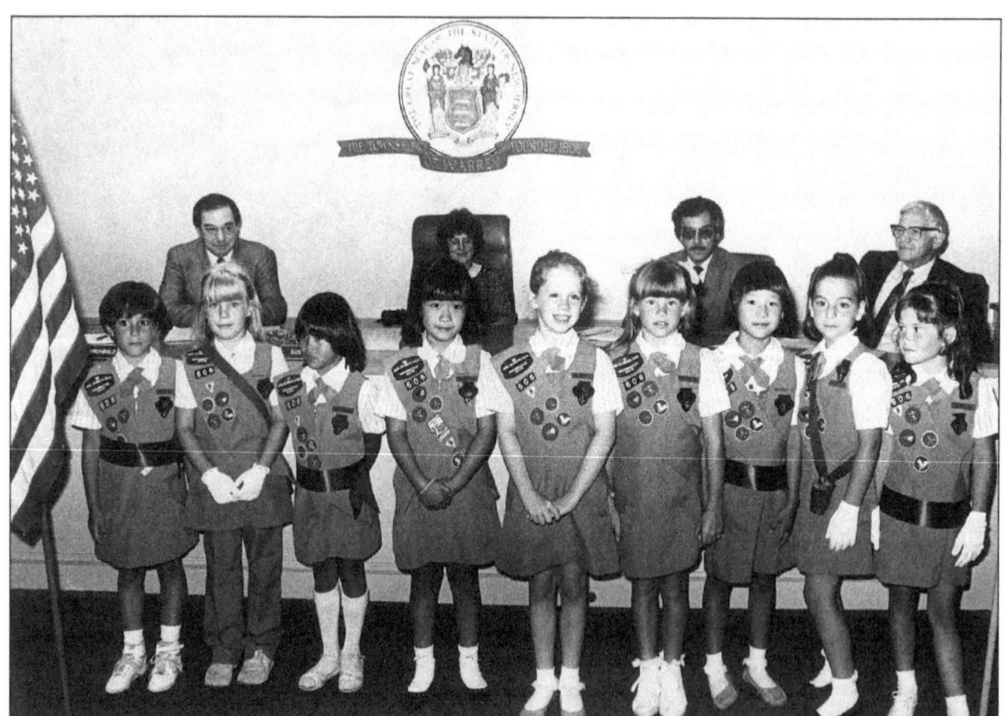

Mayor Susie Boyce and the township committee honored Girl Scout Troop 606 in this 1986 ceremony. From left to right are: Deborah Roth, Jennifer Bleeker, Sherri Marker, Jane Hsieh, Amy Siegel, Amanda Shamp, Stella Yi, Catherine Lynch, and Katherine Terins.

www.ingramcontent.com/pod-product-compliance
Lightning Source LLC
LaVergne TN
LVHW081339110826
845153LV00010B/410
* 9 7 8 1 5 3 1 6 6 0 1 7 8 *